Partitions of the Heart
Unmaking the Idea of India

HARSH MANDER

Daraja Press

Published by
Daraja Press
https://darajapress.com
Wakefield, Quebec, Canada

ISBN (softcover) 9781990263668

Cover design: Kate McDonnell

First published by
Penguin Random House, India

Library and Archives Canada Cataloguing in Publication

Title: Partitions of the heart : unmaking the idea of India / Harsh Mander.
Names: Mander, Harsh, 1955- author.
Description: International edition. | Includes bibliographical references.
Identifiers: Canadiana 20230547869 | ISBN 9781990263668 (softcover)
Subjects: LCSH: Political violence—India. | LCSH: India—Social conditions.
Classification: LCC HN690.Z9 V5512 2023 | DDC 303.60954—dc23

PRAISE FOR THE BOOK

At last a book that turns a powerful searchlight on the evil tide of hatred and violence stalking our country, where our minorities live in fear, and Muslims among us are killed under a government that has declared war on Islam. Harsh Mander started work as a civil servant and quit for reasons of conscience. He has since been the conscience of India. He reminds us of the state-sponsored massacre of Muslims in Gujarat in 2002, and the Gulberg massacre in that pogrom where the courts have yet to provide justice. He reminds us of individual Muslims—the boy Junaid and the cattle trader Pehlu Khan—who were butchered for being Muslim. He draws a parallel between India and America, showing how both governments have brought out the worst in their people. He asks why Indians have not risen against our government's inhuman policies as Americans have risen against theirs. It is a question we have to answer. Mander works among the survivors of mass violence and his karwans visit the grieving kin of murdered Indians, making him heir to Gandhi, who was one with the suffering of others. —**Nayantara Sahgal**, journalist, author of *Day of Reckoning: Stories* (2015).

Harsh Mander's is the voice of Kabir come alive in our violent times. We can hear it to our redemption, ignore it to our peril.
—**Gopalkrishna Gandhi**, former administrator and diplomat, Governor of West Bengal 2004-2009

Once again, with all the quiet passion at his command, Harsh Mander reveals what we, both as a people and a nation, have become: desensitized and brutalized. In our scoundrel times, he holds up a mirror for all of us to reflect upon and, hopefully, regain our humanity.
—**Saeed Akhtar Mirza**, screenwriter and director in Hindi films and television

I can't pay a better compliment to Harsh Mander than saying that he is perhaps what today's culture will call an anachronism. He is the conscience of this beloved and beleaguered subcontinent and carries the torch that Gandhiji, Nehru and Ambedkar lit for a secular republic. That statement may suggest that he is but an observer, one who keeps track of the goingson in a homeland in terrible turmoil. But that is missing the essence of the man. Harsh Mander is a doer, a "walking", intensely caring, and deeply committed human being: committed to the Constitution of India and the notion that every human life is invaluable. He could have stayed put as a senior IAS officer and risen to a highly prestigious rank in the national administrative service. Instead, he resigned years ago and has dedicated his life to the betterment of all those victimized by the current Hindutva mandarins at the very top and their rabid followers. Fortunately, Mander is a highly sensitive and fine writer. A quiet, sane voice instead of inflamed rhetoric is what makes his book so invaluable. Instead of generalities, he goes to the heart of the matter. He literally walks the talk by going to the homes of the murdered Junaid, Pehlu Khan and so many others who have suffered appallingly because this regime is hell-bent on treating the minority communities as second- or even third-class citizens. In case after case, he shows us how hundreds of thousands, actually it's millions, of Muslims have been deprived of a livelihood because of the Hindutva community's diabolical tactics. In his preface, he draws the most disturbing comparisons between Trump's America and the RSS-inspired BJP's India. The shocking fact, it turns out, is that the majority of the well educated and the well heeled in India don't give a damn that the current powers that be are hell-bent on a subterranean, second partition of the country. This book is absolutely mandatory reading. You owe it to the much-vaunted "motherland" which is being abused so shamelessly.

—**Kiran Nagarkar**, novelist, playwright, film critic and screenwriter

Partitions of the Heart effectively partitions the readers' hearts with a rare surgical precision and democratic insight by chronicling the chilling story of the wilful demolition of the secular backbone of the largest democracy called India. The way Harsh Mander analyses the environment permissive of bigotry, hate speech and collective vengeance in our hitherto uniquely secular nation is so searing and poignant that the book leaves our hearts ravaged by the devastating question: "What were it that we were doing at that moment of history?" A riveting documentation of the unmaking of India.

—**K.R. Meera**, Indian author and journalist, who writes in Malayalam

'Harsh Mander chillingly unravels the grotesqueness of today's India. If this book does not awaken you to the horrors of divisive politics propagated, nothing can.' —**T.M. Krishna**, Indian Carnatic vocalist, writer, activist, author and Ramon Magsaysay awardee

In memory of all those felled by hate violence,
in my land and every other.

Contents

Acknowledgments

To acknowledge my debts to the people I have learnt from over the years, for the insights that I have gained in order to be able to write this book, I would need to fill another book the same size with just their names. So instead, I offer here my silent gratitude to all these persons with whom I have walked on journeys for justice and healing after hate attacks—communal violence, atrocities against Dalits and Adivasis, and lynching.

These include firstly the survivors of communal violence in Indore and Khargone in Madhya Pradesh, where I first handled as a district official the tumult of communal violence, respectively in 1984 against Sikhs and in 1989 against Muslims in the wake of L.K. Advani's Rath Yatra. My journeys with the survivors have continued—after I left the Indian Administrative Service in 2002—for a decade with the survivors of the Gujarat massacre, and over the years with the survivors of many other communal massacres, of the 1984 anti-Sikh riots in the widows' colony of Tilak Vihar, Delhi, of Bhagalpur in the 1989 slaughter, and later the survivors of the Marad communal killings in Kerala of 2001 and 2002, the Nellie massacre of Assam in 1983, the Kokrajhar violence of 2012 and the Muzaffarnagar violence of 2013. I learnt from all of these survivors of hate violence, often attacked by their own neighbours, of their intense suffering, their unhealed wounds, the betrayals and their losses, their struggles to rebuild their lives and protect their families, and their battles for justice.

I have learnt enormously from human rights and peace workers who battled ceaselessly for justice. Their list is long as well, and I have been able to mention only some of them in the course of this book. I have learnt most of all from my colleagues at Aman Biradari, who joined the Nyayagraha struggle for justice, who taught me the generosity of fighting for others in the midst of your own unspeakable losses. Between 2010 and 2012, as a member of the National Advisory Council I co-convened with Farah Naqvi the NAC working group to draft the Communal and Targeted Violence Bill. The draft was discussed intensively, and I learnt a great deal from all my colleagues who participated in the discussions, including those who robustly opposed the law (which incidentally was never finally admitted to Parliament). I have immersed myself more and more in studying communal violence—impunity, failures of justice, suffering, healing, saving lives—in many sites, and have learnt from many colleagues in this research, such as Navsharan Singh, Pritarani Jha and Warisha Farasat. More recently, we have begun to build a people's archive of communal violence since Independence, covering the official record and the public record, with survivors' testimonies, inspired by Urvashi Butalia's Partition archives and Uma Chakravarthy's 1984 archives.

In the course of completing this book, we launched in September 2017 a journey of atonement, solidarity and conscience called the Karwan-e-Mohabbat, or Caravan of Love, to families of those hit by hate attacks and lynching across India, and the journey continues. Once again, this rather audacious enterprise built on an alternative politics of love has been supported by hundreds of people—many of whom I did not know and who now have become beloved comrades— with their money, time, solidarity and faith.

Much of the text of this book has appeared in some form in my articles, mainly for Scroll, the Indian Express, the Wire, Hindustan Times and the Economic and Political Weekly. I am grateful to the editors of each of these journals—Naresh Fernandes, Rajkamal Jha, Vandita Mishra, Siddharth Varadarajan, M.K. Venu, Sidharth Bhatia, Lalita Panicker, Kumkum Dasgupta, Rammanohar Reddy, Paranjoy Guha Thakurta, Kalpana Sharma—for creating and nurturing spaces even in difficult times for dissenting voices like mine. To my editors for this book from Penguin, Meru Gokhale and Manasi Subramaniam, I offer a very warm and special thanks. They handled my long, intense (and possibly politically fraught) manuscript—replete, I am sure, with many failings—with very special care, understanding and patience, and we became friends as we journeyed together with the many rewritings of the book. I am grateful to my young colleague Shruti Iyer for her painstaking, generous and patient support with the detailed referencing for the book, and to Anirban Bhattacharya for his research advice. I am grateful to poets Hafiz Ahmed and Jhilmil Breckenridge for permission to use their poetry for this volume.

They all brought to bear their many strengths to my imperfect text. The responsibility for the flaws that endure remains with me.

PREFACE TO THE INTERNATIONAL EDITION

A Ravaged Democracy

A few years into the first term in office of India's Far-Right Prime Minister, Narendra Modi, I wrote *Partitions of the Heart: Unmaking the Idea of India (Penguin India, 2019)*. In your hands now is the international edition of this book.

I describe in *Partitions of the Heart* an India bitterly divided on the basis of religion, one that targets particularly India's Muslim minorities with unrelenting hate speech and violence. I write of millions of partitions that have risen between hearts, nurtured and inflamed by the country's ruling leadership, the media and social media.

This new international edition of the book is being published in 2023, toward the end of Mr Modi's second term in office, and 75 years after India became free. The Indian republic is now profoundly ravaged and enfeebled. Its institutions, its democratic polity, its higher judiciary, its civil service, its independent media, its academia, its spaces for peaceful disagreement with power, its accountability, and above all its collective moral compass, each are eroded and shaky; some have visibly caved in.

※

Before his elevation as India's Prime Minister, Narendra Modi was for a dozen years the Chief Minister of the western Indian state of Gujarat. His term was scarred by a horrific massacre in 2002, mostly targeting the state's Muslim minorities. Prior to this, for all his adult life he was a *pracharak* (literally one who spreads the ideology) of the *Rashtriya Swayamsevak Sangh* or the RSS. The RSS is a mammoth countrywide Hindu supremacist volunteer paramilitary organisation – estimated to be the world's largest 'civil society' – drawing inspiration from European fascist movements.

The RSS is the lodestar of Modi's government. Since he took the reins of leadership of both Gujarat in 2002 and, in 2014, the Indian nation, Modi never distanced himself from the RSS. On the contrary, various ministers of his cabinet were directed by Modi to subject themselves to the evaluation of their performance by the RSS. Persons ideologically committed to the RSS are systematically installed in every major public institution. There can be little dispute that the RSS defines Modi's fundamental ideology and world-view. I quote from the RSS website, that its 'supreme goal is to bring to life the all-round glory and greatness of our Hindu Rashtra' (Nation). It states that 'Hindus have a "View of Life" and a "Way of Life",' and that Christians and Muslims who live in India must accept the Hindu world-view.

It was amid rivers of blood that India won freedom in 1947 from two centuries of British colonial rule. Freedom came with the violent partitioning of the country into two countries – Muslim Pakistan and multi-religious Hindu-majority India. A frenzy of blood-letting swept this ancient land, as a million Hindus, Sikhs and Muslims slaughtered each other.

India chose at that time that it would not be a country of its majority Hindu population. Instead, it would be a country that would assure equal freedom and rights as equal citizens to people of every religious identity, including its Muslim citizens. This was an idea that the RSS bitterly opposed, and was never reconciled with. The RSS believes in India as a Hindu nation, in which particularly Muslims and Christians would be second class citizens, with lesser rights, lesser belonging.

❀

Risen from the stables of the RSS, Modi's right-wing BJP (Bhartiya Janata Party) expensive shock-and-awe election campaigns made abundantly clear that it had declared war on a segment of India's citizens, its Muslim people. Since India's Constitution assures equal citizenship to all regardless of their faith and caste, this was also a war on the Constitution. It was war against the ethos of India's freedom struggle and against what is finest in India's civiliza-tional legacy: its pluralism, its accommodation of diversity.

The national elections of 2014 and 2019 were crafted by the BJP first to render the 200 million-strong Indian Muslim citizens politically irrelevant. They accomplished this seemingly impossible political feat by constructing as the common enemy India's Muslims; and by welding disadvantaged Hindu castes with privileged castes and in India's North-East even with Christians – against this 'enemy' within. These, and various state elections that came in between the elections to the federal government, saw the unprecedented political invisibilisation of the Muslim, with even opposi-tion parties reluctant to raise issues of concern to Muslims or field Muslim candidates. By 2023, the BJP wore as badge of honour that it had not a single Muslim member in either the lower or higher houses of Parliament, or any of the state assemblies.

❈

Accomplishing their political marginalisation is not the only signs of a tacit war of the Indian ruling party and ruling establishment against India's Muslims. It has penetrated deep into social relations, law, policy and the practice of the state. In these nine years, Muthe ruling establishment taught Muslims in India live with hate speech, prejudice, discrimination, and the fear that they can now be lynched at any place and any time with impunity.

There has never been a more dangerous time to be the member of a minority in India, most of all Muslim. One bellwether of this is the uninhibited and frequent resort to toxic criminal hate speech that taunts and stigmatises India's Muslims by leaders of the ruling party, and even the union government. The government refuses to rein in these voices, let alone punish these; on the contrary, the worst offenders are conspicuously rewarded with influential party or even government positions.

The speeches of Prime Minister Modi, especially in election time, are rife with dog whistles and anti-Muslim innuendo. He taunts his political adversary Rahul Gandhi in 2019 for fighting elections in a seat in which 'the minority is the majority', insinuating that this is somehow an insult both to Hindus and the nation. Since Hindus are 48 percent of the population of this constituency, Rahul Gandhi could win only by asking for votes also from Muslim and Christian residents. In his worldview, how is this illegitimate – unless we believe that Muslims are lesser citizens than Hindus?

The battle lines of the war by hate speech are drawn even more unambiguously by Modi's closest lieutenant union Home Minister Amit Shah. Shah describes India's Muslims in border states as infiltrators and 'termites.' He thunders: 'They are eating the grain that should go to the poor, they are taking our jobs.' This language is even more belligerent and crass in the speeches of the saffron-clad Chief Minister Adityanath, who rose to political power by founding a Hindu youth militia. He pits 'our' Bajrang Bali (a much-loved Hindu god) against 'their' Ali.

Social media has become colonized by anti-Muslim bigotry and hatred. Trolls are systematically organized by the BJP and its notorious 'IT Cell', with the Prime Minister himself following several toxic purveyors of hate and bigotry online. This hate has penetrated and poisoned family and friends, WhatsApp groups, living rooms and workplaces.

☀

Lynching or mass killing of mainly Muslim or Dalit men with frightening echoes of lynching of African Americans from the late 19th century in the United States has grown under Modi's watch into a national epidemic. Crowds gather and beat to death mostly Muslim or sometimes Dalit men, charging them with slaughtering cows that are sacred to many Hindus, or of 'love jihad', an extraordinary and incendiary myth that Muslim men are trained to trap hapless Hindu women into marriage romantically. These mass killings are gleefully recorded on video and uploaded – and more recently, live-streamed on Facebook – to be consumed by millions.

Convinced that the politics of hate can only be battled by the politics of love, I made a public call in the autumn of 2017 for a large citizen campaign of atonement and solidarity to resist the surge of hate attacks. A sterling assortment of people responded – students, lawyers, rights and peace activists, filmmakers, writers, trainee priests – and we came together for what we called the *Karwan e Mohabbat* or Caravan of Love. We resolved that we would go to the homes of every family who had lost loved ones to hate violence anywhere in the country. We would assure them that they were not alone, that there were many in the country who shared in their grief and pain; we would seek their forgiveness for what we have become as a country; we would assure them that we would be with them as they heal their shattered lives and their fights for justice; and we would tell their stories.

In more than 30 journeys of the *Karwan e Mohabbat* to families hit by lynching, we have found them isolated and in a situation of congealed fear, unsupported by the state administration, which instead mostly criminalized the victims, and even unsupported by local communities for reasons of either hate or fear.

The sense of siege of the targeted minorities is fed further by the ways that the lynch mobs are not just protected from punishment but are instead valorised as heroes. One union minister garlands the men convicted of lynching when they are released on bail; another wraps in the national flag the body of a victim of lynching who dies in jail; a state minister contributes money to support a man who kills a Muslim man captured on videotape; another man accused of lynching is in the front rows of election rallies addressed by senior political leaders, including those holding constitutional offices.

✻

This hateful war against Muslims manifests itself in many other ways as well. The livelihoods of Muslims are constantly under siege. This began with attacks on the beef trade, but now extends to attacks on Muslim vegetable and meat vendors, restaurant workers and even bangle sellers. Laws enabling governments to detain people who they claim threaten national security have been deployed against those in the beef trade without explaining how this threatens national security.

The names of roads and towns that reflect the country's shared heritage of Hinduism and Islam are being changed, as though to wipe out the history of 1000 years of shared living of people of different faiths in India. History books are being rewritten to advance a communalised anti-Muslim world-view to impressionable children. Even the reasons why Mahatma Gandhi was assassinated are being removed from textbooks.

Muslims are prevented by law or mob intimidation from living in apartments and settlements where Hindus reside. Muslim shrines are being razed, and crowds gather to prevent Muslims from offering Friday prayers in parks and open spaces. The scale of attacks on Christian places of worship, pastors and nuns has also risen sharply, as have gang-rapes and killings of young Dalit girls.

India's criminal justice system has long reflected a sectarian institutional bias. However, this touched new lows in the Modi years. Maya Kodnani, a minister in Modi's Gujarat government, had become, before 2014, the first senior political leader convicted for instigating and leading the most brutal massacre in Gujarat in 2002, and was given a jail sentence of 28 years. But she was given bail soon after Modi assumed power and subsequently acquitted of all charges. The men convicted for a particularly gruesome episode of mass rape of a pregnant Bilkis Bano and the murder of her young child and several members of her family, again during the Gujarat massacre of 2002 under Modi's watch, were awarded premature pardon and were garlanded like heroes after their release. Criminal cases which accused Amit Shah, union home minister, and many senior police officers convicted of extra-judicial killings, were all discharged.

People accused of terror crimes by hard-line Hindu supremacists, in a series of blasts between 2006 and 2008, in Malegoan, the Samjhauta Express train, the Mecca Masjid in Hyderabad and the Ajmer Dargah, have one by one been acquitted, mostly on grounds that the prosecution did not martial the evidence which was available to them. Pragya Thakur, accused (and still not discharged) of being one of the key conspirators of a series of terror attacks targeting Muslims, was hand-picked as the BJP candidate for Parliament in 2019 from Bhopal. She won with a convincing majority.

⁂

As I write, democracy stands more jeopardised than ever in the journey of 75 years of the Indian republic.

India has become a dangerous place for people who dissent with or resist the policies and actions of the ruling establishment. It is routine for anti-terror laws or colonial-era sedition laws to be slammed on people who struggle against the targeting of minorities, protest in places like Kashmir, fight the displacement from forests and lands of indigenous people; or uphold civic rights. Student activists, academics and human rights lawyers, even poets and priests, have been jailed indefinitely and denied bail, charged with fomenting Maoist insurgencies, but given no opportunity to establish their innocence because trials have not begun. Among these, an ageing Jesuit priest with Parkinson's, a hero who had devoted his inspiring life to fight fearlessly and peacefully against the displacement of indigenous people, was jailed, accused of being a Maoist, and died in prison. Sudha Bhardwaj, a rights lawyer of exemplary dedication who lived and worked with the most impov-erished mine workers, was forced to spend three years in prison. A Kashmiri activist, Khurram Parvez was jailed and charged with abetting militants; he is widely loved for the help he extended to thousands of families whose loved ones were disappeared during the decades of militant uprising in Kashmir.

Even reporters are not spared; a journalist Siddique Kappan was jailed for two years and charged with terror crimes; he was arrested when he was on his way to report on the gang-rape of a Dalit girl, charged with links with jihadi organizations, but he still has not been even given a copy of the charge-sheet filed against him.

When confronted with the largest and most sustained peaceful protest currently on the planet, by farmers who fear that new laws will throw them at the mercy of big capital, the state fell back on this same playlist, cheered by its radicalized and privileged supporters.

This ruinous collapse of India's democracy is not sudden. This has come to pass because too many choose not to see or resist the climate of hate and fear systematically built over Mr Modi's stewardship of what would soon be the world's most populous country.

Many Indians turn away unmoved by an alarming rise of lynching and hate attacks targeting mostly Muslims and Dalits with unspeakable cruelty, videotaped by the perpetrators confident that they will not be punished but treated as heroes of the Hindu nation. They are unmoved when a Muslim boy is thrashed for entering a temple because he is thirsty. They do not speak out when a Dalit child is thrashed to death by his teacher for his temerity of drinking water from an earthen pot set aside for his "upper-caste" teacher. They turn away as the regime targets mainly India's Muslims and left-liberal voices that stood in public defence of the rights of minorities. They ignore (or cheer) runaway hate speech by senior members of the ruling party, including cabinet ministers, chief ministers and elected representatives.

A democracy is ultimately secured by multiple assertions to prevent the runaway hubris, callousness, incompetence and corruption of the elected executive. These alternate centres of power include the political opposition, the higher judiciary, the higher civil service, the media, the university, trade unions and other collectives of working people, and peaceful resistance of the people themselves. In the years of the Modi regime, people who felt privileged by the new equations of power – the growing ranks of radicalized Hindus, big capital and the middle classes – condoned, even celebrated the destruction of these other power centres, and fuelled the politics of hate and inequality. They felt newly empowered by the growing executive power concentrated in the office of the Prime Minister and his closest partners like the union Home Minister.

Nazi Germany is an essential reminder that the majority in a democracy can turn majoritarian and ultimately fascistic if institutions are not active in the defence of the rights of minorities. In India, political opposition has been increasingly timid in fighting discrimination and violence against Muslim (and to a lesser extent Christian) minorities. The constitutional framework also places major responsibilities for this on the shoulders of the higher judiciary. But the Indian Supreme Court in recent years has repeatedly disappointed with its tardy and reluctant action on petitions concerning the restrictions of minority rights and equal citizenship. It also did not intervene effectively when approached for providing protection to informal and migrant workers who were thrust overnight by the lockdown during COVID into penury, hunger and joblessness, forced to migrate sometimes hundreds of kilometres by foot to reach a place of safety that they called home. The media, the civil services, academia, and ultimately large sections of the middle classes have also let them down.

☀

When the government introduced changes in India's citizenship law that, for the first time, created a legal hierarchy of rights to citizenship based on religious identity, discriminating against Muslims, students rose in campuses around the country in peaceful protest. "You divide, we multiply", they declared. In even larger numbers, Muslim women in low-income settlements around the country took leadership in the frontlines of these resolute protests, developing their own idiom of fighting hate with an alternate discourse of solidarity and love, holding aloft the national flag, the national anthem and the constitution as the icons of the humanist and inclusive pluralism that they sought to defend.

Yet the protests were crushed by charging young people and seniors who supported the protests with some of the gravest crimes in the statute books, of criminal conspiracy for insurrection, terror, hate and sedition. India watched impassively as many young people were jailed indefinitely for this, and the dagger of similar incarceration still stood over the heads of many senior academics and activists.

☀

There are many days when I think wistfully of Mahatma Gandhi's struggle and dreams for a very different India.

In her memoirs, veteran political leader Anis Kidwai recalls the tumult of religious violence that inflamed India and Pakistan in 1947. Her husband was tragically killed as he fought to save the lives of innocents in the carnage. She rushed to Mahatma Gandhi in Delhi to offer her services to the survivors of the Partition riots. She remembers that Gandhiji was immensely saddened by the fires of hate that burned around the country.

'My life's work is not done,' Gandhi said quietly to her, 'my life's work will be unfinished until a Muslim child is able to walk outside without fear in his land.'

How far we have strayed from the India of Gandhi's imagination.

Into which darkness have we lost our way?

PREFACE TO THE INDIAN EDITION

A Gathering Darkness

It is a darkness that keeps on swelling.
As if blood was spouting from night's every vein...

Faiz Ahmed Faiz[1]

There are moments in history when later generations will ask, what is it that you did at that time? I believe that we are living through one such moment of history.

India as we know it is fast being unmade with every passing day. In this bewilderingly changing land, hatred and bigotry risk becoming the new normal. Hate-mongering led powerfully and charismatically from the top – a kind of 'command bigotry' – creates an enabling environment for people to freely and publicly articulate their bigotry and act out their hate. In India today, Muslim and Christian people are at risk of being reduced to second class citizens. Everywhere – on the streets, in workplaces, in living rooms, in neighbourhoods, in television studios and on the internet – this permissive environment for hate speech and mob violence labels and targets Muslims, but also Dalits, Adivasis, Christians, women, people of colour, ethnic minorities from India's north-east, and liberals. A fearsome climate of everyday, mostly unspoken, dread has mounted, by the reckless stoking of embers of recurrent, divisive and considered provocative hate-speech, threats, incitement and assaults. These together seek to coerce, by intimidation, a single way of living on all Indians – a homogenised faith system and set of cultural practices, with violent prohibitions on what you can eat, what you can wear, what work you can do, who you can love and what you can think.

If this pattern of routinizing systematic hate violence is not effectively resisted, the danger is that it will spiral downwards into further and further cycles of grim and deepening strife, which will continue to target innocents

---

1 In "Poems by Faiz" (1971), translated by VG Kiernan, London: George Allen and Unwin, p 105.

and ultimately tear us apart as a people, destroying the idea of a humane, pluralist, inclusive India – an idea always imperfectly realized, but one that endures as an iridiscent collective aspiration. India already has an ancient and troubled history of socially legitimised inequality and violence against savagely oppressed castes and women, and a more recent history of horrific blood-letting in the name of religion. But it also has an iridescent tradition of pluralism, and respect and protections for diverse religious faiths that go back to the times of King Ashoka in 270 BC, and sustain – after centuries of brutal violence against Buddhists, wiping them out from the land of their birth – to include Emperor Akbar in 1556 AD and Mahatma Gandhi during India's anti-colonial freedom struggle. These endure: Jawaharlal Nehru, India's first prime minister, wrote of India as an 'ancient palimpsest on which layer upon layer of thought and reverie had been inscribed, and yet no succeeding layer had completely hidden or erased what had been written previously'.[2]

We tried to thrust behind us our history of cruelty and segregation against browbeaten, subjugated, humilated castes and women, and claim instead that part of our civilizational history that was comfortable in diversity and tolerant, as we came together and forged a compact of egalitarian unity as a pluralist, humane and inclusive democratic nation. The promise embedded in the constitution that we the people gave to ourselves, was that this nation would belong equally to all people who are born into or choose it, regardless of their faith, caste, gender and class. This equitable, democratic and humane political order would protect all people equally without discrimination, and would ensure fair and just life-chances to all people born here and those who choose to live here.

Despite frequent failures, setbacks and betrayals, there were still significant efforts – official, social, political – over seven decades of independence to live up to those promises. Successive governments have compromised cynically with secular and egalitarian principles over and over again, and thereby failed both their constitutional mandate and the people of India. But through all of this, the constitutional core of secular and pluralist democracy has still held together. These were continuously eroded battered and over past decades, but today they appear more threatened than ever before, because a central organising principle of the RSS which has a strong influence on the country's BJP-led ruling establishment is to deny certain religious minorities their right to live in India with dignity as equal citizens.[3]

2 Jawaharlal Nehru, 'The Discovery of India' (1994), Delhi: Oxford University Press, p.59.
3 The BJP is part of the 'Sangh Parivar' – the 'family' of organisations affiliated to the RSS. For more on this link, see Christophe Jaffrelot (eds.) *The Sangh Parivar: A Reader* (2005), New Delhi: Oxford

Philosopher-economist Amartya Sen has voiced his worry that this fear being faced by the minority communities in India cannot be seen as the cultivation of fraternity. Indeed, during the energetic and powerful leadership of Prime Minister Narendra Modi we observe severe contestations of many constitutional principles, but none more than fraternity.[4] The centrality of fraternity in nurturing and sustaining democracy is one of Babasaheb Ambedkar's many profound and precious insights. The word used in the constitution in Hindi is *bandhuta*, which evokes vividly ideas of comradeship and mutual belonging. That regardless of our bewildering, almost boundless multitudes of differences – of faith, caste, class, gender, language, of the ways we dress and eat, love, marry, divorce, celebrate, quarell and mourn – we are in the end one people, because we *belong* to and with each other.

India has survived as a relatively peaceful nation rebuilding itself from colonial ravages and the desperate poverty of millions of its people, because it has forestalled the path of majoritarian dominance, protected minority rights and respected difference and diversity. India's admittedly imperfect adherence to its core constitutional values has enabled India to avoid so far the enormous civil discord and violence that several other countries in the neighbourhood and beyond have experienced since their independence. Countries of the global North, like India, are witnessing the rising tide of hate. In India we see today the growing destruction of the egalitarian and humane principles of secular democracy. India as we know it – both as an idea and as its realization – stands profoundly threatened.

⁂

The people of India are not alone as they grapple with these turbulent times. These are indeed times of global disquiet as gales of hatred and bigotry are sweeping country after country around the world. Country after country is

---

University Press. The RSS is a Hindu nationalist movement, which declares itself to be working "towards the Hindu Century" (see the RSS stated vision and mission, available at http://rss.org//Encyc/2012/10/22/rss-vision-and-mission.html).. Its official website until recently openly declared its commitment to the establishment of Hindu Rashtra or Hindu nation, which stands entirely at odds with the idea of its secular democratic constitution which promises equal rights in all ways to people regardless of their faith. Even the present website contains numerous references to Hindu culture being the life breath of the Indian nation (described as Hindushtan), calling for the organisation of Hindus into a nation, and its paramount goal to raise the nation to the pinnacle of its glory through the pursuit of the Hindu dharma.

4 'Atmosphere of fear in universities threat to Indian democracy: Amartya Sen', *Hindustan Times*, New Delhi, 23 February 2017. Available at http://www.hindustantimes.com/india-news/atmosphere-of-fear-in-universities-threat-to-indian-democracy-amartya-sen/story-HbiRUK3NtJ9BKqYm-9SUtbI.html

throwing up – and people often choosing – leaders who are authoritarian, chauvinistic, hostile to immigrants, minorities and Islam, and indifferent to the poor. Authoritarian dictators are giving way to authoritarian leaders supported by sufficient sections of the electorate to allow such leaders to either assume power or, as in France, come credibly close to getting elected. Citizens of most countries with a majority of Muslim populations also tend to live under authoritarian regimes that are intolerant of political and religious dissent and of minorities. The world's two largest democracies, India and the United States – as indeed large parts of Europe – are increasingly are becoming hostile, threatening places for people with a Muslim name to live in. Being born a Muslim in too many countries around the globe today carries with it often intolerable and utterly unjust burdens of stigma, discrimination, segregation, stereotyping, exclusion and an ever-lurking fear of violence.

There is a well-known story about a frog, which when thrown into boiling water, reacts immediately by jumping out. By contrast, if the frog is placed into lukewarm water which is slowly heated, it does not react or resist even as the water gradually boils, and the frog ultimately dies. Zoologists today contest the science of this experiment, but as metaphor it vividly illustrates to me the difference between what is unfolding against Muslim minorities in the United States and India. The frog in this metaphor is of course the democratic rights to equality and freedom of minorities in both countries.

President Trump with his brash inexperience threw the frog into boiling water. Within days of his assuming office, President Trump's ban on the entry of citizens of Muslim majority countries signalled an official ideology legitimised from the top that all people of Muslim faith are suspect and potentially dangerous. The official prejudice and injustice that lay at the core of this ban was clearly apparent to all the world, and the frog also reacted. In India, the process is much more akin to a slow but lethal raising of temperatures, through countrywide cow vigilante attacks, campaigns against religious conversion, majoritarian aggression and communal innuendo in election rhetoric, and the demonising of Muslims as terrorists, sexual predators, serial divorcees and irresponsible breeders, and Christians as devious and well-heeled evangelists. Official silence as vigilante mobs tacitly or openly supported by the police routinely attack and lynch Muslim and Dalit men across India on charges that they killed cows or sexually harassed Hindu women, and hate speech hectoring and pillorying Muslims by senior political leaders of the ruling party, or when Christian places of worship are vandalized, similarly create a climate of dread for ordinary Indian Muslims, Christians and Dalits.

Observers are unable to notice the deadliness of the assault, and the sombre reality that through all of this the frog is gradually being boiled alive.

The historically dominant groups in both countries are being convinced that they are being short-changed and oppressed in their 'own' country. This creates a peculiar moral inversion when, the rhetoric led from the highest office convinces the dominant groups that it is they who are persecuted, rather than being the oppressors, or at least the relatively privileged. Thus in the United States, white Americans are persuaded that the country belongs to them, but it is being taken away by upstart and violent coloured people, alien immigrants and the untrustworthy Muslim people. In India, the message is that the country belongs to the Hindu majority, but it is being stolen – aided by corrupt 'pseudo-secular' parties – by Muslims and Christians whose loyalty lies outside this land. This moral inversion resonates in both democracies, spurring the rise of a minority persecution complex in the dominant majority.

❂

After Donald Trump's emphatic and stunning electoral success to the office of the President of the United States of America in the winter of 2016, I wrote this mail to many American friends: 'Like many around the world, I am in mourning, just as I was two and a half years back in India. I see this as the triumph once again of prejudice and hatred: this has become the current powerful public common sense globally. Love and goodwill will prevail one day. Of this I am sure. But what will happen until then?'

I received many responses. One friend wrote, 'yes we are devastated here and there are so many tears. Protests are building up daily in major cities. It is a waking nightmare'. And another, in reflective anguish, 'I am still in a bit of shock, uncertain as to what this means – what it says about the American character, what impact this will have on 'out groups' in America and the rest of the world. I truly did not think this was possible. We have essentially elevated the basest characteristics of human nature to the highest office in the land. We have vindicated vengeance, hatred and exclusion – not only that, all of those things are part of Donald Trump's mandate to govern, since he did not hide who he was. I feel physically sick at the thought of the next four years.'

Some friends wrote in rage, 'A fascist bully is going to the White House. We are also so angry at the Clinton machine for its arrogance and its utter failure to address many of the issues that Trump cynically exploited.' Another observed, 'Condolences are indeed in order around the world – Trump is a planet killer and those on the flood plains in Bangladesh will suffer more than those of us in the United States in the long run.' And yet another, 'I understand your sentiments. But, to be frank, I am not in mourning. This country had it coming; Americans got the president they deserved…'

And finally, hopeful and sombre at the same time, 'As you've said, love and good *will* prevail. We have no choice but to get stronger, become more intuitive and understanding, and let that lead our action. And to never, ever take anything for granted – the worst we can imagine can happen, and we have to prepare for it and fight through it. In India and the US, those dark days have unfortunately arrived. Now, more than ever, is the time to be alert and invigorated – we have many, many difficult days ahead of us.'

The mood of these exchanges took me back to two and a half years earlier, when the results of the 2014 midsummer Indian elections confounded liberals and minorities in India with a very similar feeling, of being shocked and distraught. Of disbelief, even mourning, identical to what large segments of the liberal American populace were in the throes of in the fall in 2016. Many friends called me then to say that they did not believe that a day could come when India's electorate would vote in a divisive majoritarian government of the kind that Narendra Modi won the mandate for. For minorities in both countries – of religion, caste, gender, ethnicity, race and sexuality – there was a mood of dread and the hurt of intense betrayal: the stunning popular vote, they believed, laid bare what the majority of caste-Hindu Indians and white Americans respectively felt about us all along, and we never suspected that they held in their hearts so much hate. We felt up to now that we belonged. But the masks are off, faith is shattered, and we realize that in this country that we love, we will always be a minority.

In his early years in the country's highest office, Prime Minister Modi distanced himself somewhat from his own surcharged communal oratory of his career as Chief Minister of Gujarat, by resort to a rhetoric of relative moderation, especially when speaking on foreign soil. His party president, ministers and legislators did not seem to don masks of restraint in their continued communal and often openly hate public provocations.[5] This divi-

5 See "BJP chief Amit Shah chargesheeted over alleged hate speech in UP", Firstpost, 11 September 2014. Available at http://www.firstpost.com/india/bjp-chief-amit-shah-chargesheeted-over-alleged-hate-speech-in-up-1706105.html. Also see speeches pointed to here, "Minorities panel tells Rajnath: Act against hate speech", *The Indian Express*, 20 September 2014. Available at http://indianexpress.com/

sion of labour was useful for those who wished to explain away their support for Modi as being for his business-friendly economic policies and not his communal agenda, which they claimed was being pursued by his aides against his will.[6]

But even the thin and unconvincing masks of moderation were set aside, with Modi's appointment in the summer of 2017, after the BJP was elected with a massive mandate to the state assembly, of saffron-clad Yogi Adityanath who had openly revelled in hate-speech and communal incitement against Muslims as the Chief Minister of India's most populous state Uttar Pradesh.[7] Adityanath is the creator of a private Hindu force (which has not been disbanded even after he assumed power)[8] in a state which, if independent, would be the fourth largest country in the world. This signalled even more unambiguously, in the words of *The Guardian*, that 'in India minorities exist mainly on the goodwill of the majority. Step out of line and there will be blood.'[9] And blood is flowing.

The differences between the two men chosen to lead their countries by voters (it did not matter in the end that the electoral majorities in both countries were in fact numerical minorities) were obvious. One was a billionaire, with a flamboyant life-style, the other from much more humble origins. In personal life, one had moved from marriage to marriage, the other had never lived with the only woman he married. One had no experience in governance, the other had led a major province of India for a dozen years. One also had no stable long-term ideological moorings in any social or political organisation, whereas the other has remained rooted deeply from his early boyhood for all his adult life in the Hindu supremacist Rashtriya Swayamsewak Sangh, the RSS, an organisation avowedly devoted to the establishment of a Hindu nation, entirely at odds with India's secular constitution. Trump was endorsed by the white supremacist Ku Klux Klan, and displayed his sympathies for it

article/india/india-others/minorities-panel-tells-rajnath-act-against-hate-speech/

6 See "Congress+SP+BSP=KASAB, says Amit Shah", *The Hindu*, 22 February 2017 Available at http://www.thehindu.com/elections/uttar-pradesh-2017/congressspbspkasab-says-amit-shah/article17347625.ece

7 See a compendium of these statements at Meghnad Bose, "New UP CM Yogi Adityanath's Tryst With Free (Hate?) Speech", *The Quint*, 19 March 2017. Available at https://www.thequint.com/news/india/new-up-cm-yogi-adityanath-most-controversial-quotes-hate-speech-or-free-speech

8 This is the Hindu Yuva Vahini. For more, see Abhimanyu Chandra, "What the Hindu Yuva Vahini's Constitution Tells Us About Yogi Adityanath's Regime in Uttar Pradesh", *The Caravan*, 27 March 2017. Available at http://www.caravanmagazine.in/vantage/hindu-yuva-vahinis-constitution-tells-us-yogi-adityanaths-regime-uttar-pradesh

9 'The Guardian view on a key poll: victory for anti-Muslim bigotry', *The Guardian*. 19 March 2017. Available at https://www.theguardian.com/commentisfree/2017/mar/19/the-guardian-view-on-a-key-poll-victory-for-anti-muslim-bigotry

after the violent Charlotteville stand-off between white supremacists and liberals during the summer of 2017, but was not a member of it. And most of all there were striking contrasts in their economic prescriptions for the failure of the economy to create jobs. One sought to reverse globalisation, the other to deepen it.

But there were overwhelming – and sobering – similarities between these two men who fought vigorously and won spectacular elections to the highest offices in the world's two largest democracies, which overshadow the obvious differences between them. Most of all, both ran vigorous and expensive 'shock and awe' electoral campaigns that mirrored and amplified popular majoritarian bigotry and chauvinism. They cynically reflected, reproduced, widely broadcast and above all legitimised the most dishonourable sentiments of prejudice and hatred. Trump's public bigotry, worn as a badge of hyper-masculine distinction, closely mirrored Modi's history of shrill and open anti-minority stances and his claim of being the only leader with a 56-inch chest.[10] These were particularly in evidence in his public addresses in his series of electoral bids to the office of Chief Minister of Gujarat after the 2002 communal carnage that targeted Muslim women and children with great cruelty, where instead of ever expressing remorse or regret, he boasted and also taunted the Muslims of his state. Modi was more restrained in his electoral speeches in 2014 as he fought his way to the country's leadership, although his speeches were still peppered with snide references to the 'pink revolution' of alleged surge in beef exports,[11] or threats to Bangladeshi immigrants in Assam that were soon followed by a brutal slaughter of Bengali Muslim women and children there.[12] These were all signals of issues of majoritarian muscle-flexing that were to rise frighteningly during his tenure (mob attacks on minorities and Dalits related to cow protection, and a dangerous convergence of anti-Muslim sentiment and chauvinistic nationalism in Assam). But his close allies like his former Home Minister, and now national party president of the BJP, Amit Shah and many others were much more open in their anti-minority rhetoric, and both their political mobilisation and public discourse

10 See Srivastava and Banol, "Will take a 56-inch chest to turn UP into Gujarat, Modi to Mulayam", *The Times of India*, 24 January 2014. Available at https://timesofindia.indiatimes.com/india/Will-take-a-56-inch-chest-to-turn-UP-into-Gujarat-Modi-to-Mulayam/articleshow/29269342.cms

11 K. Balchand, "Modi fears a 'pink revolution'", *The Hindu*, 3 April 2014. Available at http://www.thehindu.com/news/national/other-states/modi-fears-a-pink-revolution/article5864109.ece

12 See Krishn Kaushik, "The Spectre", *The Caravan*, 1 April 2016. Available at http://www.caravanmagazine.in/reportage/the-spectre-assam-elections-immigrants-fear

overtly and emphatically preyed on prejudice and hatred.[13] And the party he led, the BJP, pointedly and conspicuously did not field a single Muslim in any constituency although they constitute about 15 percent of the population, the third largest Muslim population in any country in the world after Indonesia and Pakistan. Mr Modi during his campaign donned the headgear of every community he addressed, but equally conspicuously refused only to wear a Muslim skull-cap. The message to the Muslim minority was that for us, you are politically insignificant. We can come to power without you, and therefore you don't matter to us.

Both populist leaders rose to office appealing to the basest human instincts of suspicion, distrust, fear and hate of the artificially constructed 'other'- fellow countrymen and women belonging to minorities (variously in the two countries religious, racial, ethnic, and sexual). They did this by portraying them as dangerous, parasitical, the sinister enemy within. The two politicians positioned themselves as the only alpha-male men in public life, and it was only they who had the courage to name, shame and fight these unpatriotic, anti-national and dangerous threats, in contrast to weak mendacious bleeding-heart liberals and secularists in other parties. Both cast themselves as warriors who had stormed the citadels of the liberal establishment of privilege. It helped that for both, their centrist political opponents – the Congress Party in one case and Hillary Clinton in the other – were widely seen as part of the entrenched establishment of power, and carried less credibility in their authenticity and consistency of their liberal and pro-poor credentials. But the campaigns of both Modi and Trump did not give voice to the underdog; instead they actually fed on the resentment of the relatively privileged who railed against minorities pulling themselves out of their historical disadvantage and competing with them for jobs and power. The more outrageous the pronouncements seemed to shocked liberal opinion, this only consolidated their support-base among this multitude of threatened privilege, stoking further their disaffection and loathing with each strike.

Through this, they legitimised the strange moral inversion that I spoke of earlier, in which the relatively privileged majority – in one case white Americans, and in the other upper-caste Hindus – were portrayed not as the persecutors but the persecuted. This was *their* country, yet they were being treated as second-class citizens within it. The minorities and the poor were recreated in this triumphing discourse not as the dispossessed, the persecuted, but as the persecutors, stealing away the jobs and the political and economic dominance of the legitimate citizens, and parasitical on their hard-earned tax money and their country. They thus posited a bogus hierarchy of citizenship. The country belonged to them, these denizens of threatened privilege, and the freeloading interlopers were cunningly taking over their country from them. At last now the disaffected majority had found leaders who were 'men' enough to call a spade and spade, and restore their country to those to who it actually belonged.

A new counterfeit hyper-nationalism emerged out of this freshly minted political hegemony of the privileged but resentful majority, in which both assertions of liberal inclusiveness and dissent were demonised as unpatriotic. Modi's slogan 'India First' closely foreshadowed Trump's 'Making America Great Again', the innuendo being that for their political and ideological opponents, their country did not come first, and instead they were enfeebling their nations by their faux liberalism and by pandering to minorities. Trolls and abuse were heaped on all those who questioned these leaders who promised to return the nation to the hands of those to who it really belongs.

The two leaders have also lowered precipitously – but I fervently hope not permanently – the civility and decency of public discourse at the country's highest levels. Suddenly civility and elementary courtesy became both passé and signs of political weakness. Instead we find that political opponents and dissenters are treated with an unrelenting barrage of abuse, invective and innuendo. What is more, this often coarse political hectoring is mounted as high public entertainment, as towering oratory, all made-for-television and the echo-chambers of the social media colonised substantially by the extreme right. The relatively civil opponent is depicted as ineffectual, weak, and sometimes in India actually comical. Technology facilitates this spectacle as political circus, a daily reality show, with unceasing pounding assaults of 'viral' trolls and (in India during the 2014 elections) Modi's ubiquitous holograms.

Their successful election in both countries laid bare the frightening face of two profoundly fractured, divided nations. For the first time, the electoral victories were not seen by their supporters simply as the triumphs of a political leader or party, but the conquest of and by their supporters themselves, electrified with an unprecedented sense of triumphalism. Mirroring this, their distraught opponents saw the electoral outcomes not as the defeat of their chosen political candidate or formation, but as their own personal defeat. The triumphalist victors in India were big industry, the middle-classes, the aspirational middle class and bigoted Hindu nationalists. In the United States, these were resentful white Americans, men as well as women, of the middle and working classes, but not the very poor. The distressed losers in both countries were strikingly similar: secular and liberal Indians and Americans, minorities of many kinds, and the poor. These are both leaders who did nothing – and could be expected to do nothing in the future – to bridge or heal the dangerous and painful divides in their nations. Instead they thrive precisely on these fractures. Without these hostile schisms, they have no reason to be. They work to widen and consolidate these gulfs further, making these increasingly irreconcilable, and bridge-building and healing in the future progressively difficult. They bask in the adoration of their angry and triumphalist supporters as much as in the dread and agitation of their opponents.

Each promised to fix the economy by creating millions of jobs. And both are doomed to miscarry. But what is interesting that they promised to accomplish this by diametrically opposed medicine prescriptions. Modi vowed and convinced young aspirational voters that he would lead them into the glittering citadels of the middle classes. He would do this by hastening further globalisation and structural adjustment with even more stern and undiluted market fundamentalism than his predecessors, and this would create jobs for the millions joining the workforce every month who are dreaming of a better life in a globalised world. But Donald Trump's remedy is just the reverse, of turning back globalisation with much greater protectionism. Jobs have been 'Bangalored', or outsourced to emerging economies with masses of coloured young people lining up to steal the jobs that are legitimately those of (white) Americans. However, both are bound to fail their voters profoundly. Sky-high economic growth in India has been accompanied by nearly jobless growth and the actual decline of decent work opportunities.[14] Both leaders are actually tapping into a mounting discontent created and fuelled by the unacknowledged global crisis in neo-liberalism, namely its failure to create the massive opportunities for decent work that its votaries had promised. And as they both are bound to betray this central pledge of their campaigns, the only recourse they would have to offer young people denied their legitimate dreams is of scapegoating people of greater disadvantage than them as raiders and robbers of their own chances for a better life, and of stoking further the fires of aggressive hyper-nationalism.

14 Shreya Shah, "Three years of Modi govt: Job-creation promise falls short as unemployment rate up", *Hindustan Times*, 23 May 2017. Available at http://www.hindustantimes.com/india-news/three-years-of-modi-govt-job-creation-promise-falls-short-as-unemployment-rate-up/story-NiJ519k-We56MjNCfMtgEeO.html. See also Kompier et al. "Labour Markets: Exclusion from 'Decent Work" in *India Exclusion Report 2013-14*, Bangalore: Books for Change.

Within a week of Modi taking office, a visibly Muslim computer engineer Mohsin Sadiq Shaikh was lynched on the streets of the city Pune.[15] This was only the first publicly documented instance of hate crimes that continue to scar his tenure in office. There was a similar surge in hate crimes in the US, with 1,094 bias-related incidents recorded in the month following Trump's election, targeting immigrants, people of colour, Muslims, LGBTs, Jewish people and women.[16] A high-school student felt emboldened to write to a Muslim teacher advising her to hang herself with her hijab, saying it is not allowed any more, and signing off as America.[17] Graffiti came up on walls screaming 'Black Lives Don't Matter'.[18] The license to engage in racist, Islamophobic and homophobic discrimination and violence persists through Donald Trump's tenure. The genie of hate was released from the bottle by Trump and Modi during their political campaigns, and it cannot be pushed back.[19] It has only been further fanned and nurtured with each passing month.

Alexis Okeowo, a staffer with *The New Yorker*, wrote of calling her parents, coloured people in Montgomery, Alabama, soon after Trump won his seat to his country's highest office, to make sure they were being more cautious than usual about where they pumped their gas, where they bought their groceries, whom they decided to talk to. Her Nigerian-born father immigrated to Alabama as a college student, in the 1970s. 'It wasn't unusual to see K.K.K. rallies on the street

---

15 'Muslim techie beaten to death in Pune, 7 men of Hindu outfit held', *The Indian Express*. 4 June 2014. Available at http://indianexpress.com/article/india/politics/muslim-techie-beaten-to-death-in-pune-7-men-of-hindu-outfit-held/

16 'Update: 1,094 Bias-Related Incidents in the Month Following the Election', Southern Poverty Law Centre. 16 December 2016. Available at https://www.splcenter.org/hatewatch/2016/12/16/update-1094-bias-related-incidents-month-following-election

17 'Muslim teacher receives anonymous note about her headscarf: 'Hang yourself with it'', *The Independent*, 13 November 2016. Available at http://www.independent.co.uk/news/world/americas/a-muslim-teacher-receives-anonymous-note-about-her-headscarf-hang-yourself-with-it-a7414656.html

18 Durham community cleans up 'Black Lives Don't Matter' graffiti', WNCN, 18 November 2016. Available at http://wncn.com/2016/11/10/durham-officials-to-clean-up-black-lives-dont-matter-graffiti-downtown/

19 'For hate speeches made while Modi was Chief Minister of Gujarat, see Annexure 10, Hate Speech, to Volume I of the Concerned Citizens Tribunal. Available here: http://www.outlookindia.com/website/story/hate-speech/218024. There are also multiple inflammatory speeches that he made while campaigning in the 2014 election. For statements made on beef, see Shoaib Daniyal, "How Narendra Modi helped spread anti-beef hysteria in India", *Quartz India*, 7 October 2015. Available at https://qz.com/518975/how-narendra-modi-helped-spread-anti-beef-hysteria-in-india/. Modi also made a statement saying that the Assam government was killing rhinos to make way for Bangladeshi immigrants (see "Assam government killing rhinos to make way for Bangladeshi immigrants: Narendra Modi", NDTV, 1 April 2014, available at https://www.ndtv.com/elections-news/assam-government-killing-rhinos-to-make-way-for-bangladeshi-immigrants-narendra-modi-555757). Also see "If a kabristan can be constructed, a shamshaan too should be built: PM Modi", *Hindustan Times*, 20 February 2017. Available at https://www.hindustantimes.com/assembly-elections/if-a-kabristan-can-be-constructed-so-should-a-shamshaan-pm-modi/story-obPfbdpUwPZm98wBKdZmTN.html.

then, he told me, but he tried to block out the threat as best he could. We will get through these next four years, he went on, just as black people got through more difficult circumstances. He wasn't wrong: the harassment of recent days is familiar to many African-Americans. The tragedy lies in the fact that many of us thought we had left the prospect of mass terror behind.'[20] Okeowo's words so painfully echo to me the many ways that Muslim, Christian and Dalit people are bracing themselves to learn across the land of their birth to live as second-class citizens in Modi's India. The American people gear up to endure a long bleak winter of hate, in the way the Indian people are living through a blistering dusty long summer of hate.

※

It is above all to map this systematic erosion of equal citizenship of Muslim and Christian and many Dalit people first in Modi's Gujarat and now in Modi's India that I feel compelled to write this chronicle. That this erosion and subversion of India's constitutional assurances was accomplished without adequate resistance by India's political and state institutions, courts and the media, and by ordinary Indians, causes me intense disquiet and grief.

In all of this, I see around us massive failures of solidarity. I do recognise that although this battle within has reached a decisive phase, it has long been in the making, with the so-called 'secular' parties carrying a great part of the responsibility for where the Indian people find themselves today. For these political parties, secular and egalitarian democracy has too long been an instrument of opportunism, electoral calculation and consolidation, rather than a core ethical principle.

I worry about the powerful rise in recent years of a polarising political leadership in India – similarly to those claiming power in so many countries, a leadership that does not heal or bridge divides but instead legitimises hatred and bigotry. However through all of this, I worry even more that the voices of public protest across India have been far too muted and few. In recent years of mounting organised hate-mongering against Muslims and Christains, I worry that although the majority did not join these campaigns to scapegoat, stigmatise and target their neighbours, we also did too little to resist these. We allowed cow vigilantes – and in Haryana and Uttar Pradesh uniformed policepersons –

---

20 Alexis Okeowo, 'Hate on The Rise After Trump's Election', *The New Yorker*, 17 November 2016. Available at http://www.newyorker.com/news/news-desk/hate-on-the-rise-after-trumps-election

to attack Muslim and Dalit people for rumours that they eat cow meat.[21] Fifty thousand Muslims are expelled from their villages in Muzaffarnagar by hate violence, and the only opposition we hear is from Hindus protesting that their relocation has worsened crime because Muslims spell trouble wherever they go.[22] There are reports from many parts of the country that many Muslims are too frightened to perform their annual ritual animal sacrifice on Bakra-Eid because they fear that they will be attacked for cow slaughter.[23] Muslim young men continue to be detained for years on false charges of terror violence and none can return to them the years stolen from their lives by bigotry, but we believe that the state is justified in suspecting Muslim men of terror crimes even if they are innocent.[24] Eight Muslim youth jailed in a high-security jail in Bhopal were killed at close-range in the winter of 2016 after claims that they crafted keys from toothbrushes and a knife from a spoon, yet there were no protests.[25] In the autumn of 2016, the country's security forces responded to stone throwing by students in mass protests in Kashmir with pellet guns that blinded and maimed hundreds of teenagers.[26] This muscular militarism against youthful civilian protest was applauded as patriotism.

Through this, what lessons have we learnt in India? It is imperative that people do not allow hatred and bigotry to get routinized into a new 'normal' that would have been morally and politically unacceptable publicly in the past. Solidarity with and between religious, ethnic and sexual minorities, oppressed castes and tribal peoples, women, poor and dispossessed people, immigrants and working class people, and people of colour, must be forged and strengthened. Public institutions must be defended against assaults. Public vigilance must never slacken. Never stop resisting wrong. Public dissent should be seen as the highest public duty that cannot be suppressed, even if it is stigmatised

21 'India: 'Cow Protection' Spurs Vigilante Violence', Human Rights Watch, 27 April 2017. Available at https://www.hrw.org/news/2017/04/27/india-cow-protection-spurs-vigilante-violence

22 Harsh Mander, 'Muzaffarnagar, three years later', *The Indian Express,* 7 September 2016. Available at http://indianexpress.com/article/opinion/columns/muzaffarnagar-riots-probe-muslims-in-india-shamli-communal-violence-3017199/

23 Shehzad Poonawalla, 'How the BJP and Khattar government stole my Eid', *Daily O,* 12 September 2016. Available at http://www.dailyo.in/politics/eid-ul-adha-biryani-policing-cow-vigilantism-khattar-gau-raksha-mewat/story/1/12880.html

24 See Harsh Mander, "Terror, Innocence, and the Wages of Official Prejudice", *Economic and Political Weekly*, Vol 52, No 16, 22 April 2017.

25 'SIMI activists' jailbreak: Families of killed men to move HC seeking CBI probe', *The Indian Express,* 2 November 2016. Available at http://indianexpress.com/article/india/india-news-india/simi-activists-jailbreak-families-of-killed-men-to-move-hc-seeking-cbi-probe-3731958/

26 'An Epidemic of 'Dead Eyes' in Kashmir as India Uses Pellet Guns on Protesters', *The New York Times,* 28 August 2016. Available at https://www.nytimes.com/2016/08/29/world/asia/pellet-guns-used-in-kashmir-protests-cause-dead-eyes-epidemic.html

as unpatriotic, attacked and persecuted. We should declare and forge proudly and determinedly *our* ways of loving our country, our people and indeed all peoples of all countries. And in these times of normalising hate, a new imagination must be nurtured, of people of difference within and across borders bound together by love and respect.

❈

'Beware India!' warns my friend Apoorvanand, who teaches Hindi in Delhi University. 'You are being led into a civil war. Or, you are already in it.' He speaks of the closure of slaughterhouses; the gutting of small meat shops; a hotel owned by a Muslim in Jaipur being surrounded and attacked in daylight on rumours of it selling beef, its employees beaten up by a mob, the hotel evacuated, sealed, the owner hounded, the police joining the marauders; youth being arrested for Facebook posts against the new Chief Minister in UP; thousands of Muslims in Assam being evicted from their habitats in the name of preservation of forest lands; a 16-year-old Muslim boy detained in a police station in Uttarakhand on the charge of abducting a Hindu girl, sent dead to his parents by the police; a Muslim student disappearing from a university and all that the media can do after five months is to discover that he had affinity for terrorists. The Muslim, he says, 'is feeling a prisoner of this nation called India... The feeling of the fear of living under this "legitimate suspicion" is distinctly Muslim.'

He then insists, '... This is a war on the Muslims of India. It needs to be said in these very words. And the spread is wide... Let us put it on record that India was pushed into this war by its ruling parties, the governments that they created and fostered disaffection towards a large section of society and stoked violence against them. Let it be recorded that the finest minds of the educated youth who form our civil services and the police collaborated in this with the murderers. Let it be said that we went about our lives unperturbed when our neighbours were doubling with pain and not allowed to scream even for it would sound a sectarian cry. It would be a long war and we would come out of it one day, with stories of the banality of violence and our shame of participating in it and mutilated bodies. Victims are being blamed for forging victimhood; asked to free themselves of this imaginary cage. This duplicity would be noted in some distant time'.[27]

---

27 Apoorvanand, 'The anti-Muslim pitch', *The Tribune*, 27 March 2017. Available at http://www.tribu-neindia.com/news/comment/the-anti-muslim-pitch/382700.html

In Uttar Pradesh villages posters came up after the BJP electoral triumph
in 2017 giving notice to Muslim residents to leave.[28] I waited in vain for the
day when Hindu residents of these villages would reassure their Muslim
neighbours that they are both welcome and safe. Where they would fight to
defend the security and livelihoods of tens of thousands of people threatened
by cow politics and contested abattoirs? When would students, teachers,
lawyers, doctors, workers, farmers, actors, journalists, all would join battle
against the toxic politics of baiting and scapegoating minorities?

Our silences can only signal our complicity with the brazen changing
of India into a majoritarian Hindu country. A land where minorities must
submit, else blood will flow.

Is it that we are too frightened to speak out? Or are we just indifferent?
Or is the reality that we actually support the hatred and persecution of other
Indians because of their faith and caste?

✸

Even as both India and the United States grapple with this era of 'command
bigotry' or bigotry nurtured from the top, in the middle of the second decade
of the 21st century, the most striking differences between the two countries
indeed has been the response of ordinary people to the anti-Muslim policies
of their governments.[29] Protestors gathered with welcoming signs at American airports within hours of the Presidential ban on citizens of seven Muslim
majority countries;[30] people visited their Muslim neighbours to reassure them
of their safety and welcome; judges at all levels struck down the Presidential
order; lawyers gathered at airports to offer legal aid;[31] and film actors spoke
eloquently for the rights of people of colour and minority faiths in film award
functions.

'No hate, no fear, refugees are welcome here.' This protest anthem
resounded from demonstrators who gathered outside the White House,
in front of the Statue of Liberty, and in airports across the United States,

---

28 Shehab Khan, 'India: Hindus tell Muslims to leave village immediately', *The Independent,* 16 March
    2017. Available at http://www.independent.co.uk/news/world/asia/india-uttar-pradesh-posters-an-
    ti-muslim-leave-immediately-a7633096.html
29 Portions of this section are excerpted from my *Indian Express* article titled "Unlike America",
    18 February 2017.
30 'Thousands protest against Trump travel ban in cities and airports nationwide', *The Guardian,*
    30 January 2017. Available at https://www.theguardian.com/us-news/2017/jan/29/protest-trump-
    travel-ban-muslims-airports
31 'Appeals court upholds block on Trump's travel ban; administration to appeal to Supreme Court',
    CNN, 26 May 2017. Available at http://edition.cnn.com/2017/05/25/politics/4th-circuit-travel-ban/

hours after President Trump temporarily limited the entry of Muslims from seven Muslim-majority countries on January 27, 2017. His executive order suspended the entry of refugees from any country for at least 120 days and of refugees from Syria indefinitely. It also stipulated that among refugees let into the country, Christians would be prioritized over Muslims. There were an estimated 33 million Muslims living in America who would now be subject to much harder scrutiny and insecurity.

American airports everywhere were rapidly jammed the very next day after the order with protestors gathering in strength in solidarity with Muslim travellers – refugees, spouses, parents, students, and professionals – stuck inside. CNN reported that airport officials accommodated protestors by closing security checkpoints and diverting traffic. Demonstrators waved banners displaying slogans such as 'No wall, no ban' and 'You are welcome.' One even said, 'We are all Muslims.' Muhamad Moustafa, a Syrian training to be a doctor was distraught when his wife was put on a plane back to Qatar, although she had lived in the US for almost a year and had a J2 visa given to spouses of immigrants. He told CNN that he did not know what he could do to help his wife. 'I was hopeless, but seeing this'- the crowds at Washington DC airport of people holding welcome signs – 'this gives me hope.' In some airports, immigration lawyers established a makeshift legal clinic with volunteer lawyers who gathered with their laptops to help travellers arriving from the banned countries. [32]

Judges across the country stood up against the ban. Federal judges in New York and then Massachusetts and Boston immediately blocked parts of the order. Trump defensively said, 'This is not about religion – this is about terror and keeping our country safe.'[33] Former President Barack Obama responded that he 'fundamentally disagrees with the notion of discriminating against individuals because of their faith or religion.'[34] US District Court Judge James Robart blocked the ban nationwide. Others were to follow. The President unveiled a revised order on March 6. The District Court Judge Hawaii blocked

32 Emanuella Grinberg and Madison Park, '2nd day of protests over Trump's immigration policies', *CNN*, 30 January 2017. Available at http://edition.cnn.com/2017/01/29/politics/us-immigration-protests/
33 Chiara Palazzo, ''This is not about religion – this is about terror and keeping our country safe' – Donald Trump defends executive order and attacks the media', *The Telegraph*, 30 January 2017. Available at http://www.telegraph.co.uk/news/2017/01/30/not-muslim-ban-donald-trump-defends-executive-order-attacks/
34 Dan Merica, 'Obama 'fundamentally disagrees' with Trump's immigration order', *CNN*, 31 January 2017. Available at http://edition.cnn.com/2017/01/30/politics/obama-donald-trump-travel-ban-statement/

this as well countrywide hours before it would have been operational. A frustrated President said the decision was 'an unprecedented judicial overreach.'[35]

There was also a massive outpouring of protests against Trump's ban by Christian and Jewish faith leaders. Stosh Cotler of the Bend the Arc Jewish Action, declared 'As Jews, we know what it's like to be scapegoated and we will not be silent now'.[36] J Street representing another progressive Jewish organisation said that 'The fact that President Trump's order appears designed to specifically limit the entry of Muslims evokes horrible memories' of Jews turned away during World War II. 'Most ultimately perished in the Holocaust. That episode remains a blot on the conscience of the United States. It is a terrible irony that today, the same day on which this order is to be signed, is also International Holocaust Remembrance Day.'[37]

The Catholic Relief Services president said that 'denying entry to people desperate enough to leave their homes, cross oceans in tiny boats, and abandon all their worldly possessions just to find safety will not make our nation safer... We have a moral obligation to 'welcome the stranger'.' A Baptist priest added that bans on Muslim refugees based on religion gives a 'message that there are second-class faiths...A threat to anyone's religious liberty is a threat to everyone's religious liberty.' Rev. Paul Raushenbush proclaimed that the ban echoes 'fears that guided past discrimination against other religious communities such Catholics, and, disastrously, Jews in the years before Nazi Germany'.[38] Reverend Dr. Peter J. M. Henry from Detroit's Grosse Pointe Memorial Church said 'Jesus was an internally displaced person.' He said 'Every person in the Bible has an ancestor that was a refugee.'[39] The Archbishop of York said, 'In Christ, we are called to welcome the stranger especially when in desperate need.' (Sadly, though I searched and searched, I could not find reports of such statements by American Hindu or Sikh faith leaders).

Even former Secretary of State Madeleine Albright, known for her hawkish

35 Steve Almasy and Darran Simon, 'A timeline of President Trump's travel bans', *CNN*, 30 March 2017. Available at http://edition.cnn.com/2017/02/10/us/trump-travel-ban-timeline/
36 Jack Jenkins, 'Faith groups across the country condemn Trump's ban on refugees and immigrants from Muslim countries', *ThinkProgress*, 26 January 2017. Available at https://thinkprogress.org/faith-groups-country-immigrants-muslim-b22798233c90
37 Laura Koran, 'Jewish groups pan Trump for signing refugee ban on Holocaust Remembrance Day', *CNN*, 28 January 2017. Available at http://edition.cnn.com/2017/01/27/politics/trump-refugee-holocaust-remembrance-day/
38 See Jack Jenkins, 'Faith groups across the country condemn Trump's ban on refugees and immigrants from Muslim countries', *ThinkProgress*, 26 January 2017. Available at https://thinkprogress.org/faith-groups-country-immigrants-muslim-b22798233c90
39 Laura Rena Murray, 'How Christians Across America Are Fighting Trump's Refugee Ban', *The Development Set*, 14 March 2017. Available at https://thedevelopmentset.com/what-are-american-churches-doing-to-help-refugees-d2641de62ee6

militarist policies, tweeted: 'America must remain open to people of all faiths and backgrounds.' 'I was raised Catholic', she said in another tweet, 'became Episcopalian & found out later my family was Jewish. I stand ready to register as Muslim in #solidarity.'[40]

One of Hollywood's most respected actors, Meryl Streep, said this in her 2017 Golden Globe award acceptance speech: 'This instinct to humiliate, when it's modelled by someone in the public platform, by someone powerful, it filters down into everybody's life, because it kinda gives permission for other people to do the same thing. Disrespect invites disrespect, violence incites violence. And when the powerful use their position to bully others, we all lose.'[41] Actor Seth Rogen tweeted that 'one of the many reasons I am opposed to the #MuslimBan is because my family immigrated to North America after fleeing wars in Russia. One of the other reasons I oppose the #MuslimBan is that I feel it›s prime effect is persecuting innocent refugees.' CBS›s 'The Big Bang Theory' held a sign reading, 'Refugees welcome'. Henson said while accepting the cast award for 'Hidden Figures' at SAG Awards said, 'We win. Love wins every time.' 'I thought I had walked into a nightmare,' said Dev Patel. 'Of course, the first thought in my head was women and children turning up to these shores with so much hope in their eyes being turned away. I can›t imagine the pain they must be going through and for those families that are being separated, that voice of negativity and divisiveness at times like this. It›s terrifying. What gives me hope is all the people out there, those courageous human beings in the streets, in the airports, trying to spread positivity at least.' Ashton Kutcher said, 'I am a citizen of the world. Everyone in airports belong in my America. You are a part of the fabric of who we are, and we love you, and we welcome you.'[42] Members of the entertainment industry called upon people to donate to the American Civil Liberties Union. The effect was that the ACLU raised a record $24 million to help immigrants who were detained at airports.[43]

40 Eugene Scott, 'Madeleine Albright: Trump's ban 'just flat anti-American'', *CNN*, 31 January 2017. Available at http://edition.cnn.com/2017/01/26/politics/madeleine-albright-muslim-executive-order/
41 Daniel Victor and Giovanni Russonello, 'Meryl Streep's Golden Globes Speech,' *The New York Times*, 8 January 2017. Available at https://www.nytimes.com/2017/01/08/arts/television/meryl-streep-golden-globes-speech.html
42 'Celebrities react to Trump's 'un-American' immigration ban with outrage' in *Business Insider*, 30 January 2017. Available at http://www.businessinsider.in/Celebrities-react-to-Trumps-un-American-immigration-ban-with-outrage/Seth-Rogen/slideshow/56878561.cms
43 Joseph Pimentel and Susan Abram, 'Southern California Muslim, Jewish, Latino leaders blast Trump travel ban', *Los Angeles Daily News*, 31 January 2017. Available at http://www.dailynews.com/government-and-politics/20170130/southern-california-muslim-jewish-latino-leaders-blast-trump-trav-

Reports also came in from mixed neighbourhoods across the United States of Christian and Jewish residents reaching out to their Muslim neighbours with reassuring messages of friendship and acceptance. A retired teacher, stood on a sidewalk with a welcoming message 'No matter where you are from, we're glad you're our neighbour'.[44] Other slogans included: 'If you build a wall, we will raise our children to tear it down'; 'Love not hate makes America great'; and 'We are all immigrants.' Two women held a poster showing the Star of David with a crescent inside it, and the words 'Never again.' One of them affirmed 'Never again for the Holocaust – this means never again for the Jews, never again for any group that's being marginalised.'[45]

The dark foreboding that enveloped me with Donald Trump's election lightened considerably with this luminous spontaneous public display of solidarity and empathy with targeted Muslims by millions of ordinary Americans. A politics of hate – however powerful – can never triumph if people, with individual and collective acts of compassion, defy attempts to divide them with bigotry and fear.

This led me to reflect if we, in India, have adequately resisted the fear and animosity that has been systematically fostered against the Indian Muslim minority in present times. India is home to more Muslims than any other country in the world except Indonesia and Pakistan. Its constitution promised that they would enjoy equal rights in every way, yet they are being pushed by triumphalist majoritarian politics into second-class citizenship. Have Indian people reached out to defend and reassure their Muslim neighbours in ways that Americans have?

The systematic hate propaganda against Muslims, people of colour, Latinos and immigrants in the United States was resisted among white Americans mostly by those who had benefited from a college education. By striking contrast in India, the greatest support of divisive hate ideologies[46] lies with people with the highest levels of education and privilege. I find much greater instinctive willingness for peaceful and respectful co-living between people of difference in India among people who have been denied education and bene-

el-ban

44 Ali Harb, 'Women's March on Washington: Solidarity comforts anxious Americans', *Middle East Eye*, 22 January 2017. http://www.middleeasteye.net/news/womens-march-washington-solidarity-comforts-anxious-americans-1152160639

45 Ibid.

46 See Modi at Fatehpur: If land is given for kabristan, shamshaan must get it too, India Today, 19 February 2017. Available at http://indiatoday.intoday.in/story/narendra-modi-fatehpur-uttar-pradesh-elections/1/886614.html

fits of economic growth. This illuminates worryingly what higher education does to those who benefit from it in India: far from building liberal values or scientific temper, it seems only to nurture a sense of selfish entitlement and prejudice against minorities of various kinds and the poor.

These differences endure even when these privileged and educated Indians migrate to the United States. Newly emigrated Sukhada Tatke observes in an article in *Firstpost* the glaring absence of voices of fellow Indians in street demonstrations and protest marches as well as on social media feeds after Trump's election. She speaks of her California cousin who wondered why she was so distraught. 'Nothing he does is going to affect you, he had said. Is that any consolation? I snapped back.' Later, only after new moves in the president's immigration policy did he slowly begin to speak out against the dangers of a Trump presidency, only because he felt threatened himself by it.[47] Many of us with relatives and friends working and resident in the United States have similar stories to tell.

American protestors against Trump's anti-Muslim policies invoked the words engraved on the Statue of Liberty: 'Give me your tired, your poor, your huddled masses yearning to breathe free.' To turn them away, they declare, is to lose the very soul of our great nation. In India today are we doing enough to defend the soul of *our* great nation?

✲

Legendary police officer Julio Ribeiro (of Christian faith) wrote in great anguish, 'Today, in my 86th year, I feel threatened, not wanted, reduced to a stranger in my own country... I am not an Indian anymore, at least in the eyes of the proponents of the Hindu Rashtra...It is tragic that these extremists have been emboldened beyond permissible limits by an atmosphere of hate and distrust....I was born in this country. So were my ancestors, some 5,000 or more years ago. If my DNA is tested, it will not differ markedly from Bhagwat's (the RSS supremo). It will certainly be the same as the country's defence minister's (Parrikar) as our ancestors arrived in Goa with the sage Parshuram at the same time. Perhaps we share a common ancestor somewhere down the line. It is an accident of history that my forefathers converted and his did not... (I) hope that ordinary Hindu men and women will not be swayed by an

---

47 Sukhada Tatke, 'Donald Trump's devious anti-Muslim immigration policies should serve as a wake-up call for Indians', *Firstpost*, 3 February 2017. Available at http://www.firstpost.com/world/donald-trumps-devious-anti-muslim-immigration-policies-should-serve-as-a-wake-up-call-for-in-dians-3264426.html

ideology that seeks to spread distrust and hate with consequences that must be avoided at all cost'.[48]

In a similar mood of despondence and foreboding, another former civil servant Abdul Khaliq says that 'there is a deep sense of disquiet bordering on despair within the Muslim community. A massive communalisation of society is taking place, no longer subterranean or secretive, but in your face... (T)here are over 57,000 shakhas operating at 36,729 places with a daily attendance of lakhs. In the capital, the war-like khaki trouser drills have become more intense and regular, and havans and elaborate rituals are now being organised even in public parks. Against whom are these intense preparations of martial intent being made? I fear that the masculine demonstrations of power and desh bhakti are obliquely directed at the Muslim, who has always been demonised in shakhas. Soon after the UP elections, posters signed by 'Hindus' appeared in a Bareilly village, ordering Muslims to leave by the end of the year. Is this a portent of things to come? An irresistible, self-aggrandising Hindu majoritarian wave, which is not just dismissive of, but positively hostile to minority concerns is sweeping the land.' He quotes a recent study by the Centre for the Study of Developing Societies (CSDS) which showed that only 13 per cent considered Muslims to be patriotic. 'Is it any wonder then that Muslims are running scared?' he asks. 'There is a volcano seething below the surface. The nation cannot achieve social harmony or development on the basis of a hierarchy of citizenship that condemns 180 million Indians to second-class status.'[49]

Journalist Ajaz Ashraf found across Uttar Pradesh after the 2017 elections that 'Muslims fear the communal cauldron that Uttar Pradesh has become will be kept on the boil. But this is not what worries them. Not because they think the Bharatiya Janata Party in power will change its stripes, but because they fear Muslims will feel so cowered that they will recoil, and live in submission.' 'Our agony arises from being reduced to second-class citizens, of becoming politically irrelevant,' another journalist Asif Burney said to him. 'Look at the (UP election) results,' former Rajya Sabha MP Adeeb cried angrily. 'But for Jatavs, Yadavs, and a segment of Jats, most Hindus voted [for] the Bharatiya Janata Party.' Ashraf reports that his anger soon

48 Julio Ribeiro, 'As a Christian, suddenly I am a stranger in my own country, writes Julio Ribeiro', *The Indian Express*, 17 March 2015. Available at http://indianexpress.com/article/opinion/columns/i-feel-i-am-on-a-hit-list/

49 Abdul Khaliq, 'Anniversary appeal', *The Indian Express*, 27 May 2017. Available at http://indianexpress.com/article/opinion/columns/anniversary-appeal-4675563/

segued into grief and he began to sob, 'I am an old man', he said. 'I don't want to die in a Hindu rashtra.'[50]

In Assam, the persecuted and isolated Bengali-origin Muslim is disparagingly called Miya. A whole body of protest poetry is growing in response, which Bengali-origin Muslims defiantly call Miya poetry. One such poet, Hafiz Ahmad, writes:

Write
Write Down
I am a Miya'
My serial number in the NRC[51] is 200543
I have two children.
Another is coming
Next summer.
Will you hate him,
As you hate me?

Write
I am a Miya
I turn waste, marshy lands
To green paddy fields
To feed you.
I carry bricks
To build your buildings
Drive your car
For your comfort
Clean your drain
To keep you healthy.
I have always been

50 Ajaz Ashraf, 'The fear of Hindu Rashtra: Should Muslims keep away from electoral politics?' in *Scroll*, 14 March 2017. Available at https://scroll.in/article/831693/the-fear-of-hindu-rashtra-should-muslims-keep-away-from-electoral-politics
51 The NRC is the National Register of Citizens – an effort used by the Assamese government to determine who is an Indian citizen and who is not. In 1985, Rajiv Gandhi signed the Assam Accord which held that anyone who entered Assam after March 24, 1971 would be classified as a foreigner. This is part of an effort to disenfranchise electorally undocumented migrants into the state, purportedly from East Bengal (Bangladesh). It remains unclear how many Muslims in Assam are from Assam, West Bengal, or Bangladesh. See Harlarnker, "As Millions Try To Prove Citizenship in Assam, One Man's Story Reveals Perils of Proof", *India Spend*, 28 October 2017. Available at http://www.indiaspend.com/cover-story/as-millions-try-to-prove-citizenship-in-assam-one-mans-story-reveals-perils-of-proof-41869

In your service
And yet
you are dissatisfied!

Write down
I am a Miya...

PROLOGUE

Junaid, My Son[1]

Hafiz Junaid was my son.

I did not know him when he lived. But in his death, in the way he died, I mourn him like a son.

His dreams were unfamiliar to my agnostic world. He wanted to become a scholar and teacher of the Quran, and perhaps one day an imam. For this, from the age of six, he was sent to study in a madrassa in neighbouring Nuh, Haryana. He was a sincere and bright student, who had memorised the Quran, all 80,000 words of the holy text. He was declared a hafiz in recognition of this achievement. Hafiz in Arabic means both one who remembers, but also one who is a custodian of the sacred words of the Quran.

In other ways, Junaid was like any other boy of his age. His friends recall that he was fond of flying kites, playing marbles, and most of cricket. 'He was an all-rounder – best in batting, best in bowling, best in fielding', one of his friends fondly recalls. He wanted to buy a second-hand bike one day. He loved to bathe in the village pond. He did not use swear words, and liked new clothes and perfumes.[2]

He would return to his home only once a year, during the month of Ramzan. The Ramzan of 2017 he proudly recited the entire Quran from memory, to pious gatherings of his own village, over twenty days. He had completed this recitation of the Quran one day before he was to die. In appreciation, the villagers had made small offerings of money to him. His father added his contribution, and with a total sum of fifteen hundred rupees he set out with his brothers to the old city of Delhi to purchase new clothes, prayer mats and some gifts.

1 This chapter is derived from an article I authored for *The Indian Express*, "Junaid, my son", 1 July 2017. Available at http://indianexpress.com/article/opinion/columns/junaid-my-son-4729828/
2 Somya Lakhani, "A boy called Junaid", *The Indian Express*, 2 July 2017. Available at http://indianexpress.com/article/india/faridabad-lynching-train-beef-ban-a-boy-called-junaid-4731198/

He wore jeans, unusual for him, for his shopping adventure to the big city. But he also wore a skull-cap on his head. This was to be his fatal undoing.

I travelled with a band of my friends to his village Khandawali in Faridabad district of Haryana. We felt compelled to say to his bereaved family that we grieved with them after Junaid's brutal lynching. We knew that these words may mean little to a family that has been so brutally dispossessed, but for whatever they may be worth, we felt that these words still must be spoken. Just two months earlier, we had made a similar journey to share in the same way in the pain of the family of cattle trader Pehlu Khan in Nuh who had been lynched by mobs claiming that he was smuggling cows for slaughter. I wondered how many such journeys – of solidarity? of atonement? – will we have to make. Before we resolve to say as a country – no more. Until then, we need at least to say to those devastated by hate violence – We share your anger. We share your sorrow. It does not make your pain less. But know at least that you are not alone.

We went to the village a day after a sombre and melancholy Eid was observed in the village, as in many parts of India. Men had gathered soberly in mosques to offer the traditional Eid prayers together. But some wore black bands on their sleeves as token of their anguish. Even those who did not – uncertain if a mark of protest was fitting in a festival of love and peace – still carried hurt, fear and bewilderment in their hearts. What has happened to our country? What is our place in this country? We always believed we were equal citizens of the country we love. Were we wrong?

We found crowds outside their modest village home. Junaid's father, Jalaluddin, less than fifty years old, looked both numb and stunned as though he still could not comprehend or accept what had happened. He was unused to the milling guests from the city. In one corner, a plainclothes local police inspector was grilling his sons about the details of the incident, but curiously writing nothing in his notebook. A village official came in and said peremptorily to Jalaluddin that he must clean up his house because a senior politician, a former Chief Minister, would be visiting later in the day.

Jalaluddin accepted our words of condolence wordlessly. 'My sons are very frightened', he only said. 'I hope my older boy Shakir who is in hospital gets well soon. He has two small children.' The women in our group went in and sat with Junaid's mother, who was inconsolable. CPM leader Subhashini Ali was also with her. 'My son Junaid was too young to understand that he should not have worn a skull cap,' his mother Saira Begum mourned. My friend John Dayal went into the women's chamber and said to Saira that he had brought a prayer from his wife for her. They prayed together.

We sat on string cots outside. People spoke of how frightened everyone is of travelling outside their village, walking, on trains or in buses. Frightened of wearing a skull cap, a beard, a burka. Frightened of looking Muslim.

Hashim, Junaid's 18-year-old brother, who wore a beard and skullcap, and was also knifed in the train, spoke to us haltingly of the horrors of that evening. Both brothers studied in madrassas, Hashim in Surat and Junaid in Nuh. They were home for Ramzan and Eid on their annual vacation. The family was poor, and their father and brothers survived variously by cultivating their small piece of land, driving a taxi, and casual labour. These two brothers had set out a different path for themselves of studying the Quran and becoming imams.

After their Eid shopping at Jama Masjid that day, on 24 June 2017, the three brothers Shakir, Hashim and Junaid took a local train from the Sadar Bazar station and found seats. Crowds entered in Okhla, and Junaid gave up his seat to an old man. A group of 15 men asked the others roughly to vacate their seats. When they refused, they slapped and beat them, threw off their skullcaps, pulled the beards of the older boys, abused them for their faith, and called them Pakistanis, beef-eaters and a vulgar slang for the circumcised.

Seeing the situation worsen frighteningly, one of them managed to call their brothers in the village, urging them to come to their rescue to Ballabh-garh station where they were to alight for their village. The station came, but the men did not allow the boys to leave the train. The brothers who had come to their rescue were also pulled in.

In the nine minutes from Ballabhgarh to the next station Asaoti, the men took out knives and stabbed the three brothers several times, even as they screamed for help. Not one person came to their rescue. A few took videos and pictures on their phones instead, as the compartment filled with blood. Several egged on the lynch mob. These included the old man to who Junaid had given his seat.

At the tiny rural station Asaoti, the three boys were thrown off the train. Some of the killers may have also got off in the melee. The train stopped just for a minute and then went ahead on its journey. The brothers were desperate, but no one at the station came to their rescue. No passenger, no rail staff, no policepersons, and none of the vendors and shopkeepers at the station. Junaid bled to death, his head cradled in his distraught brother's lap. Two other brothers also lay wounded. They carried the boys across the tracks to the entrance of the railway station. One of the brothers managed to contact a private hospital in Palwal. Its ambulance came after 45 minutes. Junaid was declared dead when they reached the hospital.

My colleagues and I drove to Asaoti station after we left the family in their grief. We spoke to the rail officials at the station, and to the shopkeepers around the station. We heard only these words from every one of them – We saw nothing at all that evening.

The railway officer who was on duty at that time admitted, 'The guard did send a message about a corpse being thrown off the train.' But he added, 'I was at the controls. I could not leave my table. I have too little staff. I saw nothing.' The shopkeepers just at the entrance of the station – with a vantage of all the platforms – insisted they saw neither the injured and dead boys, nor the arrival of the ambulance. Just one Muslim shop-hand whispered to us that the body lay at the entrance of the station visible to all for 45 minutes. But he did not have the courage to say this publicly.

Junaid was my son. He was son and brother also to the people on the train compartment of his last journey, and those at the railway station where he breathed his last breath.

And yet we let him die.

CHAPTER ONE

Whatever Happened in Gulberg Society?[1]

Ahmedabad, 1969. Nishrin's earliest memories are of their house which had been burned by a terrifying mob. Her father is running desperately with her wrapped protectively in his arms in pitch darkness along a railway track near her gutted home. She was at that time less than five years old.

She remembers the relief camps in a stadium where they lived for several months under a tent. She recalls standing in line for her food at the camps.

Before the 1969 carnage, her father Ehsan Jafri used to help her grand-father, a doctor, to run his small medical clinic. They lived in a small two-room house beside the railway line in a Hindu majority colony in Ahmedabad called Chamanpura. In the afternoons he would cycle to a law college to study to be a lawyer.

Nishrin recalls that her father's best friend, a Hindu shopkeeper in their neighbourhood Rama Seth, grieved to watch their distress in the relief camp, and insisted that they leave and instead move in with him in a small single room behind his shop. Nishrin's family set up home once again in that tiny room with a few German silver utensils and old clothes that people had donated to them in the relief camp. They had lost everything. Her mother's greatest sense of loss was that the only pictures she had of her wedding had also burnt with their first house.

Violence against Muslims recurred sporadically through the years in Ahmedabad. Gradually most Muslims shifted to the safety of Muslim ghet-toes. But her father Ehsan Jafri refused stubbornly to seek safety in numbers. 'Everything I believe in would lose meaning if I felt I could be safe only among Muslims', he would often declare. Had he done so, he might still have been alive.

---

1 Portions of this section are adapted from an article I authored for *Scroll*, "Gulberg Society case: When justice chooses to be blind and the victim gets blamed", 7 July 2016.

He completed his law studies, set up a successful law practice, and in a few years bought a piece of land between the shop and the railway track. It was here that he established a housing colony called Gulberg. He was attracted to socialist ideas, and formed a union of head-loaders. He joined the Congress Party, and in 1977 when the Congress Party lost most seats, was elected to Parliament from Ahmedabad.

Whenever communal riots now broke out, the residents of Gulberg Apartments felt assured that they were safe. This was because the now influential Ehsan Jafri would call the Chief Minister and the head of police each time, and a security picket would be posted outside their gate. Even in 1985, during the largest communal conflagration after 1969 – when what began as an anti-reservation movement spiralled into attacks against Muslims taking nearly 300 lives – Nishrin recalls looking through binoculars with her brother from the terrace of their home at angry mobs with lighted torches at a far distance. But their colony was guarded by men in uniform and remained unharmed.

In 2002, however, Gulberg Apartments were burnt down, and their residents slaughtered. Nishrin was by then married and living in the United States.

2002 was the year when large parts of Gujarat were ripped apart by one of the most brutal and bloody communal massacres since India attained freedom, Following the death by burning of 58 Hindus returing from Ayodhya in a train compartment in a small railway station Godhra, a malign tempest of hate violence engulfed 20 out of the 25 districts of Gujarat for several weeks, persisting in some places for months, as state authorities did little to stem or control it. More than 1000 persons – unofficial estimates are as high as 2000 – the large majority of whom were from the minority Muslim community, were slaughtered. The killings were exceptional for their soul-numbing brutality and the extensive ruthless targeting of women and children. Mass rape, public sexual humiliation of women, and the battering and burning alive of girls, boys, women and men, marked those dismal days. Tens of thousands of homes and small business establishments – petty shops, wooden carts, auto-rickshaws, taxi jeeps, eateries and garages – were set aflame, and cattle and lifetime savings looted.[2] This resulted in the long displacement and enduring pauperisation of more than two hundred thousand terrified

---

2 See "We Have No Orders To Save You: State Participation and Complicity in Communal Violence in Gujarat", *Human Rights Watch,* 2002. Available at https://www.hrw.org/reports/2002/india/gujarat. pdf

and hapless people.[3] More than half of these were actively prevented – by fear, intimidation and social and economic boycott – from ever returning to their homes, resulting in their permanent expulsion from the villages and colonies of their birth. Hundreds of religious shrines were desecrated and destroyed in this carnage.[4]

The first major slaughter in the city of Ahmedabad occurred in the Gulberg Colony where Nishrin's parents lived in 2002. Even as the city of Ahmedabad once again was engulfed in flames of hatred, the residents of Gulberg Apartments were certain that Ehran Jafri would still be able to save their lives and homes once again. But that was not to be. On February 28, Jafri was gruesomely murdered by a feverish mob. Slaughtered along with him were around seventy other women, children and men who had taken shelter with the man who they had believed was influential enough to save their lives from a colossal armed mob baying for blood. He was their only hope. But he was dragged away by the horde, his limbs were cut off from his body before he was burned. His family could not even locate his remains. A mass grave contains what was left of many like him from Gulberg Society and Naroda Patiya, whose families could not find even the charred bodies of their loved ones.

✸

It took fourteen years and an epic, spirited battle led by Jafri's valiant ageing widow, Zakia Jafri, for the courts to pronounce their judgment about who are guilty for the second largest slaughter during the carnage that tore through the state of Gujarat in 2002. Zakia Jafri was firmly convinced that her husband died because of a conspiracy that went right to the top of the state administration, beginning with Chief Minister Narendra Modi, and including senior ministers, police officers and leaders of Sangh organisations closely associated with the ruling party.[5] The court, in its judgment running into more than thirteen hundred pages, disagreed. It did indict eleven people for the murder, but they were just foot soldiers. Judge PB Desai was convinced that there was no conspiracy behind the slaughter, and that the police and administration

---

3 Shabnam Hashmi, "The Uprooted, caught between Denial and Existence: A Document on the State of the Internally Displaced in Gujarat", *Centre for Social Justice and Anhad,* Ahmedabad, 2005, p.5.

4 See "We Have No Orders To Save You: State Participation and Complicity in Communal Violence in Gujarat", *Human Rights Watch,* 2002, p. 31. Available at https://www.hrw.org/reports/2002/india/gujarat.pdf

5 The Special Investigation Team report dated 27 April 2009, "Enquiry Report in SLP (Crl.) No. 1088" contains a summary of these allegations. Full report available here https://cjp.org.in/sit-enquiry_report_in-zakia-case/

did all they could do control it. He affirmed that a mob of more than ten thousand people did gather around the tenement building the morning after 58 people were burned alive in a train in neighbouring Godhra the earlier morning. But he concluded that what provoked the crowd to kill Jafri and other residents of the building society was Jafri himself, who fired into the crowd with his licenced rifle.[6] This is what Chief Minister Modi also had publicly claimed.[7] Jafri, by the judge's reckoning, and that of Mr Modi, was responsible for his own slaughter.

The story that the survivors told the judge over prolonged hearings in the special court in Ahmedabad was consistent. Foreboding had set among the residents of Gulberg Society once news of the burning of the train compartment in Godhra on 27 February 2002 filtered in, and the television screens and newspapers were full of speeches of rage of leaders of the ruling party and the Hindu community. The residents of Gulberg Society were mostly Muslim, with an odd Parsi home, and they were surrounded by predominantly Hindu settlements. Recurring episodes of communal violence in the city in past decades had altered the city's demography steadily. The city came to be uncompromisingly divided into Hindu and Muslim areas, and Gulberg was one of the few remaining 'Muslim' settlements in the 'Hindu' section of the city.

Because a man of Ehsan Jafri's standing lived in their midst, the other residents of Gulberg, as we have seen, were confident that they would be safe during storms of communal adversity. He had a hot-line to people in authority who had never let them down in earlier communal attacks. It was this assurance that calmed them a little as they observed, with dread, tension mount palpably in the city during the hours after the train compartment burned in Godhra station near Ahmedabad on 27 February 2002. Jafri reassured them that he had applied in writing for police protection to the nearest police station, and the police assured him that they would protect them. However, their disquiet grew exponentially when the Vishwa Hindu Parishad called for a massive state-wide bandh the next morning to protest the deaths on the train – which Chief Minister Modi and the VHP were convinced was a deliberate and pre-planned act of Islamist terror. On the morning after the train burning, activists of the VHP started forcefully closing down shops, and

6 Satish Jha, "No larger conspiracy behind 2002 Godhra riots: SIT court", *The Indian Express*, 18 June 2016. Available at http://indianexpress.com/article/india/india-news-india/no-larger-conspiracy-behind-2002-godhra-riots-court-2859809/

7 Vidya Subrahmaniam, "SIT says Ehsan Jafri 'provoked' murderous mob", *The Hindu*, 11 May 2012. Available at http://www.thehindu.com/news/national/SIT-says-Ehsan-Jafri-%E2%80%98provoked%E2%80%99-murderous-mob/article12874780.ece

raising chilling, aggressive anti-Muslim slogans. The crowd began to multiply rapidly, and they beat two Muslim men who ran a cycle shop, and set fire to some auto-rickshaws. Some senior police officers drove to the site, including according to some witnesses, the Commissioner of Police PC Pande. After they left, the crowd swelled menacingly like a monsoon flood after a cloudburst. By 1.30 pm it had expanded into ten thousand people, maybe more, raising furious, threatening slogans against Muslims. Many of them were armed. They attacked the homes and shops of Muslims who lived outside the boundaries of the Society, and their residents too ran for safety to the colony, expecting that Jafri would be able to protect them.

The housing society was bound by tall walls and its gates were locked, as its residents and others who had run into it for refuge cowered in fear within. The incensed crowds surrounded the colony, and threw burning rags, stones and acid bombs at the houses in the colony. There were chemicals in the rags that led to the rapid spreading of fire. People in the society ran to Jafri's home for protection. Many were injured. They crowded his library and living room, others went to the first floor where Zakia Jafri also was hiding.

To breach the thick cement wall topped with broken glass that surrounded the housing society, both at the rear and front walls, men lined up gas cylinders and exploded these. As the wall fell the throng then surged into the apartment complex. Many of them were armed with daggers, swords, iron pipes, acid bombs as well as petrol and kerosene cans. Some had firearms. They began to damage and burn the vehicles parked on the ground. Burning rags with incendiary chemicals fell inside Mr Jafri's home, and as the house started burning, panicky women and men ran outside where the crowd fell upon them. They attacked all the people they could find – men, women and children – and hacked them to pieces, setting their bodies on fire. Men in the crowd also reportedly caught some women and girls, stripped them naked and raped them, and then killed them and set their bodies on fire.

From morning and through all of this, many witnesses testified that Jafri desperately kept calling senior police officers and political leaders, including reportedly even Chief Minister Modi, but to no avail. Some claimed on oath that Jafri said that Mr Modi had answered his call with abuse.[8] Through the afternoon, as the slaughter continued, the small contingent of around 20 police personnel was not further augmented, and these policepersons did

---

8   Vinod K Jose, "'Try To Find Out If In The Past Jafri Has Been In The Habit Of Opening Fire': On The Gulberg Society Massacre", *The Caravan*, 3 June 2016. Available at http://www.caravanmagazine.in/vantage/gulburg-society-massacre-jafri-modi

little to intervene and control the rampaging and murderous crowds. It was only around 4.30 pm in the evening that a larger armed police contingent arrived, dispersed the mob with tear gas and firing, and rescued the persons who were still surviving.

Before this, Jafri decided that as a last bid to save those who had taken shelter in his home, he would go out and personally plead with the crowd to spare those who had gathered in his house for protection. Many appealed to him not to go out as the crowd would not spare him. Reportedly he still went out, hands folded, begging the crowd to have mercy, offering that they should kill him if they must but in return they should spare the others. Some reports are that he offered the crowd money in return for safety. But all of this was to no avail. Men in the crowd pounced on him. The crowd dragged him away. All that his son could find of his father later was one sandal. By the time the police rescue team arrived, his home and its surroundings was littered with corpses, several badly burnt. The bodies of many of the dead women were naked.

✳

None of the witnesses could describe exactly what the mob did with Ehsan Jafri except that even his body or remains could not be located later among the burned and dismembered corpses that the police recovered in the aftermath from the ravaged colony. But a chilling idea of what could have happened to him emerged from a very different source. A daring young journalist Ashish Khetan some five years after the carnage posed as a writer sympathetic to the Hindutva cause, and secretly recorded explosive conversations with many Hindutva leaders and activists. Among them were the clandestinely recorded testimonies of three VHP activists Mangelal Jain, Prahaladji and Madanlal Raval, who described graphically the events connected with the Gulberg killings.

They were triumphant and unrepentant as they gloated about the massacre to Khetan. These men ratified to Khetan that Jafri made frantic calls to police officers and political leaders. But when nothing worked, they say that Jafri in desperation opened fire on the mob and injured a few people. When even this was ineffectual in controlling the crush of men who had entered the complex grounds and were attacking and raping people and throwing burning rags into the houses, Jafri offered the mob money pleading for them to spare him and the other residents of Gulberg. At this, according to the men who spoke to Khetan, the mob demanded that he come out of the house with the money. He stepped out, dropped the money on the ground and tried to rush back. But the mob pounced on him. 'Five or six people held him, then someone struck him with a sword... chopped off his hand, then his legs... then everything else... after cutting him to pieces, they put him on the wood they'd piled and set it on fire... burnt him alive...'. After murdering Jafri, the mob fell upon the terrified people hiding in his home, or trying to flee from it in panic, and slaughtered them and set them on fire.

Their version confirmed many other parts of the testimonies survivors gave in court. They said that VHP and Bajrang Dal activists gathered in that area in large numbers early that day to enforce the bandh called by the VHP. Many activists carried tridents in their belts, and others also had sticks and carted in their cars. Some also carried fire-arms. They began by setting on fire a shop owned by a Muslim, and then they surrounded Gulberg Society, in which Muslim families lived, and poor Muslims from adjoining slums had also taken shelter within the compound. They also confirmed that their men brought gas cylinders, lined these along the boundary wall at the front and the rear of the society, and set these on fire, resulting in loud explosions, breaching the wall from the front and the rear. Others scaled the walls with ropes.

Through all of this, the activists told Khetan, the police not only gave them a free hand, but also exhorted the rioters to kill Muslims. They claimed that the police inspector in-charge of Meghaninagar police station, KG Erda, told the rioters that they had three to four hours to carry out killings. The police would do nothing to restrain them during these hours. It was only around 4.30 in the evening that additional police forces came in and they finally dispersed the mob and rescued the survivors.

※

However, the special court Judge PB Desai chose to disregard the evidence in the conversations secretly taped by Tehelka reporter Ashish Khetan. His reasons are brief. These conversations with accused persons from the VHP and Bajrang Dal certainly supported the theory that there was indeed a plan to collect, incite and arm the mob to undertake the gruesome slaughter in the housing colony in Ahmedabad. The judge admitted that superior courts have ruled that whereas a person cannot be convicted exclusively based on evidence collected in such 'sting operations', such evidence is certainly admissible as corroborative proof. But he chose to disregard this evidence, not because there was proof that these video recordings were in any way doctored or false, but simply because the Special Investigation Team (SIT) appointed by the

Supreme Court of India chose to ignore this evidence. Because the investigators did not pursue this in greater depth, he concluded that the 'recordings cannot be relied upon as trustworthy or substantial evidence and establish any conspiracy herein.'

After listening to all the statements of the witnesses and the accused and the arguments mustered by the lawyers of the men accused of the carnage and the survivors, Judge Desai rejected out of hand the charge that there was a pre-planned conspiracy, supported by senior state leaders and officials and the police, to slaughter people in Gulberg Society as collective revenge for the burning alive a day earlier of Hindu persons in the train compartment in Godhra.

Instead, he concluded that the gathering of ten to fifteen thousand persons, many of them armed, was the result of a collection of individual decisions with no collective planning. He also believed that the police did their duty that day and were in no way partners in a conspiracy of mass killings, rape and arson. He also was convinced that this crowd had no intention of conducting the massacre, and it was only the provocation of Ehsan Jafri by firing on the mob that led to an understandable collective rage in the mob, and it was this that plunged them into the gruesome slaughter.

The reason he offered for rejecting the conspiracy theory is that until 1.30 pm, the crowd did gather, and did attack some Muslims and burn their shops and vehicles, and did throw stones and burning rags into the houses of the Society, but they did not actually kill people from 9 in the morning when they began to gather, until 1.30 when the slaughter began. The judge was convinced by the argument of the defence lawyer that if the crowd was intent on committing the massacre, and was assured that the police would not prevent them, they would have pulled down the walls and broken into the grounds of the Society and perpetrated the killings in the morning itself.

His reasons for rejecting the claim that the police officers deliberately delayed by several hours the bringing in of reinforcements and intervening to disperse the crowds and rescue the besieged residents of Gulberg Society are given in one brief paragraph, remarkable for its terseness in a judgment that runs into over 1300 pages. 'In my opinion', the judge says, 'much attempts have been made to rake up this issue time and again...and such proceeding have been found to be without merit by all Courts at all levels...therefore it would be *unsafe* (emphasis mine) and unfair to have even further discussion on this aspect. The controversy in my opinion has been laid to rest and is required to be given its due burial.'

The judge instead went on to ask why 'all of a sudden, things got ugly after 1.30 pm, as if some tap was turned on which resulted in a flood of water and the carnage was perpetrated'? He felt that from the evidence presented to his court that it is conclusively established that a crowd which was largely confined to stone throwing and damaging properties of Muslims 'suddenly turned into an ugly mob which indulged in the massacre' only because they were gravely provoked by the resort by Ehsan Jafri to 'private firing' from his licenced weapon into the crowd. The firing is said to have resulted in one death and fifteen injuries. The judge regreted what he describes as the selective amnesia of most survivor witnesses about Jafri's shooting. He relied instead entirely on the evidence by police personnel who were present at the spot who were unanimous that it was only because of Jafri's gunfire that the crowd 'went out of control'.

Baldly, the learned judge agreed with the defence lawyer and all the police witnesses, that the person centrally responsible for the massacre of Ehsan Jafri and nearly seventy people who took shelter with him was Ehsan Jafri himself. If he did not provoke them by shooting into them, the crowd of ten to fifteen thousand people would have dispersed after some acts of arson and looting.[9]

Judge Desai's conclusion that it was Jafri's action that provoked the mob into attacking him and others in Gulberg Society, was supported by both the Special Investigation Team and, influentially, Chief Minister Modi. In the closure report concluding that there was no prosecutable evidence against Narendra Modi for Gulberg and other massacres in Gujarat, the SIT declared: 'In this connection, it is to be stated that Shri Narendra Modi has clearly stated in his Zee TV interview that it was late Ahesan (sic.) Jafri, ex-MP, who first fired at violent mob and the provoked mob stormed the society and set it on fire. In this interview, he has clearly referred to Jafri's firing as "action" and the massacre that followed as "reaction". It may be clarified here that in case late Ahesan (sic.) Jafri, ex-MP, fired at the mob, this could be an immediate provocation to the mob, which had assembled there to take revenge of Godhra incident from the Muslims.'[10]

※

---

9 "Judge Buys Police, SIT's Claim that Private Firing by Ahsan Jafri Triggered the Gulberg Society Massacre", *Sabrang India,* 19 June 2016. Available at https://sabrangindia.in/indepth/judge-buys-police-sit%E2%80%99s-claim-private-firing-ahsan-jafri-triggered-gulberg-society-massacre?page=1

10 Vidya Subrahmaniam, "SIT says Ehsan Jafri 'provoked' murderous mob", *The Hindu,* 11 May 2012. Available at http://www.thehindu.com/news/national/SIT-says-Ehsan-Jafri-%E2%80%98provoked%E2%80%99-murderous-mob/article12874780.ece

Judge PB Desai's and Mr Modi's conclusions about what happened in Gulberg Society on 28 February, 2002, resulting in the second largest toll among the innumerable episodes of killing, rape and arson that unfolded on that day and for weeks thereafter, largely conform to a popular – and I believe communally highly charged – narrative about what causes mass communal violence in the country more generally. According to this version, it may be true that Muslims suffer most losses of life and property and sexual violence in most episodes that are described as communal riots. But it suggests that it is Muslims themselves who provoke Hindus into these acts of bloodshed and arson, by their own resort to unprovoked violence and perfidy, against Hindu temples, women and cows, and as in both Godhra and Gulberg Society, against basically peace-loving Hindu people.

In the case of the Gulberg massacre, the learned judge of the special court is prepared to accept that a crowd of ten to fifteen thousand people spontaneously gathered outside the housing complex of predominantly Muslim residents. He is convinced that no one planned the slaughter, nor did anyone facilitate the killings by arming the crowd with weapons, daggers, swords, acid bombs, firearms, cans of petrol and kerosene and large numbers of cooking gas cylinders. Although they gathered in such large numbers, and raised menacing slogans calling for the killing of Muslims, the judge strangely still concludes that they had no intention to actually kill Muslims, and only proposed to set a few properties owned by them on fire and return to their homes peacefully.

On that day – and in the weeks that followed – the slaughter and rape of several hundred Muslim children, women and men was unfolding across Ahmedabad and indeed in 20 or more districts of Gujarat. This is well known. But still Judge Desai was convinced that the crowd that gathered in Gulberg was somehow different. They had no intention to kill or rape. It was, according to him, only Ehsan Jafri's shooting at them that led them, again spontaneously, to muster and deploy a range of weapons, gas cylinders, petrol, kerosene and other inflammable materials, against the housing society and its residents, with arson, cruel slaughter and rape.

Judge Desai also concluded that the charge of grave police complicity in the massacre has appropriately been given a 'due burial', because of which he does not need even to consider the merits or the evidence regarding this charge. Gulberg Society is located in Chamanpura in central Ahmedabad, one kilometre from the police station and two kilometres from the office of the Commissioner of Police. This housing complex with mostly Muslim residents was located in a predominantly Hindu section of a city in which residence is sharply divided in communal lines. It is elementary to even basic policing that at a time of such communal sensitivity, adequate police forces should have been deployed in advance to protect the Society. It is also not disputed that senior police officials, including disputably Police Commissioner PC Pande, visited the location at around 10.30 am that morning, witnessed the gathering violent crowd, but although they were accompanied by a striking force of armed policepersons, this was not deployed at the spot.

It is also not disputed that the time that elapsed between when the crowd began to gather at 9 am and the deployment of sufficient forces to disperse the mob and rescue the survivors at 4.30 pm was a full eight and a half hours. If sufficient police forces were deployed in the morning, and timely curfew declared and imposed at that time, the crowd could not even have gathered in the numbers that it did. If the police force and action that was undertaken at 4.30 pm had taken place three or four hours earlier, the lives of most of the seventy people could have been saved, and the rapes prevented. Instead only around twenty four policepersons were deployed right until 4.30 pm, and they did little to prevent the crowds from their marauding. And it is their statement that Judge Desai chooses to rely upon while concluding that Jafri was responsible for inciting the mob into enraged slaughter.

As a district officer, I have handled major communal massacres in 1984 and 1989, as well as studied many communal massacres of recent decades. I have no doubt that if the police administration is committed to controlling even the largest of communal conflagrations, it is entirely possible for them to accomplish this in a matter of a few hours. Their failure to do so reflects either criminal incompetence or, as is much, much more likely, their criminal and culpable compliance with political directives from senior levels to allow the communal bloodletting to continue. Judge Desai does what many judges, in courts and judicial commissions, have done before him: to accept uncritically the version of the police, and to turn his face away from the criminal culpability of the police deploying the device of deliberate inaction, and the political leadership on whose command they do this.

※

The learned judge did not pay any attention to statements by every survivor witness that Jafri did call, repeatedly and desperately, numerous senior police officers and other persons in authority, including allegedly Chief Minister Modi, to send in police forces to disperse the crowd and rescue those against who the mob had laid a powerful siege. Senior journalist Kuldeep Nayar in an article affirms that Jafri even telephoned him in Delhi, begging him to contact someone in authority to send in the police or the army to rescue them. 'When Jafri was surrounded by the Hindu mob, he rang me up, seeking my help to rescue him from the frenzied crowd that surrounded him. I rang up the Home Ministry in Delhi and told them about the telephone call. They said they were in touch with the state government and were "watching" the situation. As I put down the telephone, it rang again and Jafri was at the other end, beseeching me to do something because the mob was threatening to lynch him. His cry for help still resounds in my ears.'[11]

The judge ignored evidence that this man in his seventies did all that was possible within his power to protect those who believed that his influence would shield them from the rage of the mob, including begging them to take his life instead, and courageously going out to plead and negotiate with the armed and angry crowd. When he realized that no one in authority would come in for their protection, he also did pick up his licenced fire-arm and shot at the crowd, as a final vain bid to protect the people for whose safety he felt personally responsible.

Instead, the judge agreed with the defence lawyers, the police witnesses, and indeed the SIT investigation, that Jafri's final resort to firing was not a legitimate action- even less one of rare courage and humanity as he tried single-handedly to defend the women, children and men who had sought his protection – but an indefensible act of the gravest provocation.

In this, he echoed the position taken repeatedly by Narendra Modi that the killing of Jafri by the mob violence was only a 'reaction' to his 'action' of shooting on the mob. In interviews to the press, Modi said that investigations revealed that the firing by the Congressman played a pivotal role in inciting the mob. Asked what could have led him to open fire, he said it was 'probably in his nature' to do so.[12] As a *Times of India* report of one such interview with Modi puts it, 'in the case of the lynching of former Congress MP Ahsan Jaffrey (sic.), he was quick to point out that it was Jaffrey (sic.) who had first fired at the mob. He forgot to say what a citizen is expected to do when a menacing mob, which has already slaughtered many, approaches him and the police has deliberately not responded to his pleas.'[13]

---

11 Kuldip Nayar, "Travesty of justice", *Deccan Herald*, 23 June 2016. Available at http://www.deccan-herald.com/content/553774/travesty-justice.html
12 See Annexure 10, Hate Speech, to Volume I of the Concerned Citizens Tribunal. Available here: http://www.outlookindia.com/website/story/hate-speech/218024
13 'Newton' Modi has a lot to answer", *The Times of India*, 2 March 2002. Available at http://timesof-india.indiatimes.com/india/Newton-Modi-has-a-lot-to-answer/articleshow/2599766.cms

It is as though even when they are being attacked and surrounded by an armed mob shouting vicious slogans threatening to murder them, and with acid bombs and burning rags flung at them, a 'good Muslim' victim should do nothing except plead, and this would ensure that the crowd would not attack them. I am reminded the advice of some religious leaders after the gang-rape of the young physiotherapist called Nirbhaya in Delhi on 16 December 2012. They said that if the victim had not offered resistance to her rapists, and just folded her hands and called them her brothers, her life would have been spared.[14]

✺

Ehsan Jafri's family was devastated by the court's judgment, particularly the blame it places on Ehran Jafri for his own murder and that of his neighbours. His son Tanveer Jafri declared in anguish, 'This is not only a complete insult to the life, work and memory of my father, Ehsan Jafri who worked and lived among his people but it makes a mockery of the sacrifice he gave of his life to save the life of others. What were the 24 police officers present doing for four hours, watching the show? The judgement not only appears to have ignored the violent build up but appears to have been standing some of the evidence on its head. We will soldier on till we get justice,' he added.[15]

The fourteen years prior to the judgment his mother, Jafri's widow, the ageing Zakia Jafri, had been preoccupied with little else except this battle for justice. She attended every court hearing, refusing even to visit her daughter abroad, or to rest and move on as so many counselled her to. She lived with her son Tanveer in Ahmedabad. Even as her health declined, she refused to give up on her legal battle. After Judge Desai read out his judgment, she was disconsolate. 'My husband was a good and kind man. I will never give up my fight for justice, for him and thousands like him.'[16]

✺

Ehsan Jafri's library, his house, indeed all the tenements in this middle-class housing cooperative in Ahmedabad are still in ruins, standing forlorn, empty,

14 Palash Ghosh, "Delhi Gang-Rape: Prominent Religious Leader Blames Victim", *IB Times*, 1 July 2013. Available at http://www.ibtimes.com/delhi-gang-rape-prominent-religious-leader-blames-victim-997912

15 See Kuldip Nayar, "Travesty of justice", *Deccan Herald,* 23 June 2016. Available at http://www.deccanherald.com/content/553774/travesty-justice.html .

16 Harsh Mander, "When justice chooses to be blind – and the victim gets blamed", *Scroll,* 7 July 2016. Available at https://scroll.in/article/811250/gulberg-society-case-when-justice-chooses-to-be-blind-and-the-victim-get-blamed

savaged as they were at the time of the slaughter. The peeling walls even today are still black with soot, the floors still piled with rubble and burned remains of people's belongings. No one lives there, none of the houses have been rebuilt or restored. The grounds are overgrown with weeds, and stray dogs sleep in the verandas. Within the walls of the six houses and eighteen flats in Gulberg Society today are only memories and ghosts. And the secrets of what indeed transpired there on that fateful day, 28 February 2002.

Nishrin is married and lives in the United States. She and her children would visit her parents in Ahmedabad every summer. There is one memory that her son Tauseef Hussain, now in his twenties, still cherishes of his grandfather Ehsan Jafri. They would visit him in Ahmedabad from his home in the United States during his summer vacations. He would sit in his grandfather's library in the stifling summer heat. His grandfather – lawyer, poet and politician – had taped over the switches and would stubbornly not allow anyone to turn on the ceiling fans. He did not want the nesting baby sparrows who flew through their apartment to hit the fans and die.

CHAPTER TWO

The Ethics of Collective Vengeance

In the BJP parliamentary party meeting in Delhi in December 2002, the then prime minister, A.B. Vajpayee, lamented in a thinly disguised rationalization of the 'Hindu anger' manifested in the violence that followed the alleged torching of the train, 'Why didn't people of the Muslim community condemn the Godhra incident? Even today, there is no repentance that we committed a mistake or that this should not have happened and that it was a crime.'[1] Expressing regret for the post-Godhra violence, he went on to ask in April 2002, '*Lekin aag lagayi kisne*? (Who lit the fire?)'[2] The poet-prime minister suggested that Muslims as a whole should seek forgiveness for the crime that some of their co-religionists had allegedly committed; and that because they did not, the massacre that followed was regretful but understandable.

Indeed ever since the train compartment burned in the wayside railway station of Godhra that late-winter morning in 2002, intolerably heavy burdens of vicarious guilt have been thrust upon the shoulders of the entire Muslim community in India for the outrage allegedly commmited by a few who shared their religious identity in Godhra. The slaughter, rape, loot and arson that followed were widely perceived as righteous, or at least a reasonable and explicable reaction to the 'barbaric crime' of 'the Muslims.'

Some of the most brutal mass crimes in recent history are those of collective vengeance wreaked against an entire community for the real or imagined crimes of a few of its members. The blood of thousands of innocent Sikhs flowed in 1984 in one of the two biggest communal slughters after the Partition riots of 1947 (the other was in Nellie in Assam in 1983), as a reprisal against the acts of two Sikh guards who assassinated Indira Gandhi. Terrorist attacks on the twin towers in New York have been used to condone inde-

---

1 'Muslims are not repentant for Godhra: Vajpayee', *Rediff*, 17 December 2002. Available at http://www.rediff.com/news/2002/dec/17pm1.htm
2 Praful Bidwai, ''But who lit the fire?'', *Frontline*, 22(3), February 2005. Available at http://www.frontline.in/static/html/fl2203/stories/20050211001909200.htm

fensible military attacks on civilian populations in faraway Afghanistan and
Iraq. Each terror strike in Paris inevitably makes the entire Muslim population in France (and for some across the world) culpable in many eyes.

The same dangerously warped and morally flawed logic was used to
condone the merciless bloodletting that mortally wounded Gujarat in 2002.
Without evidence, Chief Minister Modi described the gruesome incident at
Godhra as a pre-planned 'one sided collective terrorist attack by one community...' In a speech telecast on 28 February 2002 on Doordarshan, the government owned channel, he said, 'Yesterday in Godhra, an inhuman tragedy
took place. More than 40 women and children were burnt alive and 18 men
were also burnt alive. In all 58 persons were burnt alive together in a railway
compartment by cannibals. In the history of mankind, such a heinous crime
will bring tears to the eyes of even the hardest of men. This heinous crime,
cowardly and inhuman crime, has taken place in Gujarat. It cannot be justified in any civilized society. A crime that can never be forgiven.'[3] He has to
date, of course, made no remotely comparable speech expressing anguish at
the gruesome killings and rapes of several times more Muslims that followed
after the Godhra train burning, or indeed for Muslims killed by lynch mobs
in his tenure as Prime Minister.

For many people anger and violence against all Muslim people was
comprehensible, if not actually righteous, because some Muslims were alleged
to have deliberately set fire to a compartment filled with Hindu women, children and men. Even if there was evidence that this had indeed occurred, it
is important to defend the ethical principle that this would not justify the
killing, rape and looting by mobs of Muslim people. But the facts of what
happened in Godhra railway station that fateful morning is far from settled.
Terming the (Godhra) attack as a 'pre-planned, violent act of terrorism', Mr
Modi said that state government was viewing this attack seriously,[4] indicating
that he assumed that the train burning was a deliberate conspiracy and that
too a crime of cross-border terror, in effect, he ruled out the possibility that it
could have been an accident, before there was any forensic evidence to confirm
this one way or the other. and this was the essential spark for the retributive

3 A video of this speech is available on YouTube, here: https://www.youtube.com/watch?v=4Ci-
uBBKJ30Q
4 Quoted from a Gujarat government press release in Manoj Mitta, ''Preplanned inhuman collective
violent act of terrorism':What Modi got away with in the Godhra case', 27 February 2017. https://scroll.
in/article/830319/preplanned-inhuman-collective-violent-act-of-terrorism-what-modi-got-away-with-
in-the-godhra-case

mass killings especially targeting Muslim women and children that followed.[5] Also without evidence, he charged that this was a terror act planned by Pakistan's ISI executed.[6] The claim of Pakistani involvement was not sustained even by the state government's own charge-sheet about the incident later.[7]

Modi's statement without any proof that the burning of the train compartment was a terror crime involving the Pakistani intelligence was used by widely and powerfully by local newspapers and members of the state government to incite hatred and violence against the Muslim community. False and inflammatory stories appeared in local newspapers claiming that Muslim people had kidnapped and raped some Hindu women. The Editors Guild of India later criticised the role of local newspapers *Sandesh Gujarati* and *Gujarat Samachar*. It was of the opinion that *Sandesh* carried headlines which would provoke, communalize and terrorise people. The newspaper even used a quote from a VHP leader as a banner headline, 'Avenge with blood.'[8]

Chief Minister Modi influentially justified by implication the violence by the Hindus as understandable (and even justified) after the provocation by the Godhra train burning with several of his statements. An annexure to the Concerned Citizens Tribunal report documents these statements.[9] (The Concerned Citizen's Tribunal investigated the 2002 carnage, and comprised retired and highly respected senior judges of the Supreme Court, senior advocates, social scientists and activists – Justice VR Krishna Iyer, Justice PB Sawant, Justice Hosbet Suresh, Justice Lone, KG Kannabiran, Dr. KS Subramanian, IPS (Retd.), Dr. Ghanshyam Shah, social scientist; Aruna Roy, MKSS, and Dr. Tanika Sarkar, historian).

"With the entire population of Gujarat very angry at what happened in Godhra much worse was expected', he said in a Press Conference in Gujarat, Feb 28, 2002.[10] He also stated that he was 'absolutely satisfied' with the way in

5 In Annexure 10, Hate Speech, to Volume I of the *Concerned Citizens Tribunal*. "Asked about the violence, Modi quoted Newton's third law – 'every action has an equal and opposite reaction' – to virtually justify what is happening. — *The Times of India*, March 3, 2002" Available here: http://www.outlookindia.com/website/story/hate-speech/218024

6 See "Crime Against Humanity: Volume II. An Inquiry into the Carnage in Gujarat – Findings and Recommendations", *Concerned Citizens Tribunal*, Gujarat 2002. Available at https://www.sabrang.com/tribunal/tribunal2.pdf

7 See *Gujarat, the Making of a Tragedy* (2002), ed. Siddharth Varadarajan, p. 6. New Delhi: Penguin Books.

8 Dionne Bunsha, "Peddling hate", *Frontline*, Vol 19, No 15, July 20-August 2 2002. Available at http://www.frontline.in/static/html/fl1915/19150130.htm

9 See Annexure 10, Hate Speech, to Volume I of the *Concerned Citizens Tribunal*. Available here: http://www.outlookindia.com/website/story/hate-speech/218024

10 Quoted in Annexure 10, Hate Speech, to Volume I of the Concerned Citizens Tribunal. Available

which the police and State Government handled the 'backlash' from Godhra incident and 'happy' that violence was largely contained... 'We should be happy that curfew has been imposed only at 26 places while there is anger and people are burning with revenge. Thanks to security arrangements we brought things under control.' When asked that not a policeman was visible in most areas where shops were looted and set on fire, he said he hadn't received any complaint.'[11]

Former Commissioner of Police, Ahmedabad, PC Pande echoed the same rationale, even for the role of the police, by stating: 'Police were not insulated from the general social milieu... (When) there's a change in the perception of society, the police are part of it and there's bound to be some contagion effect.'[12] In a study of the Gujarat 2002 massacre, the Centre for Equity Studies found based on a records obtained through right to information applications – that a majority of First Information Report recorded by the police all across Gujarat, start with words to the effect that 'Enraged by the burning of the train in Godhra, a mob...' and only then describe the crimes that the mob committed. This follows the moral lead of Chief Minister Modi and his Ahmedabad police chief that somehow the first alleged crime created a moral rationale for the torrent of mass crimes that followed

The *Times of India* reported that Modi quoted Newton that every action has an equal and opposite reaction to virtually justify the massacre of Muslims.[13] This hugely controversial statement was hotly denied later, but the Supreme Court appointed Special Investigation Team confirmed that Mr Modi did make this statement in a television interview. The SIT report further says that the exact quote was, '*Kriya pratikriya ke chain chal rahi hai. Hum chaete hai ke na kriya ho, aur na pratikriya* (A chain of action and reaction is going on. We neither want action nor reaction).' When the correspondent asked Modi about widespread violence in Gujarat post-Godhra, the latter replied, '*Godhra main jo purso hua, jaha par 40 mahilao aur bacho ko zinda jala diya, is main desh main aur videsh main sadma pauchna swabhavik tha. Godhra ke is ilake ke logo ki criminal tendencies rahe hai, in logo ne pehle mahila teacher ka khoon kiya and ab ye jaghanya apradh kiya hai jiski pratikriya ho rahi hai.*' (What happened in Godhra day before

here: http://www.outlookindia.com/website/story/hate-speech/218024

11 Quoted in Annexure 10, Hate Speech, to Volume I of the *Concerned Citizens Tribunal*. Available here: http://www.outlookindia.com/website/story/hate-speech/218024
12 Ibid.
13 "'Newton' Modi has a lot to answer", *The Times of India,* 2 March 2002. Available at http://timesof-india.indiatimes.com/india/Newton-Modi-has-a-lot-to-answer/articleshow/2599766.cms

yesterday, where 40 women and children were burnt alive, this country and even foreign countries are shocked. People of that area of Godhra have criminal tendencies, they had earlier killed a lady teacher and now have committed this heinous crime, reaction to which are being felt).[14]

The SIT however maintained that these words are not sufficient to make out a case against him: 'In this connection, it is to be stated that Shri Narendra Modi has clearly stated in his interview that it was late Ehsaan Jaffrey (sic.), ex-MP, who first fired at violent mob and the provoked mob stormed the Society and set it on fire. In this interview, he has clearly referred to Jaffrey's (sic.) firing as 'action' and the massacre that followed as 'reaction.' It may be clarified here that in case Jaffrey (sic.) fired at the mob, this could be an immediate provocation to the mob, which had assembled there to take revenge of Godhra incident from the Muslims.'[15]

It is particularly instructive that this doctrine of collective communal responsibility for crimes of individuals is applied only selectively. For the gruesome killing of Dalits in Tsundur in 1991, Jhajjar in Haryana in 2002 and Khairlinji in Maharashtra in 2006, or indeed in instances of brutal and murderous atrocities on Dalits and sexual violence against Dalit women that shame every generation of Indians through the centuries, the upper-caste Hindu majority are never held collectively responsible. Nor are they pronounced jointly guilty for the massacres of 1984 and 2002. Even less are all men held responsible for the violence, crimes and subjugation of women by men through history in most parts of the world. Such collective responsibility seems apportioned only to religious minorities, to Sikhs in the 1980s, to Christians in tribal regions where missionaries work (and therefore provoke violence by sometimes coverting people to Christianity), and most of all to the Muslim people.

The Railway Minister of the UPA Government elected in 2004, Laloo Yadav, appointed the UC Banerjee Committee to probe what caused the Godhra train burning. The judge's interim report concluded that the Sabarmati Express at Godhra in 2002 was not deliberately set on fire. Instead, the forensic evidence suggested that the fire was accidental. This UC Bannerjee report was judicially challenged in the Gujarat High Court, which struck it down in 2006, as unconstitutional and void. This was done on only the

14 'Modi 'action-reaction' statement not sufficient to make a case: SIT', *The Indian Express,* 11 May 2012. http://archive.indianexpress.com/news/modi-actionreaction-statement-not-sufficient-to-make-a-case-sit/948186/
15 Ibid.

technical ground that the setting up of the commission violated the provisions of the Inquiry Act and the Indian Railway Act because an existing commission, namely the Nanavati-Shah Commission, was already probing the matter. Legal experts however disagreed, as there is no legal bar to two complementary probes running alongside. The challenge to this order by the central government was withdrawn after the BJP-led government came to power in Delhi in 2014. And there it rests.

The judicial commission headed by Justice Nanavati (and Justice Shah, who subsequently passed away) in 2008 came to a conclusion completely at variance with that of Justice Banerjee. He submitted Part 1 of his Report in 2008, which endorsed the government's version of what caused the fire in the train in Godhra, accepting the theory of a pre-planned conspiracy by Muslims (but did not support the claim that Chief Minister Modi had made that this conspiracy was planned by Pakistan's ISI). It claimed that Maulvi Husain Haji Ibrahim Umarji, a cleric in Godhra, and a dismissed Central Reserve Police Force officer named Nanumiyan were 'masterminds' behind the operation.

The official version of the government of Gujarat was also pressed before the trial courts, interpreted through nine charge-sheets. This was that a conspiracy was hatched at a guesthouse in Godhra, the night before the fire, to kill the kar sewaks returning from Ayodhya, by setting aflame coach S-6 of the Sabarmati Express. For this, 140 litres of petrol were said to have been procured. The next morning, on 27 February 2002, the train was halted at Godhra station by the conspirators, by repeatedly pulling the alarm chain. It was alleged in the police version that a kar sewak misbehaved with a Muslim girl which led to tension and confusion. It was further charged that taking advantage of the confusion the conspirator cut through the canvas of the vestibule, and allowed the petrol to leak in coach number S-6 and then set it aflame.[16]

In February 2011, after a tortuous journey of the case through many courts, the trial court accepted that the train-burning was a 'pre-planned conspiracy', and it convicted 31 people and acquitted 63 others based on the murder and conspiracy provisions of the Indian Penal Code. It awarded the highest penalty of death to 11 men, and 20 were sentenced to life imprisonment. The cleric Maulvi Umarji, who the Nanavati-Shah Commission had

---

16 The entire prosecution theory presented to the trial court is detailed in V. Venkatesan, "Busting a conspiracy theory", *Frontline*, Vol 22, No 13, June 18-July 1 2005. Available at http://www.frontline. in/static/html/fl2213/stories/20050701003303800.htm

deemed to be the prime conspirator, was acquitted along with 62 others for lack of evidence. The Gujarat High Court upheld the acquittals, and reduced the dealth penalty to life imprisonment.[17]

However, the evidence before the Banerjee judicial commissions, and reports of independent experts, seem to completely debunk the police theory. Lawyer scientist Mukul Sinha pointed out that there is no explanation as to how the alleged conspirators came to know that kar sewaks were travelling by the Sabarmati Express on that fateful day, when the police and intelligence departments themselves consistently claimed they had no such advance information.[18] It is established that it was not Muslims but the kar sewaks who pulled the chain to stop the train, because several passengers were left behind on the platform. The theory of petrol being poured into the bogey also collapses because none of the seventy or more passengers who escaped from the bogey had any burn wounds below their waist. Manoj Mitta, in his surgical analysis, points out that not a single Hindu survivor from the ill-fated compartment endorsed the police claim that Muslims tore through the vestibule and poured large quantities of petrol into the compartment.[19]

The last word has not been spoken about what indeed caused the fire in the train compartment in Godhra on 27 February, 2002. Activists on both sides of the divide hold firm onto their own sinister conspiracy theories. The scientific and forensic evidence at present seem to support the conclusion that it probably was an accident. But one judicial commission and the courts have concluded otherwise.

It is important for us to know conclusively the answer to this question. Right from the start, Prime Minister Vajpayee, Chief Minister Modi, many officials, the police records, one judicial commission, and significant sections of Hindu middle-class opinion in India suggest that somehow the carnage that followed was understandable, even morally justified, because of the train burning allegedly by a cruel conspiracy by Muslims.

But I feel it is morally perilous for us to argue that that anything at all can justify the mass retaliatory killing and rape of other human beings, even

17 Mahesh Langa, "Godhra train burning case: HC commutes death sentence of 11 to life", *The Hindu*, 9 October 2017. http://www.thehindu.com/news/national/other-states/live-updates-verdict-on-appeals-in-godhra-train-burning-case/article19827239.ece

18 Mukul Sinha, 'What if Sabarmati Express had arrived at Godhra at the scheduled time of 2:55am on 27th February 2002?', *Truth of Gujarat*, 27 February 2014. https://www.truthofgujarat.com/sabarmati-express-arrived-godhra-scheduled-time-255-m-27th-february-2002/

19 Manoj Mitta, "'Preplanned inhuman collective violent act of terrorism':What Modi got away with in the Godhra case", 27 February 2017. https://scroll.in/article/830319/preplanned-inhuman-collective-violent-act-of-terrorism-what-modi-got-away-with-in-the-godhra-case

less those who are unconnected in any way from the alleged crimes. Even if some Muslim people had indeed set the train compartment on fire that fateful morning in Godhra station, there is no justification whatsoever for the 2002 massacre of minorities in Gujarat. After all, it is undeniable that Prime Minister Indira Gandhi was killed by her Sikh bodyguards in 1984, but that fact still does not justify the taking of a single Sikh life. No community can be allowed to be held collectively culpable for the crimes, alleged or actual, of individuals. And civilians have no right –legal or moral – to cause any physical violence even to those who might have directly perpetrated a heinous crime.

I do not know if we will ever be sure how the train compartment S6 in Godhra station actually caught fire on the morning of 27 February 2002. But it is certain that despite many years in power, the state has not been able to establish that the fire was lit as part of a pre-planned terrorist conspiracy, even less a cross-border terrorist act, as rashly and dangerously claimed publicly by then Chief Minister Modi, which helped fuel the chain of events that led to the deadly massacre.[20] This unsubstantiated but incendiary claim contributed greatly to dangerously inflaming public anger among Hindus across the state of Gujarat that resulted in the carnage.

The massive evidence of extensive advance planning of the carnage is intensely worrying. The fire in the train, possibly accidental, was not the cause, the flashpoint, but the excuse for the massacre that followed.

Despite this, the same 'logic' reverberates to this day in middle-class living rooms across the country. The reasoning of understandable collective vengeance chokes the flow of human sympathy for the brutalized, bereaved and homeless survivors of the Gujarat communal carnage. Unlike the Bhuj earthquake in Gujarat a year earlier and tsunami two years later, there was no jostling of celebrities, no star-studded concerts, no media houses and newspaper houses competing to raise money for the victims, only a shaming silence. The unstated sub-text was that it was somehow fitting that a gravely tainted community was left to deal with the consequences of its supposed collective transgressions. 'They had it coming.'

---

20 See the press statement quoted in Bunsha, "The mystery of the Godhra fire", *Frontline*, Vol 20, Issue 6, March 2003. Available at http://www.frontline.in/static/html/fl2006/stories/20030328003203700.htm

CHAPTER THREE

Borders in Gujarat

As the years pass, in villages and towns of Gujarat, survivors of the 2002 communal pogrom live with their aching memories, yet have adapted themselves to the new lived everyday reality of second class citizenship. The India of the aspirations of Madhavrao Golwarkar, the second Sarsanghachalak or national head of the RSS from 1940 to 1973, who dreamed of an India in which religious minorities would be allowed to live only as second-class citizens, can be glimpsed in the Gujarat of today.

Across Gujarat, I observe what I regard to be the 'Dalit-isation' of the Gujarati Muslim. Dalits for centuries have suffered appalling segregation, discrimination and violence, the most shameful scourge of our collective civilizational legacy, along with the subjugation and violence against women. Like Dalits, Muslims in Gujarat today also live in segregated settlements, socially devalued and economically ostracised. They are routinely discriminated in schools and police stations; deprived of basic public services like roads, water, electricity, drainage and sewerage; discouraged in both private and public employment; and excluded from social intercourse such as wedding and birth celebrations. Dalits have endured these social and economic disabilities for centuries. But the process of pushing Muslims to the same humiliating margins of Gujarati society as Dalits was compressed into a period of history of just a decade and a half. This is the enduring legacy of the politics of hatred and division which has triumphed in Gujarat (and one that is asserting itself nationally). This is at the heart of the Gujarat model.

Muslims in Gujarat today do not live in the expectation of another imminent orgy of mass violence like the one in 2002. But they stoically survive daily discrimination as an incontrovertible element of daily survival. Markers of Muslim identity are rapidly fading from Gujarati public life. In many villages, one of the conditions imposed on Muslim residents who wished to return, was that the call of the *azaan* from their mosque should no longer resonate in the village. Muslim eateries have adopted culturally neutral names like Ekta,

Tulsi and Jaihind, and no symbols of Muslim faith decorate their walls.

Memories of how life was before the storm – most survivors describe the events in 2002 as the *toofan* or tempest – haunt the survivors each day even after many years have passed; of all that they lost which can never be reclaimed. More than half the two hundred thousand people who fled murderous mobs and burning homes in 2002 can never return to the lands of their birth. Entire villages have been 'cleansed' of their erstwhile Muslim residents. Based on over a dozen years of work and research in Gujarat, I estimate that over a hundred thousand people have been permanently ejected from their erstwhile demographically mixed neighbourhoods of 2002, these settlements 'cleansed' of Muslim residents. A quarter of these internally displaced persons survive in austere underserved relief colonies, established after the carnage by various Muslim organisations, initially as temporary settlements of refuge, but now their permanent homes.

Others who could afford it have moved into the safety of numbers in crowded poorly serviced Muslim ghettoes. They were forced to sell their lands and properties at distress rates to their Hindu neighbours. The state remains openly hostile to these Muslim settlements, and discriminates in providing basic public services like drinking water, roads, electrification, sewerage, schools and health-centres. Some have fled the state forever.

After the carnage in Gujarat in 2002, I have worked intensively with the survivors for a dozen years, including relaocating to Ahmedabad to assist in legal justice work for nearly a year. In these years, in Ahmedabad, as in many parts of the state today, I heard people routinely speak of 'borders'. I found that the capital city of the state after the carnage of 2002 has been socially divided into two parts, one occupied by Muslims and the other by Hindus. People of both communities often speak to me in my visits of feeling unsafe on the other side of the 'border'. The Muslim segment of the city includes the crowded inner-city settlements and slums of the old city, and Muslim ghettoes like Juhapara that have swollen to twice or thrice their original size with refugees who have escaped or been expelled from the mixed villages and city settlements that were their homes before 2002. From what I have seen, these are conspicuously under-resourced and under-served, in noticeable contrast with the Hindu parts of the city, which are glittering and up-market.

Doctoral scholar Charlotte Thomas wrote in 2015 of Juhapara as emblematic of what it means to be Muslim in Modi's India. She describes in Juhapara 'the absence of public infrastructure and services present in other neighbourhoods of Ahmedabad. In Juhapura, there is no street lighting, gardens or parks, no asphalt roads beyond the four-lane axis crossing the ghetto [...] there are no sealed roads. The inhabitants,' she observes, are all 'victims of what local doctors call the 'Juhapura cough', a consequence of the dust. More serious problems come from the water delivered each day, which is almost unfit for consumption.' The doctors she interviewed spoke to her of the many respiratory and digestive illnesses that arise from the intensely unsanitary environment of the ghetto. 'Public hospitals are also nonexistent, and the four public schools here barely cover 10% of the educational needs of the ghetto's inhabitants.' The residents speak to her of 'the administrative 'harassment' that they suffer from police forces, the only representatives of public power visibly present in the ghetto. Arbitrary arrests are a frequent sight, notably of young men, or frequent car searches, *a fortiori* as Eid draws near – in order to find meat that was illegally introduced in the ghetto.' She concludes dispiritingly, 'Although formally Muslim citizens have the same rights as their Hindu counterparts, in Ahmedabad and even more in Juhapura, their ethnicity disqualifies them from an effective form of citizenship.'[1]

'Hindus and Muslims have traditionally lived adjacent to each other instead of in the same building or even the same lane. Their lifestyles, including their food habits, accounted for this separation', notes Christophe Jaffrelot insightfully. 'There was an element of self-segregation in this ancestral arrangement – which, however, did not preclude interaction.'[2] In Ahmedabad, this living side by side began to get eroded with the first major communal carnage of 1969, and again in 1985. But this separation was greatly accelerated after 2002, when even middle-class and richer Muslims like former MP Ehsan Jafri were targeted. Muslims, rich and poor, were forced to find safety in numbers in Muslim localities like Juhapara. 'In Juhapura, former judges, retired IAS and IPS officers and other middle-class representatives have ended up living in the same locality as individuals in much more precarious circumstances', Jaffrelot notes.[3] Living arrangements with a voluntary mixing of classes is welcome, but what we see here is a forced co-living of people who would not otherwise choose to live together but are forced to do so because they can only feel safe among people of their own religious identity. '[A] ghetto is also defined by the absence of public facilities. Indeed, in Juhapura, the state has

1 Charlotte Thomas, 'What Juhapura Tells Us About Being Muslim in Modi's India', *The Wire*, 28 May 2015. Available at https://thewire.in/2606/what-juhapura-tells-us-about-muslims-in-modis-india/
2 Christophe Jaffrelot, 'The Juhapura model', *The Indian Express*, 25 April 2014. Available at http://indianexpress.com/article/opinion/columns/the-juhapura-model/
3 Ibid.

not developed roads, schools or public hospitals the way it has elsewhere – in spite of the fact that this locality has a population of more than four lakh, and has, at long last, been included in the Ahmedabad Municipal Corporation's jurisdiction.'[4]

I have observed that there are 'borders' everywhere within the state now, not just in the capital city, but in all cities and many villages. People speak routinely of 'borders' and of fear of the 'other' community if they cross these borders. These borders have become normal. Survivors spoke to me often sections of professionals like doctors and lawyers, as well as traders, who boycotted Muslim clients, refusing to serve them. Muslim employees spoke to me of their services abruptly terminated after the communal upheaval, with many never restored. I have heard Gujarati Hindu middle-class men and women boast of their refusal to engage even a rickshaw with a Muslim driver. People from the minorities tell me how today it is nearly impossible to rent houses in segments of the city outside their own ghettoes. Even opening a bank account is difficult if one carries a Muslim name. Mothers advise their Muslim sons to shave their beards. National newspapers published reports that Muslims altered their names when admitting themselves in hospitals or travelling in trains, because they feared so desperately for their safety. However, inhabitants on the other side of the borders of the shining cities claim to me that nothing changed for them after the 2002 violence except perhaps that they take new roads to work–roads that by-pass the 'dangerous' Muslim ghettoes, roads that Muslim rickshaw pullers do not want to ply on for they are built over their razed shrines.

For those who could return to their homes, life after the *toofan* is one of segregation, isolation and penury. They survive as second class citizens, shunned by their neighbours. They are no longer welcome in weddings and funerals. People employ them only when there is no one else available. Despite the pain that throbs all the time deep inside, the survivors nonetheless immerse themselves in the simple struggles, the everyday drudgery of just living on.

Their wounds left by the *toofan* could possibly have healed a little with demonstrations of remorse and justice. But this does not happen – the merci-lessness of the original slaughter is matched by the determination, sustained for all these years, of both the state and their neighbours – to block efforts of the victimised people to rebuild their old lives; to refuse to express regret; and to strenuously subvert justice.

4 Ibid.

Many persons who filed charges against their neighbours for the crimes of 2002, found themselves embroiled in false criminal charges, and some even spent months and years in jail.[5] They dropped their charges as this was the price they were coerced into paying to be freed from jail and relieved from the false criminal cases against them. Young Muslim men also lived in fear that they will be picked up for terrorist crimes. Many were forced to spend bleak hopeless years behind prison walls on flimsy charges, of which they were ultimately acquitted. But who could return to them the lost years of their lives? And of those of their loved ones who wait out these years outside in penury and despair?

Moyukh Chatterjee accompanied my colleagues, justice workers and lawyers of Aman Biradari from the Nyayagrah (Justice First) campaign and the witnesses. He observed acutely the ways that second-class citizenship of Muslims was reproduced by and within even the courts of Gujarat. 'Judicial proceedings in the aftermath of 2002 were polarized along the same religious lines that allowed a one-sided attack against Muslims in the first place. The atmosphere inside the courtrooms captured the paradox of legal activism: the Hindu accused were neither remorseful nor afraid, they walked in and out of the courtroom with the swagger of those who did not really care for the rituals performed in front of them; while Muslim complainants were tense, fearful, and needed to be cajoled and escorted by the [Nyayagrah] paralegals. The demeanour of the accused inside and outside the court, the tone and tenor of Hindu defense lawyers who often shouted at witnesses is an important part of victims' experience of what it means to fight for 'justice' in the aftermath of Gujarat 2002. Ironically, while the accused roamed around unrestrained inside the premises of the court, Muslim witnesses and (Nyayagrah) paralegals exercised caution and restraint in the courtroom. ...Since most cases ended in acquittals, the confidence of the accused was not misplaced.' He remarks aptly: 'The courtroom in Gujarat transformed into an official space to unmake the witness; sending a [...] robust message about the subordinate status of religious minorities, especially Muslims, within a Hindu nationalist regime of rule.'[6]

⚘

---

5 See Harsh Mander, *Looking Away: Inequality, Prejudice and Indifference in New India* (2015), Speaking Tiger Books: Delhi, p. 350-52.
6 Moyukh Chatterjee (2016), "Against the Witness: Hindu Nationalism and the Law in India," *Law, Culture, and the Humanities*, p. 1-18.

In fifteen years after the carnage, I have not met a single survivor who has been able to rebuild livelihoods to regain levels of living before the 2002 mass violence. This is partly the result of meagre state support, but more so because of the organised economic and social boycott that persisted even years later against the Muslim community. I have not been able to locate any comparable campaign in the aftermath of any riot in India prior to Gujarat, or any other contemporary account of ethnic conflicts, in which a boycott of this scale is organised and sustained for so many years against the members of a targeted community as has been accomplished in Gujarat. In this sense, Gujarat witnessed an on-going genocidal project. The first phase saw blood flow on the streets; the years that have followed have been the bloodless phase of the genocide, in which the spirit, social standing and economic strength of a community has been systematically destroyed; and when they have been rendered politically insignificant, second class citizens in every way.

Their spirit is broken by this sustained and systematic economic blockade in rural Gujarat of a scale never seen before in the aftermath of the many communal conflicts that the country has witnessed. In the months after the people who were driven out of the village or fled in terror, when they took refuge in relief camps, upper-caste Hindu village leaders organised alternative competitors for as many of the vocations pursued by the Muslim residents as possible. Upper caste Hindus, especially Patels – who were the strongest community behind the massacre – opened shops to compete with the businesses earlier run by Muslims. When the Muslims returned eventually, they found that the shops which some of them gradually reopened were boycotted by the Hindu residents of the village. They could sell their wares now only to the depleted numbers of impoverished Muslims who had returned to the village. To make matters worse, wholesalers who earlier sold them goods on credit refused now to do so, but instead extended this credit to their new Patel competitors. Therefore typically the numbers of Muslim shops are reduced today to a fraction of those which prevailed earlier, whereas twice or more this number of Patel shops thrive.[7] The surviving Muslim shops complain of earning less than half of what they earned earlier.

As I wrote in *Fear and Forgiveness*, 'In many small towns and villages, people returned after months in relief camps only to find that on the govern-

---

Sohini Das, 'A slice of Vibrant Gujarat for the state's Muslim businessmen', *Business Standard*, 3 October 2015. Available at http://www.business-standard.com/article/current-affairs/a-slice-of-vi-brant-gujarat-for-the-state-s-muslim-businessmen-115100300913_1.html

ment land on which their humble cabins selling cigarettes, paan or general provisions had stood for decades, tribal or Hindu shop owners had now established their enterprises. There is no one, government officials or village elders, to whom they could turn for help or justice. Those who have re-started their petty businesses are helpless today if people refuse to pay.'[8] I recall Akhtar Hussain, barely recovered from a police bullet that pierced his face and destroyed one eye and eardrum, had re-opened a small non-vegetarian dhaba in Daboi village with the help of his brother. But hardly a day passed without a gang of hoodlums eating a hearty meal and then threatening to pull down his shop again if he has the temerity to ask for the bill to be paid.

I observed that the economic boycott worked in many other ways as well. 'For decades, Muslim traders from Salia and Natapur bought and sold cattle and goats, and thrived on the small profits that they made from these transactions. After the carnage, no one would either buy from or sell animals to any Muslim trader. Tenants are evicted from agricultural land. Farmers are unable to cultivate because their borewells are stuffed with stones, their pump houses destroyed. No one could rent a house except from another Muslim. In Pavagarh, traditionally Muslim catering establishments served Hindu pilgrims who worshipped at a revered local temple. These dhabas were torched during the violence of a year ago, and their owners were not allowed to reconstruct these anywhere in the vicinity of the temple.'[9]

For other vocations which caste Hindus would avoid due to caste taboos, such as those of masons, blacksmiths, drivers, tailors, factory workers, even farm labour, Dalit and Adivasi competitors were invited to the village, and patronised by the upper castes. In one village, we even found a Hindu was invited to replace the Muslim butcher. This strategy killed two birds with one stone: it further impoverished the already stricken and broken Muslims, and recruited as junior partners Dalits and Adivasis in this on-going organised social enterprise of hate. It is the Una struggle after the public lashing of Dalit boys in 2016 that resulted in the first welcome signs of Dalit-Muslim solidarity against upper-caste oppression in Gujarat, a story that I will come to in a later chapter.

Muslim families struggled and coped, by resort to unskilled labour, often migrating long distances, sometimes to anonymous cities or even outside the state. Children dropped out of school, and women stepped out of their

---

8 Harsh Mander (2009), *Fear and Forgiveness: The Aftermath of Massacre*, New Delhi: Penguin, p.84.
9 Ibid, p.85.

homes to earn wages, to hold the family together. Many looked for self-employment which was not dependent on local Hindu clients.

I observed that for the majority of families who had been forced to turn their backs for all time on the villages of their birth, survival was a daily struggle. 'Many women, who in the past tended their own homes or shops, today beg for work, cleaning dishes or sweeping floors in the wealthy homes of the towns in which these internal refugees have gathered for shelter. Rehana was compelled to pull her two sons out of school, and send them to work in road-side restaurants. 'One little boy brings back ten rupees a day, another fifteen. In this way alone, we are able to eat.'[10]

Despair occasionally does slip through the cracks. Saira, still in a refugee camp in Kalol with forty more families, broke down when I met her years ago: 'I wish they had also killed us,' she lamented. In their village, forty lives were lost, and many young girls and women were raped. Their own shop was looted. 'We are paying five hundred rupees as rent for a small room. My husband now pushes a small hardcart in the town. What can he earn from this? I have four small children. They are always hungry. The people of my village do not even let us enter our village. Whenever I look at our humble handcart, my heart breaks. We used to own such a big shop ... our shop was my entire life. It is lost forever.'[11]

The Concerned Citizens Tribunal also reported:

In many villages, especially in Mehsana, Gandhinagar, Panchmahal and Dahod districts, Muslims who have returned to their battered homes were facing a strictly enforced economic boycott by the dominant castes and communities through their refusal to buy milk products from them, to hire them as labour on their fields, etc. A near permanent loss of livelihood, and therefore a reduction to penury, was an imminent and serious likelihood.[12]

In the moving description of the PUDR report, '[b]ack in their village the victims huddle in the burnt out shells of some houses, in the midst of row upon row of desolate charred structures. The guilty roam free. This is what normalcy looks like this Gujarat summer.'[13]

---

10 Ibid, p.85-6.
11 Ibid.
12 See Concerned Citizens' Tribunal (2002), "Crime Against Humanity Volume II: An Inquiry into the Carnage in Gujarat, Findings and Recommendations", p.129. Available at https://www.sabrang.com/tribunal/tribunal2.pdf
13 See People's Union for Democratic Rights, *Maaro! Kaapo! Baalo!* : State Society, and Communalism in Gujarat", Delhi: PUDR, 2002, p.47. Available at http://www.pucl.org/Topics/Religion-communalism/2002/maro_kapo_balo.pdf

The silver lining was that the boycott was substantial, but never total. It was breached by individual Hindus who opposed this social ideology as unacceptable hate against their innocent neighbours. Over time, after some years, Dalits and Adivasis began to brave the wrath of the dominant caste landlords and returned to their former Muslim traders, because they were able to buy from them very small amounts of wares, and access credit, denied by the Patel shopkeepers. They cited other benefits as well, such as that they could barter eggs and chickens for goods in the shop to Muslim traders, but not with the vegetarian Patels. Also even upper caste Hindus began to invite back Muslim artisans and skilled labour, after five or six years of boycott, because they found that those who replaced them were unable to repair their agricultural instruments, or build and repair their homes as skilfully and cheaply as the Muslims. The transport business has also been restored substantially to Muslims in many rural areas.

The consequences of economic boycott was to make everyday survival for people savaged and displaced by hate violence a daily challenge. But their social boycott was the source of even greater grief for many rural people battered by the violence. Earlier no one needed to invite people on festivals in the village: it was understood that all festivals would be celebrated together. In the past, Muslims contributed willingly for the installation of the beloved Hindu deity Ganesh; today they tell me that they grieve that no one comes to them to ask for *chanda* or donations. It was routine for Hindus and Muslims to attend weddings at each other's households, and give the couple gifts of 51 or 101 rupees; today no one invites them, and, I've been told that if they do, the invitation is so cursory as to communicate that they will not be missed if they do not come. In Vijaynagar in Sabarkantha, I met Muslims who, in desperation, printed two wedding cards, one with Muslim symbols for Muslim guests, and the other with a picture of Ganesh for the Hindus guests. A Muslim invitation with Hindu religious symbols was unheard of until then, but such was their desperation for their Hindu neighbours to attend their wedding celebrations that they even crossed this threshold. But to no avail. Even this did not succeed in bringing in any Hindu guests.

Amina bahen, a middle aged widow weeps often in the loneliness and austerity of her one room tenement in a relief colony in Himmat Nagar. She was married into her village Khumapur when she was 16 years old. 'Where have those good times gone? It was a village where, when my son fell from a tree and hurt himself, Jayanthibhai Patel drove his scooter at a crazy pace 8 kilometres distant, to fetch an auto-rickshaw to take him to the hospital, as

though his own son had been injured. It is the same village where my neighbours attacked my house, and we barely escaped with our lives. Today I only
have my son. If we return and he is killed, then I will have no one. So I have
become a stranger to my home.'

There was a continuous sense of loss in big things, and small. My
justice worker colleague Usman Sheikh recalls an evening in Pahada village
in Sabarkantha, when the elderly matriarch gave five rupees to a *faqir* who
was begging at their threshold. She then began to weep inconsolably. They
worried that they had stirred some painful memories. She explained: 'Earlier
Allah had given us so much that I would never send away *faqir* for less than
50 or 100 rupees, and I would have given him a meal. Today I could only place
five rupees in his out-stretched hand.'

The loss could be even more intangible, and yet no less profound. A
group of college interns from Delhi came to spend a month in summer, and
we housed them with survivors who welcomed them, despite their empty
homes. One day, the women were sitting together and applying make-up. One
elderly woman said she looked like the legendary beauty, film actress Madhu-
bala, when she was young. Maybe the student's face fleetingly reflected her
disbelief. 'I had photographs which would have shown you how beautiful I
was. But these too burnt with our house', she sighed. She mourned the loss
of evidence of her beauty and youth. All interns and our community workers
remarked at how almost *every* conversation with survivors always must go
back to: 'It was not always like this. Before the *toofan*, before 2002...'

※

The brutal assaults on Muslim men, women and children after 58 people
tragically lost their lives in the train fire at Godhra on February 27, 2002 was
intended *and* perceived as a punishment and a warning to the entire Indian
Muslim community. Around this time, Chief Minister Narendra Modi
said in rallies that only he had a '56 inch chest'.[14] It was not just vengeance
against the allegedly 'criminal-minded' Ganchi Muslim residents of Godhra;
it was retribution for an entire community for what the militant Hindutva
vision of history portrays as a millennium of Muslim subjugation, violence
and treachery. Mr Modi himself when he was elected to be Prime Minister

14 Rajiv Srivastava and Anjumand Banoi, "Will take a 56 inch chest to turn UP into Gujarat, Modi to
    Mulayam", *The Times of India*, 24 January 2014. Available at https://timesofindia.indiatimes.com/
    india/Will-take-a-56-inch-chest-to-turn-UP-into-Gujarat-Modi-to-Mulayam/articleshow/29269342.
    cms

spoke in Parliament of a thousand years of slavery, signalling that he too felt that India was enslaved not just by British colonialists but equally by Muslim leaders who ruled India for the greater part of a millennium.[15]

I interacted with innumerable gatherings of Muslim people – in cities, towns and villages across India and with Indian Muslims in many countries in the world after 2002. Muslim people are very diverse, with the same multiplicity of class, language, caste, gender, age and belief, which one encounters among Hindus. They have as little community with each other across classes as Hindus. And yet each time I met different gatherings of Muslim people, I was struck by the extent to which they grieved with the suffering of the victims. The meta-narrative of the pregnant woman whose womb was slit open and the foetus set aflame[16] was repeated and recalled as though it was experienced by a known loved one, as were numerous gruesome stories of rape, arson and murder. Each grieved with a personal sense of loss, each time a new mass grave was discovered, or when a Muslim was killed by the police in a faked encounter. I met non-resident Indian Muslims, who have not returned to India for years, but who lapsed into clinical depression after the Gujarat carnage. Many wept and held my hands, even years later, like people unable to come to terms with an enormous personal tragedy.

More than anything else, I encountered in the hearts and minds of Indian Muslims after 2002 the anguish of intense *personal* betrayal. Each recounted his or her memories of childhood and youth, peopled by close Hindu friends, who they believed loved them without chauvinism: with whom they comfortably shared the spaces of home, play and school, who were an intrinsic presence in moments of joy, celebration and sadness. But after 2002, and with Modi's election three times as the state's Chief Minister, they felt variously stricken. By the open support of their childhood comrades for Hindutva ideologies, or by their deafening silences, their failures to condemn the injustice of holding them culpable only because of their separate religious identity. They would wonder what has changed between them, or were they only fooling themselves that their bonds were untainted by prejudice. And with the election of the person they perceived to be the chief architect of the

15 Debobrat Ghose, "1,200 years of servitude: PM Modi offers food for thought", *Firstpost,* 13 June 2014. http://www.firstpost.com/politics/1200-years-of-servitude-pm-modi-offers-food-for-thought-1567805.html

16 This refers to what allegedly happened to Kauser Bano, a victim of the Naroda Patiya massacre. Babu Bajrangi claimed to have done this. See "Even demons have shame: Kausar's husband", *The Indian Express,* 29 August 2012. Available at http://archive.indianexpress.com/news/even-demons-have-shame-kausar-s-husband/994966/

slaughter to the office of the Prime Minister of the country, cheered on by most of the country's leading industrial leaders, led them to wonder if the pledges of the Constitution, that no person in this country is the child of a lesser god, were in the end a sham.

But although there was a sense of this shared suffering, this did not ensure enduring solidarity with the victims of the 2002 massacre. Since the state government refused to establish relief camps for around two hundred thousand people who had been displaced by the conflict – and the secular humanitarian organisations who came forward to reach out a hand were too few to meet the colossal need for succour to the people who had been critically traumatised and dispossessed – it was mainly the Muslim community which had to support a massive relief and reconstruction effort. Donations poured in from Indian Muslims from across the country and the world over: religious organisations, overseas Indians, rich business houses and probably even the mafia filled the gap left by the abdication of the State and large segments of secular civil society. This gigantic self-help collective enterprise of extending relief and rebuilding homes was admirable and epic: many unknown heroes emerged in these times.

But the modes and institutions for distributing this colossal assistance were built around conventional notions of charity, which were intrinsically inegalitarian and patriarchal. The survivors were never informed or consulted about the funds raised for them, or the plans made for rebuilding their futures. They were not involved in the management of the camps, and even less in the construction and management of relief colonies. In virtually every relief colony, run mostly by diverse religious organisations, residents report that demands were made for them to pay large sums of money – from ten to twenty five thousand rupees – to secure allocation of the homes. They paid this with great difficulty, collecting money from relatives and private moneylenders – and I am sure that the donors were never informed about these demands – but in no colony have they received papers of title to these homes. They live even fifteen years later, at the time I write this book, in constant fear of eviction. The managers of many of these colonies emerged as local tinpot dictators, who could eject dissenters from their homes at will; and single women often complained of sexual harassment and targeting. And they were uniformly hostile to single and independent women.

There is one murky area that needs further sensitive investigation, and this is the alleged role played by crime mafias in 'assisting' and recruiting foot soldiers from direct survivors of conflict, when they were socially and economically broken. In Gujarat I came to hear that some of the major relief camps were funded by the local building and liquor mafia in Ahmedabad. This is an open secret among the survivors. This should not come as a surprise, because when the State and most secular humanitarian organisations abdicate, those in the community who have a lot of money to donate will fill the vacuum. In the Muslim community, which has a very small wealthy middle class, big money can be found from three sources: religious organisations, non-resident Indian Muslims, and the mafia. Each played their role when the community was battered, but each came with their agendas. It is whispered that many affected youth were later recruited by the mafia in cities like Ahmedabad for criminal activities like bootlegging (Gujarat is a state with complete prohibition, in which illegal liquor can be easily procured); but I have no way of verifying these claims.

And compassion wearies. Donors within and outside India increasingly became unwilling to contribute to the survivors' struggles for justice, or to rebuild their homes and livelihoods or educate their children. Conventional class suspicions overtook their view of the impoverished survivors, who they saw to be parasitical and unreasonably dependent on further external support.

Even within Gujarat, there was an almost unbreached communal divide between lawyers of different religious identities, with only rare Hindu lawyers willing to pursue criminal charges against accused people of their own religious faith. But leading Muslim lawyers were also unwilling to fight the cases of Muslim survivors unless they were paid extraordinarily high fees. Survivors gossiped that the greatest beneficiaries of the carnage and the fight for justice that ensued have been local lawyers, whose fortunes have risen from two-wheeled scooters to luxury cars. To make matters worse, even with these high fees, in our work with the survivors of the carnage, we found that many of these Muslim lawyers negotiated behind the backs of their clients 'compromises' with the Hindu accused, in which they agreed to prevent the witnesses from recording truthful statements, in return for money which was shared unequally between the lawyer, sometimes the judge, and the witnesses. We also found that former relief camp managers made their own compromises with authorities: they told me that since they have businesses to run, and properties to preserve, they could not afford to antagonise local politicians and officials.

The more privileged victim survivors also tend to be far more willing to surrender to forms of second-class engagement with the majority community. A large number of Bohra shopkeepers have returned to their villages – and some even supported the ruling BJP government in elections – and wealthy owners of truck companies and garages in cities resumed their livelihoods, accepting the condition that they would not give evidence to the police or courts against any of their attackers. But within, the betrayal does rankle even those who tactically choose silence.

The owner of a transport company with nearly a hundred trucks in Ahmedabad confided to me that the Hindu partner of his company had himself organised the loot and arson of his properties. But months after the carnage, he resumed business with the same partner, as though nothing had happened. However, he met us one late night on his request. He wanted to secretly support another witness who was willing to give evidence against his partner. He was unwilling to openly proceed against his partner, but was happy if someone else facilitated his punishment. But publicly he demonstrated only goodwill to his partner.

※

Since communal violence targets people only because of their religious identity, symbols of this identity are attacked with special viciousness, such as places and books of worship, or cemeteries and cremation grounds. In 2002, bodies were pulled out of recent graves and set aflame. Women's bodies were seen as the 'property' of the community, and therefore violated. In both homes and places of worship that were desecrated, stones with saffron paste were planted, or statues of Hanuman installed which rioters called *Hullad Hanuman* (or Hanuman of the riots), as symbols of Hindu occupation and domination. In many of these locations, these installed symbols remain embedded years later, and some survivors are fighting legal cases to vacate these spurious 'temples' from their properties.[17] In one village, women each morning would collect cowdung. A portion of it was for their homes for fuel or to mix with clay and hay to plaster their walls; but some they set aside every day to throw into the Muslim cemetery as a daily ritual of desecration.

The conflict impacts hard on identity anxieties and aspirations of targeted religious minorities. In the event of a threat, there are two rational responses: to flee or to fight. In response to attacks on one's religious identity, people can respond in two binary opposed ways. One is to try to hide one's identity, and the other is to assert it more aggressively. I find the individuals and communities who are impacted by threats to their identity tend to respond in complex

---

17 Parvis Ghassem-Fachandi, *Pogrom in Gujarat: Hindu Nationalism and Anti-Muslim Violence in India* (2012). New Jersey, USA: Princeton University Press, p. 287.

ways, with elements of both 'safe' assimilation into the mainstream identity, and proud, self-conscious, aggressive, even foolhardy identity assertions.

In a continued climate of fear which prevails just below the surface in Gujarat, there is a much greater effort to hide identities by Muslims in cities of Gujarat. Markers of identity like beards, skull-caps and veils (if they are used, which is not common) remain relatively unchanged among those who live in villages, possibly partly because in the more intimate social economy of a village, it is impossible to hide your identity in the way that is feasible in the anonymity of cities. However, all persons who have returned to their villages after the carnage report that they have had to suppress identity expressions and celebrations. Many have 'voluntarily' disconnected the loud-speakers from mosques which relayed the *azaan* or the traditional call for prayer five times a day. They abstain from celebration of festivals like Bakra-Eid which involve the ritual sacrifice of goats, and if they wished to celebrate, they did so with relatives in Muslim ghettoes in cities. I saw the same 'voluntary' abstention from ritual sacrifice on Bakra-Eid in Mewat in 2016, and heard reports of this from many parts of India.

In Gujarati cities, there are intensified identity expressions, but mostly within the safety of Muslim ghettoes. However, poorer victims often struggle with 'safer' identities in the wider society. After 2002, in cities, especially in the practice of livelihoods, I observe a conscious masking of religious identities. Many of the eateries in the highways are owned by Muslims, but it would be hard except for a trained observer to detect this. The eateries are pure vegetarian, and have names – as I mention earlier – like Ashish, Tulsi and Bhagyodaya, Sanskritised names usually preferred by Hindu businesses, or patriotic names like Jaihind. It is conventional in other parts of India for owners of eateries to decorate their walls with religious symbols and pictures, to bless their business, but none of these are visible in these eateries. The same is true of auto-rickshaws, drivers of which have a partiality all over India to pictures of gods to keep them safe in their risky vocation, alongside pictures of film actresses or actors. But in cities like Ahmedabad, I can detect that an auto-rickshaw is owned by a Muslim only by the fact that it carries no religious symbols.

But in all of this, there are always striking, sometimes dramatic, exceptions. I met in a shanty in Ahmedabad a Sikh truck driver who lived with a Muslim woman for many years. Their home, with those of their neighbours, were targeted and destroyed in the carnage of 2002. This so infuriated him, that he converted to Islam and aggressively wears his newly assumed Muslim identity.

I have observed the least religious orthodoxy among working class and poorly educated Muslims in Gujarat, compared both to the non-resident community of Indian Muslims, and the smaller numbers who have improved their economic status within India. Overseas, there is a growing number of Muslims of Indian origin resort to the headscarf and beard as assertive markers of identity, and resort to orthodox versions of their faith. But most of the working class Muslims in Gujarat worship devoutly at dargahs. Like other Gujaratis, they love to dance the *garba*. They are partial to sentimental and usually Hinduised television soaps and loud film music. Few wear the veil. Contrary to stereotypes, women are assertive even among men, and engage in banter and teasing between genders. There is also scepticism against religious orthodoxy. Some youthful residents of the one of the colonies described the fundamentalist Tableeqi Jamaat – which calls for return to strict Islamic orthodoxy, including the veil and abjuring of music – as *Allah Miyan ke Police* (the police force of Allah). This attracted much merry laughter and approval.

But now, in relief colonies – which thousands of the poorest and most dispossessed of the survivors have been forced to accept as their permanent homes – they are under intense pressure by the religious organisations which established these colonies to follow orthodox religious practices; to wear the *burqa* or at least the headscarf or *hijaab*;[18] and to abandon traditional Indian Sufi forms of worship and prayers at dargahs; and to stay away from television, the radio and 'non-Islamic' celebrations like the *garba* dance.

It is also simultaneously a fact that because they live segregated and under daily threat – discriminated on the basis of their identity and ghettoized to live in the security of neighbourhoods populated with people of their own religious identity– there is in general a tendency common in such persecuted communities anywhere to look more inwards for solutions. This in turn is fertile ground for orthodoxy to gain more willing ears. A large section of working class residents, however, still do not accept these restrictions without a fight, but worry that they may be ejected if they dissent too raucously. The worst hit are single women, who are taunted by colony managers and even male neighbours if they work outside their homes, claiming that they have lapsed into clandestine sex work. Some are offered remarriage to much older men, often with children who are as old as them. Many resist, but some tire of the daily struggle and derision and accept these loveless unequal matches.

18 Soutik Biswas, 'The brave Muslim women of Gujarat', *BBC News*, 27 March 2012. Available at http://www.bbc.com/news/world-asia-india-17508814

In these ways, different identity aspirations and responses prevail between vicarious and direct victims, and between working class and more wealthy survivors. These fault lines lead to potential conflict within religious communities after conflict. Many unite against single women, both colony managers and residents. Residents of relief colonies sometimes sullenly resent that donors invest more in places of worship than in public services; they are angered by non-transparent demands for money for house allocations; the residents of many colonies still have no house title deeds; and they are sullen about restrictions on TV cable and radios. We observe a sharp rise in domestic violence after communal conflicts, displacement and loss. Women are truly the stronger gender; men tend to crack up in these times of crisis, and either slip into depression, or assert their masculinity by drinking or beating their wives. Women by contrast tend to take charge of their families, protect their children, struggle to bring food to the table, and hold their shrunken broken households together.

The most worrying re-assertions of identity are not of orthodoxy, but when they are of hatred of the 'other' identity. In many villages, particularly which have succeeded in driving out all the erstwhile Muslim residents, there are boards at the entrance announcing that the village is a Hindu village in a Hindu Rashtra (country). In some of these, there is a local 'ritualisation' of hate: statues have been erected of 'martyrs' in village Moghri; these are men who died when a house was set on fire after the Muslim residents had fled, and the men were still inside looting, unknown to the arsonists. Each Hindu marriage procession in the village goes and bows before these statues of 'martyrs' to the Hindu cause.[19]

In cities, children are growing up in ghettoes, in which they rarely encounter children of the other community. For those who try to cross the new 'borders', there are often saddening repercussions. We heard the story of a Muslim schoolgirl of an upper-middle class who invited her friends to her home for her birthday party. When they saw the address, in Juhapara, all their parents refused to send their children to the party in the biggest Muslim ghetto in Ahmedabad. Muslim children dropped out of school in large numbers after 2002, to assist their families in times of economic hardship, and their only schooling was in *maqtabs* or informal religious schools in mosques. Children who still are able to study in mixed schools report occa-

---

19 See Harsh Mander, "Conflict and Suffering: Survivors of Carnages in 1984 and 2002", *Economic and Political Weekly*, 45 (32), August 7-13 2010.

sional discrimination from teachers. Students are wary of them as they eat meat and eggs. A Muslim boy was told by a teacher, 'Why do you bother to study, if you are going to end up as a mechanic in a garage?'

But as an entire generation of Muslim and Hindu children are raised with little or no contact with children of the other community, identity assertions, prejudices and even hatred are likely to deepen and coagulate with time. This outcome of seemingly irreversible ghettoization is the greatest victory of those who designed the communal project. I am still haunted by a conversation recorded by film-maker Rakesh Sharma with a six year old Muslim schoolboy in his film 'Final Solution':

> Sharma: *What will you be when you grow up?*
> Boy: *A soldier. Then I'll burn them.*
> Sharma: *Who?*
> Boy: *Hindus'*
> Sharma: *Why?*
> Boy: *Because they did the same'*
> Sharma: *Why do you want to do bad things like them?*
> Boy: *I'll definitely kill them. I won't spare them.*
> Sharma: *Are all Hindus bad?*
> Boy: *Yes'*
> Sharma: *Why?'*
> Boy: *Because they use bad words.*
> Sharma: *What bad words?*
> Boy: *I won't tell you as I don't use bad words.*
> Sharma: *I am a Hindu as well. Will you kill me?*
> Boy: *(Silence)... You are not a Hindu. You are a Muslim.*

☀

It is natural for concerns for security – which minorities typically harbour even in normal times – to surface even more troublingly after outbreaks of mass communal violence, both for members of targeted religious communities and with far greater urgency for those who are the direct victims.

The unsaid dread among the direct victims of the carnage in 2002 in Gujarat, and even other Muslims who lived in the state but were not attacked the last time, was of not even just the possibility of recurrence of communal violence, but the heart-breaking *certainty* that it would recur. Therefore they needed to plan their futures in a scenario in which they were certain that they would be attacked again.

This is not surprising, because the state remained openly hostile to the community; it was seen to be protecting its tormentors, and persecuting the community on frequently trumped up terror charges. Every cricket match, inter-community love affair, festival, or clash between individuals of different faiths are still seen as potential sources of fresh tension. There is large- scale movement away to homes of relatives and friends in Muslim ghettoes, of Muslims who still live in mixed colonies or of residents of colonies which lie in the vicinity of Hindu settlements, when cricket matches are played between India and Pakistan. If India wins, hordes crowd outside their homes and taunt them; if India loses, they are accused of siding with Pakistan and the crowds vent their anger against them.

My colleagues and I, based on our work for over a dozen years among the survivors, estimate that half or more of the affected persons have not returned to their original villages. Many waited vainly for people of their village to invite them back from the relief colonies, but no one came. Some returned uninvited, and recall the grief and fear of returning to their homes with no greeting or helping hand from their neighbours. There were taunts by day and threats by night; and many lost heart and returned to the relief colonies.

Those who did not return live in nearly 90 relief colonies that were built mainly by Muslim organisations, but without the security of title, or of work. Those who were even slightly better off tried to rent or purchase properties in Muslim ghettoes, which are burgeoning with growing numbers of these refugees from hate. But we already noted the dangers of such ghettoes – where people from large numbers of now ethnically cleansed settlements gather to live – to interactions of understanding, trust and respect between people of diverse faiths, which for centuries have defined the civilisational ethos of this ancient land.

Those who still chose to return did so because there was no work in the relief colonies – often built on graveyards or agricultural land near Muslim settlements – where there was no work to be found, or too many people now chasing too few opportunities to earn. They swallowed their pride and returned to guard and cultivate their fields, or try to reopen shops or eateries, or run jeep taxis, all in a continuing climate of economic boycott. Some returned only to be able to sell their lands at some price, but eventually gave it dirt cheap to buyers who knew they had no choices left. In many families, we find that old parents or the oldest sibling returned to the village, but left behind the young to the safety of Muslim ghettoes. The aged would look after the properties, but wanted the young to be safe. Even with the attendant dangers, the older people missed the soil of their homelands. As an elderly woman said to me, holding back her tears: *gaonda to gaonda hi hai, bhai.* 'One's village, after all, is one's village, my brother.'

But each of these village returns had to be negotiated with village elders, and they laid down several humiliating conditions. The foremost of these was they would have to abandon all claims for legal justice, by not testifying against any resident before the police or the courts. Other requirements could include spatial segregation, and muted religious and cultural activities. Their return to their homeland is thus under coercive conditions of segregation, surrender and humiliation.

By agreeing to the condition of abandoning claims to legal justice, many survivors realised that they were placing themselves at greater risk the next time, because they would be perceived as weak sitting ducks. They realised that their best chances to secure non-recurrence was to force the accused to face the police and courts, and hopefully steward them into jail incarceration. This is why witnesses in 250 criminal cases registered after the carnage opted to work with Aman Biradari in its Nyayagrah enterprise, a community based mass legal action campaign that I described in my book 'Fear and Forgiveness'. But those who wished to return to their homes, and many of the relatively wealthy survivors who wished to restart their businesses dependent on the goodwill of the majority, found themselves in a cruel bind. To negotiate immediate safety, they had to give up the longer-term security – and dignity – of the legal battle against their attackers. The assurances of India's secular constitution seemed feeble, powerless in the predicament in which they found themselves.

⁂

A widely shared assumption is that after the electoral endorsement months after the carnage in 2002 and repeated and categorical electoral victories in 2007 and 2012, 'normalcy', economic prosperity and peace were restored to the ravaged state of Gujarat. But I have made repeated journeys almost every month for over a decade into Gujarat over these past years – and for nearly one year I relocated to Ahmedabad to try to help the survivors fight for justice. I observed through these many years the frightening face of this counterfeit peace, built on a resigned social acceptance of settled fear, unequal compromises and the culture and practices of enforced second-class citizenship. There is peace in Gujarat today, but that is because the Muslims of Gujarat have learnt that they must accept everything that comes their way – the denials of justice, stigma, confinement to under-serviced ghettoes, discrimination, state hostility, arrests – and not complain or protest. This second-class citizenship extends in many ways to Christians, Dalits and tribal people in Gujarat as well, and for the latter two groups has an even older history.

As Siddharth Varadarajan argues, Modi, the BJP, and the fraternal organizations of the right-wing RSS, have succeeded in establishing a hierarchy of suffering – between that of the immediate victim community (the Muslims) and the allegedly long-suffering majority community of the Hindus. This aims at creating a moral universe in which questions of official accountability and justice could be postponed indefinitely or actually erased so that the manifest failure of the state to provide security to all is condoned.[20]

It is for this reason that I regard even more terrifying than the sustained and state-enabled mass hate crimes of 2002, to be what followed in the dozen years and more after. These years passed between the hate carnage and – borrowing the words of Bertolt Brecht – Mr Modi's 'resistible rise' to the office of the leader of the world's largest democracy. Much water flowed through the Sabarmati River in the capital city of Ahmedabad which saw the most extensive violence in 2002, during these years. The city, as much as the state of Gujarat, remains bitterly – and I fear now permanently – divided. Muslims are forced to live in segregated ghettoes which are poorly serviced by public utilities and infrastructure. There is this new normalcy of Gujarat, in which Muslims have learnt to live separately, submissively and fearfully, as second-class citizens, much like Dalits have been forced to exist for centuries.

20 Siddharth Varadarajan, '1984, 1989, 2002: Three narratives of injustice, and the lessons for democracy', *Scroll*, 27 February . 2015. Available at https://scroll.in/article/709834/1984-1989-2002-three-narratives-of-injustice-and-the-lessons-for-democracy

CHAPTER FOUR

Nationalising the Gujarat Model

In the India led by Prime Minister Narendra Modi, many of us are dismayed when we observe what was accomplished in Gujarat, under his leadership: the systematic reduction of the Muslim and Christian minorities into second class citizens, by a brutal massacre in 2002 of Muslim children, women and men, without remorse, justice or healing; by boycott, segregation and fear. This indispensable part of Modi's now-fabled 'Gujarat model', is being vigorously nationalised to the entire country, the 'domestication', the 'taming' of the country's religious minorities, their systematic reduction to submitting to second-class citizenship.

However many commentators, including those who were otherwise opposed to Modi's majoritarian track-record in Gujarat, suggested after he was elected to office that we are seeing a new Modi, one who has firmly thrust his past behind him, as he rises to lead the Indian republic. What he would bring to India from his years in Gujarat, would be 'development' and not the baiting of Muslims and Christians. Ashutosh Varshney, for instance, accomplished political scientist, in an important series of essays in the Indian Express, assesses the ideological moorings of Prime Minister Narendra Modi, his idea of India. He argues that domestically two ideas of India have long competed: one based on caste and religion, the other on economic development. He believes that Modi, like India's first Prime Minister Nehru, strives to construct an inclusive and pluralist idea of India built upon the master-narrative of economic development.[1] He admits to the reality of hate battles around religious conversions and beef-eating during the period of Modi's stewardship of the nation. But he regards these only as 'inconsistencies' born from conflicting ideological, political and constitutional imperatives, and is optimistic that Modi's moderate and progressive vision will prevail.

1 See Ashutosh Varshney, 'Modi's Idea of India- 2', February 16, 2016. Available at http://indianexpress. com/article/opinion/columns/modis-idea-of-india-2/

My evaluation of Modi's ideological moorings varies sharply from that of my friend Varshney. Modi's vision for India, and his leadership, are in fact in every way the anti-thesis of that offered by Nehru. For Nehru, secularism and socialism were non-negotiable political and ethical convictions, and he propelled India's economic development by installing the state at the commanding heights of the economy. Modi's vision in contrast is tenaciously majoritarian, hostile to religious minorities, equivocal about social equality for Dalits, and committed to accelerating economic growth driven by mega-private business that is patronised and subsidised from the public exchequer.

Before his elevation as Gujarat's Chief Minister in 2002, Narendra Modi for most of his adult life was a *pracharak* (literally one who spreads the ideology, or organiser) of the Hindu-supremacist Rashtriya Swayamsevak Sangh or RSS.[2] He joined the RSS in 1958, as an eight-year old, and has remained closely bound to it all his adult life. The RSS, today arguably the largest cadre-based social organisation in the world – was founded in 1925 combining Hindu revivalism with racial theories popular in the West and drawing inspiration from the Italian Fascists and the Nazis.[3] As a child, his family lived by selling tea at the railway station in a small Gujarati town called Vadnagar, and pressing oil. He was married early, but never lived with his wife. He left home and started a tea-stall in Ahmedabad, before he became a full-time *pracharak* of the RSS.[4] The RSS assigned him to the BJP in 1985, and he held many positions in it and rose to the position of General Secretary, until he took the reins of power in Gujarat in 2002.

As Chief Minister of Gujarat, as much as during his tenure as the Prime Minister of India, Modi has never distanced himself from the RSS. On the contrary, various ministers of his cabinet were directed by Prime Minister

2 Narendra Modi, as the Prime Minister, has floated his own website and an interactive 'Narendra Modi' software application (as 'app', as it is colloquially called). Under a section titled 'Dedicated Life' on his personal website, it says: 'With this background, an almost 20-year-old Narendra arrived in Gujarat's largest city Ahmedabad. He became a regular member of the RSS and his dedication and organisation skills impressed Vakil Saheb and others. In 1972 he became a Pracharak, giving his full time to the RSS. He shared his accommodation with other Pracharaks and followed a rigorous daily routine. The day began at 5:00 am and went on till late night. In the midst of such a hectic routine Narendra completed a degree in political science. He always valued education and learning. As a Pracharak he had to travel all over Gujarat. Sometime between 1972 and 1973 he stayed at the Santram Mandir in Nadiad, which is a part of Kheda district. In 1973 Narendra Modi was given responsibility of working for a massive summit organised in Siddhpur where he met top leaders of the Sangh.' See http://www.narendramodi.in/the-activist-3129

3 Siddhartha Deb, "Unmasking Modi", *New Republic*, 3 May 2016. Available at https://newrepublic.com/article/133014/new-face-india-anti-gandhi

4 Ibid.

Modi to formally subject themselves to the evaluation of their performance by the RSS.[5] Persons ideologically committed to the RSS are being systematically installed in every major public institution,[6] although many of them have singularly mediocre credentials. There can be little doubt that the RSS defines Modi's fundamental ideology and world-view.

I looked up the RSS website, and quote from it that its 'supreme goal is to bring to life the all-round glory and greatness of our Hindu Rashtra' (Nation). It states that 'Hindus have a 'View of Life',' and that Christians and Muslims who live in India must accept the Hindu world-view.[7] Significantly this is not very different from the position the RSS took in 1947. We are not witnessing a reinvented RSS tempered by the imperatives of India's constitution. Its openly stated objectives even today defy India's secular democratic constitution, with its alternate vision of India as a majoritarian Hindu Rashtra.[8]

The RSS organ *Organizer* in its issue on the eve of India's Independence, rejected the whole concept of a composite nation[9]. 'Let us no longer allow ourselves to be influenced by false notions of nationhood. Much of the mental confusion and the present and future troubles can be removed by the ready recognition of the simple fact that in Hindusthan only the Hindus form the nation and the national structure must be built on that safe and sound foundation [...] the nation itself must be built up of Hindus, on Hindu traditions, culture, ideas and aspirations.'

In a book titled *Jyotipunj* (Beams of Light) Modi wrote about the people he admired most. Significantly *every single* person on his list was a member

5   On September 2, 2015, at an RSS review meeting, the top Ministers in Modi's cabinet made presentations before the RSS and the Vishwa Hindu Parishad. See "At RSS review meet, top ministers make presentations", *NDTV*, 4 September 2015. Available at http://www.ndtv.com/india-news/at-rss-review-meet-top-ministers-make-presentations-1213617

6   Radhika Ramasheshan, 'Sangh Core 9 out of 20', *The Telegraph*, July 5, 2016 Available at https://www.telegraphindia.com/1160706/jsp/frontpage/story_95099.jsp#.WGzNuBt97IW

7   See M S Gowalkar, 'Bunch of Thoughts'. Full text available on the RSS website, here: http://www.rss.org/Encyc/2015/4/7/334_03_46_30_Bunch_of_Thoughts.pdf

8   See "India's a Hindu rashtra, says RSS chief Mohan Bhagwat", *Times of India*, 22 January 2018. Available at https://timesofindia.indiatimes.com/india/indias-a-hindu-rashtra-says-rss-chiefbhagwat/articleshow/62597063.cms; see also "RSS rallies for a 'Hindu rashtra' at Jammu and Kashmir meeting", *India Today*, 31 July 2017. Available at https://www.indiatoday.in/magazine/up-front/story/20170807-rss-in-kashmir-mohan-bhagwat-hindutva-sangh-social-development-1026631-2017-07-31; see also "India will become 'Hindu rashtra' by 2024, says Uttar Pradesh's BJP MLA Surendra Singh", *Firstpost*, 14 January 2018. Available at https://www.firstpost.com/india/india-will-become-hindu-rashtra-by-2024-says-uttar-pradeshs-bjp-mla-surendra-singh-4302275.html

9   Quoted by Shamsul Islam in "Anti-National RSS: Documentary Evidence From RSS Archives", *Countercurrents*, 17 January 2017. Available at https://countercurrents.org/2017/01/17/anti-national-rss-documentary-evidences-from-rss-archives/#_edn2, excerpted from RSS Organiser dated 14 August 1947, under the editorial titled 'Whither'

of the RSS.[10] His greatest hero was Madhav Sadashiv Golwalkar who led the RSS from 1940 for more than 30 years. In his essay on Golwalkar, the longest in the book, Modi compared him to Buddha, Shivaji and Bal Gangadhar Tilak, concluding, 'We are not capable of knowing or analysing Guruji's life. This is a humble attempt to recount those beautiful moments of his life.'[11]

Golwarkar was open in his admiration for Hitler's beliefs in race supremacy. 'To keep up the purity of the Race and its culture, Germany shocked the world by her purging the country of the Semitic Races – the Jews', he wrote in 1939. 'Race pride at its highest has been manifested here. Germany has also shown how well-nigh impossible it is for Races and cultures, having differences going to the root, to be assimilated into one united whole, a good lesson for us in Hindusthan to learn and profit by.'[12] He wished to model India as a Hindu nation on Hitler's fascist imagination: 'It is worth bearing well in mind how these old Nations solve their minorities [sic] problem. ... Emigrants have to get themselves naturally assimilated in the principal mass of the population, the National Race, by adopting its culture and language and sharing in its aspirations, by losing all consciousness of their separate existence, forgetting their foreign origin. If they do not do so, they live merely as outsiders, bound by all the codes and conventions of the Nation, at the sufferance of the Nation and deserving no special protection, far less any privilege or rights. There are only two courses open to the foreign elements, either to merge themselves in the national race and adopt its culture, or to live at its mercy so long as the national race may allow them to do so and to quit the country at the sweet will of the national race.'[13]

Given Golwarkar's powerful, even paramount influence on Modi's thinking, it is instructive also to look more closely at his views on Muslims and Christians who live in India, and their fit status in an India which is a Hindu Rashtra. 'It has been the tragic lesson of the history of many a country in the world,' he writes in his Bunch of Thoughts, 'that the hostile elements within the country pose a far greater menace to national security then aggressors from outside.'[14] It is no wonder that the RSS never

10 Siddhartha Deb, "Unmasking Modi", *New Republic*, 3 May 2016. Available at https://newrepublic.com/article/133014/new face-india-anti-gandhi
11 Quoted in Hartosh Singh Bal, "The Instigator", *The Caravan*, 1 July 2017. Available at http://www.caravanmagazine.in/reportage/golwalkar-ideology-underpins-modi-india
12 MS Golwalkar (1939), *We Or Our Nationhood Defined*. Nagpur: Bharat Publications, p. 35.
13 Ibid., p. 47.
14 MS Golwalkar (1996) *Bunch of Thoughts*. Bangalore: Sahitya Sindhu, p. 177.

participated in the freedom struggle.[15] He never trusted the patriotism of Muslim Indians. 'It would be suicidal to delude ourselves into believing that they have turned patriots overnight after the creation of Pakistan. On the contrary, the Muslim menace has increased a hundredfold by the creation of Pakistan which has become a springboard for all their future aggressive designs on our country.' '(I)n practically every place', he charges, 'there are Muslims who are in constant touch with Pakistan over the transmitter...'[16] His paranoia of the religious minority as the enemy within the country also extends to Christians. '(S)uch is the role of Christian gentlemen residing in our land today, out to demolish not only the religious and social fabric of our life but also to establish political domination in various pockets and if possible all over the land.'[17]

To resolve what he calls the 'minority problem' in India, the pathways he suggests closely follow what he celebrates from Hitler's Germany. 'From this stand point, sanctioned by the experience of shrewd old nations, the foreign races in Hindusthan must either adopt the Hindu culture and language, must learn to respect and hold in reverence Hindu religion, must entertain no idea but those of the glorification of the Hindu race and culture, i.e., of the Hindu nation and must lose their separate existence to merge in the Hindu race, or may stay in the country, wholly subordinated to the Hindu Nation, claiming nothing, deserving no privileges, far less any preferential treatment not even citizen's rights. There is, at least should be, no other course for them to adopt. We are an old nation: let us deal, as old nations ought to and do deal, with the foreign races who have chosen to live in our country.'[18]

No wonder that historian Ramchandra Guha describes him as the "guru of hate,"[19] while the title of a book by political scientist Jyotirmaya Sharma on Golwalkar's ideology is *Terrifying Vision*. Senior journalist Hartosh Bal observes, 'Today, when the RSS wields more control than it ever has over Indian politics and society, matching or perhaps even exceeding the Congress at its zenith, the India that we are dealing with, for better or worse, does not make sense without making sense of Golwalkar.'[20]

15 Ram Puniyani, "Did RSS Really Participate in the Freedom Movement?", *The Wire*, available at https://thewire.in/communalism/did-rss-participate-in-the-freedom-movement
16 MS Golwalkar (1996) *Bunch of Thoughts*. Bangalore: Sahitya Sindhu, p. 185.
17 Ibid., p. 193.
18 MS Golwalkar (1939), *We Or Our Nationhood Defined*. Nagpur: Bharat Publications, p. 47-48.
19 See Ramachandra Guha, "The guru of hate", *The Hindu*, 26 November 2006. Available at https://thewire.in/communalism/did-rss-participate-in-the-freedom-movement
20 Hartosh Singh Bal, "The Instigator", *The Caravan*, 1 July 2017. Available at http://www.caravanmagazine.in/reportage/golwalkar-ideology-underpins-modi-india

For the RSS, India (or their preferred name Hindusthan or the nation of the Hindus) belongs only to its Hindu residents (and to its Sikh, Jain and Buddhist minorities who it sees as offshoots of Hinduism rather than the independent, indeed dissenting religious traditions that they are). Commentators like Jaffrelot and Dibyesh Anand underline that the raison d'être for the idea of Hindutva is to privilege the Hindu community in the territory of India, unlike the rival Gandhi-Nehru-Congress civic nationalism, which asserted that India belonged equally to all its residents irrespective of their religious affiliation.

Dibyesh Anand in his book *Hindu Nationalism in India and the Politics of Fear* points to this dominant strands of the RSS ideology and the ways it is geared to creating a climate of fear for India's minorities. Treating all Muslims with the same Islamophobic brush, Hindutva plays a game of fear with many strands—Islam by its very nature is fundamentalist (the idea of moderate Muslims to them is an oxymoron); the history of Muslim rule in India is nothing but a catalogue of crimes of violence, plunder, and rape of Hindus; Muslims are solely responsible for the partition of *Akhanda Bharat* (united India) and those Muslims who stayed back in India did so because they were not satisfied with a separate Pakistan but desired the Islamization of the whole of India; Muslims, with the active backing of Pakistani and Gulf money, are waging a continuous war against Hindu India. Terrorism, violence, genocide of Kashmiri Hindus, conversion, illegal infiltration by Bangladeshi Muslims, seduction and rape of innocent Hindu girls, and over-population are all conjured up as weapons used by the traitorous Muslims to overwhelm Hindus in India. Christians are said to collude in this war by seducing poor Hindus into conversion and by encouraging separatism in the north eastern regions. By stereotyping Muslim and Christian minorities as the irredeemable anti-Hindu, anti-India Other, Hindu nationalism generates a politics of fear.' It is this politics of fear that we see playing out in India today.

As Ananya Vajpeyi observes, 'Instead of egalitarianism, the Hindu right believes in an archaic arithmetic of adhikaar and bahishkaar, entitlement and exclusion, based on caste, religion and gender ... Onto this unequal social order of considerable vintage would be layered a deadly neo-Fascist majoritarian politics that arises out of the Hindutva imagination of the modern nation.'[21]

---

21 Ananya Vajpeyi, "Ancient prejudice, modern inequality", *The Hindu*, 20 January 2016. Available at http://www.thehindu.com/opinion/lead/dalit-student-rohith-vemula-suicide-ancient-prejudice-modern-inequality/article8124315.ece

Hindus will 'allow' Muslims and Christians to live in Hindu India only if they consent to subordinate themselves to Hindu culture and religious beliefs, and seek no privileges: not even citizen rights. This is the complete anti-thesis of the idea of India embedded in its Constitution, which guarantees equal rights to all persons regardless of their faith, caste, gender, language and ethnicity, and also the freedom to both practice and propagate their faiths. No wonder that Golwarkar rejected India's Constitution as 'just a cumbersome and heterogeneous piecing together of various articles from various Constitutions of the Western countries. It has absolutely nothing which can be called our own. Is there a single word of reference in its guiding principles as to what our national mission is and what our keynote in life is? No!'[22]

Even today, Haryana's Chief Minister who was virtually unknown as a politician before he was hand-picked by Modi and Amit Shah to lead the state,[23] and had served the RSS loyally for 40 years, uses the same language of 'allowing' Muslims to live in India as long as they respect Hindu sentiments. 'Muslim rahein, magar is desh mein beef khaana chhodna hi hoga unko. Yahan ki manyata hai gau (Muslims can continue to live in this country, but they will have to give up eating beef. The cow is an article of faith here),' Khattar said when asked to respond on how he viewed the Dadri incident in which a Muslim man was lynched by his neighbours based on rumours that he stored beef in his refrigerator.[24] He said the Dadri incident was the 'result of a misunderstanding' and said 'both sides' had committed wrongs. 'It should not have happened – from both sides.'[25] (I am reminded of President Donald Trump who also blamed 'both sides' for violence against liberal demonstrators by white supremacists in Charlottesville.)[26] Khattar is reported by the *Indian Express* to 'have compared the incident with a man who sees his

22 MS Golwalkar (1996) *Bunch of Thoughts.* Bangalore: Sahitya Sindhu p. 238.
23 See "From RSS pracharak to Haryana CM: Meet Modi loyalist Manohar Lal Khattar", *Firstpost,* 21 October 2014. Available at http://www.firstpost.com/politics/from-rss-pracharak-to-haryana-cm-meet-modi-loyalist-manohar-lal-khattar-1766931.html. Also see "Profile: Haryana Chief Minister Manohar Lal Khattar", *The Indian Express,* 27 October 2014. Available at http://indianexpress.com/article/india/politics/haryana-cm-manohar-lal-khattar-profile/
24 Varinder Bhatia and Nirupama Subramaniam,"Muslims can live in this country, but will have to give up eating beef, says Haryana CM Manohar Lal Khattar", *The Indian Express,* 16 October 2015. Available at http://indianexpress.com/article/india/india-news-india/muslims-can-live-in-this-country-but-they-will-have-to-give-up-eating-beef-says-haryana-cm-manohar-lal-khattar/
25 "Beef remark: Now a denial from Haryana CM Khattar", *India Today,* 16 October 2015. Available at http://indiatoday.intoday.in/story/never-said-muslims-have-to-give-up-beef-clarifies-haryana-cm/1/500230.html
26 Andrew Rafferty, Marianna Sotomayor, and Daniel Arkin, "Trump Says 'Two Sides' Share Blame for Charlottesville Rally Violence", *NBC News,* 16 August 2017. Available at https://www.nbcnews.com/news/us-news/trump-defends-all-sides-comment-n793001

mother being killed or his sister getting molested, and his anger against the perpetrator getting the better of him. He said even if the person was committing an offence under the law for which he should be punishable, "we have to go behind the incident and examine his manyata. We have to understand why he did what he did".'[27]

※

It is possible to understand Modi's record of treatment of minorities in Gujarat and India in the light of his life-long and open admiration for Golwarkar and the organisation both men served for most of their lives, the RSS. I have elaborated how the doctrine of second-class citizenship of minorities was realized in not just the brutal communal massacre of 2002 in Gujarat but in the systematic state hostility and discrimination against minorities in the dozen years that followed the massacre. I will argue that this same ideological frame influences Modi's worldview and policies even after he assumed the leadership of India.

The complicated yet complementary relationship between the BJP (and its predecessor the Jan Sangh) and the RSS and the range of organisations that the RSS is associated with, is what makes the BJP unique, argues Suhas Palshikar.[28] When the BJP was not strong enough or was out of power, the organisational network of the Sangh kept on consolidating itself. But when the BJP suddenly revived in 2014 and began to surge ahead after that, this unique organisational arrangement could achieve three things. One, many of the RSS affiliates and 'voluntary' organisations registered under the Seva Bharati began to ideologically sustain and control the new regime by deputing their personnel to the formal tasks of the party and/or the government. Second, these organisations came forward to extend support to the various decisions of the new government. He identifies three critical moments in the first three years of Modi's government –the returning of awards by eminent intellectuals, scientists and artists; demonetisation; and the unfolding failure in Kashmir. On each of these issues, many voices from 'outside' the party have emerged from this larger organisational network and joined the debates on behalf of the regime; a mass of new writers and columnists is thrusting itself forward into public discourse,

27 Varinder Bhatia and Nirupama Subramaniam,"Muslims can live in this country, but will have to give up eating beef, says Haryana CM Manohar Lal Khattar", *The Indian Express*, 16 October 2015. Available at http://indianexpress.com/article/india/india-news-india/muslims-can-live-in-this-country-but-they-will-have-to-give-up-eating-beef-says-haryana-cm-manohar-lal-khattar/
28 Suhas Palshikar (2017), "What Makes BJP Really Different", *Economic and Political Weekly*, Vol 52, No 19, 13 May 2017.

just as many persons not directly associated with the party have been occupying the cultural space. And, most crucially, the many organisations of the Sangh network are 'independently' raising many issues and shaping public debates, steering the public discourse unmistakably towards the idea of Hindutva. 'Thus, for instance, love jihad or ghar wapsi were not formally pursued by the party in power. For the record, the Prime Minister assured all minorities full protection, while public debates were revolving around these sensitive issues because there was enough organisational space within Hindutva for such 'fringe' elements to exist and push their own agenda. The vigilantism associated with gau raksha is also an instance of the same confusion between the mainstream and the fringe. Again, the Prime Minister has chastised the vigilantes, but street action and shrill rhetoric both continue because of the organisational space available to them.'[29]

Varshney knows all of this and is as opposed to hate politics as I am. Nonetheless he based his initial optimistic assessment of Modi's new-found moderation and pluralist vision for India partly on occasional statements made by the Prime Minister, most often made on foreign soil to global audiences, extolling India's diversity or calling for social equality. However, I believe that far more reliable markers of his vision for India are his many calculated and calibrated silences within India, and in the belligerent and bigoted hate-speech and conduct of his cabinet and party leaders, and his Chief Ministers especially Khattar and Adityanath. As a result, under his leadership, the country stands dangerously divided and polarised.

❁

Campaigns for *ghar wapsi* or 'home-coming' of Christian and Muslim converts to Hinduism, suggest that only the Hindu faith is 'home' and prod-igals straying by converting to other faiths need to be brought back. Equally strident crusades against beef-eating and 'love jihad', and abusive hate-speeches by Modi's senior colleagues against Muslims; have generated fear and dread among India's religious minorities. Ghar wapsi is a campaign driven by RRS affiliate organisation the Vishva Hindu Parishad (VHP) which is committed to a return to a glorious Hindu past – as their charter says, 'If at all there is any eternal society, it is Hindu *Samaj* [community] alone.'[30]

---

29 Ibid.
30 Sandhya Gupta, "India's Concerning 'Saffron' Tide", Tony Blair Institute for Global Change, 7 April 2015. Available at https://institute.global/insight/co-existence/indias-concerning-saffron-tide

India's Constitution took care to defend not just the right of faith of religious minorities but also their right to propagate their convictions. Contrary to its spirit, there is influential public advocacy for a national law barring religious conversions, which I will talk about in a later chapter. A rash of high-decibel programmes were organised in which converts to Islam and Christianity were 'welcomed back' into Hinduism. 'Politicians everywhere (do say) outrageous things to attract and retain public attention. But in India, the hot air is accompanied with poison gas. Senior political leaders not only say that Indian Muslims should go to Pakistan, they also have been known to compel Muslims to renounce Islam through conversions, thereby violating their constitutionally protected right to freedom of religion. With public encouragement from the RSS chief, mobs of Hindu nationalists in North India forced hundreds of Muslims to 'reconvert' to Hinduism in late 2014. These Muslims, the hardline Hindu groups argue, have strayed from their path and are returning home to the Hindu fold.[31] True to form, Modi had nothing to say about these forced reconversions. Months after they began, he paid lip service to 'complete freedom of faith' in India.'[32]

Dhruv Munjal describes the fate of one such ghar wapsi program in Agra in December 2014. Those brought 'home', he reports, were mainly migrants from Bangladesh who eke out a living as rag pickers, scrap dealers and rickshaw pullers. 'A priest applied *tilak* on their foreheads, tied a red thread around their wrists and sprinkled *Ganga jal* on them. After a *havan,* they were asked to hold aloft an idol of Goddess Kali, under the gaze of the members of the Dharm Jagran Samiti – an organisation affiliated to the Rashtriya Swayamsevak Sangh that was sponsoring the event.' They told him later that they participated in the programme because they were promised Aadhaar cards and ration cards meant for those below the poverty line – citizenship documents for which they were desperate as they were undocumented immigrants. These did not materialise. Munjal reports that after news of the ghar wapsi spread, Muslim clerics descended their colony, and admonished them and said they would be brought back to the faith.

31 'RSS chief Bhagwat says conversions will continue,' *The Hindustan Times,* 21 December 2014. Available at http://www.hindustantimes.com/india/rss-chief-bhagwat-says-conversions-will-continue/story-6OWItkUyzprKIT1fZbGbDL.html

32 'PM Narendra Modi breaks silence on attacks on Christians, ghar wapsi, threatens crackdown against extremists,' *The Financial Express,* 17 February 2015. Available at http://www.financialexpress.com/article/india-news/in-wake-of-attacks-on-christians-ghar-wapsi-pm-narendra-modi-breaks-silence-threatens-crackdown/43933/ See also Shanoor Seervai, "The Rising Tide of Intolerance in Narendra Modi's India", *Kennedy School Review,* July 27, 2016. Available at http://ksr.hkspublications.org/2016/07/27/the-rising-tide-of-intolerance-in-narendra-modis-india/

A mosque in Sultanpur sends a Maulvi to the area daily to allay fears of them converting to Hinduism. *Namaaz* is offered five times a day and religious texts are read out with all members of the colony in attendance. The Maulvi also teaches English, Arabic and Hindi to the 30-odd children who live in the area. The residents say that in their hearts they never changed their religion.[33] Once again, soon after Adityanath's elevation as Chief Minister of UP, RSS activists claimed to convert 43 Muslims to Hinduism in an Arya Samaj temple in Faizabad, on April 23 and May 20, 2017.[34]

The same cultural legitimacy only of majoritarian upper-caste Hinduism underlies first Maharashtra government's ban on both selling and eating beef, criminalising dietary traditions of not only many non-Hindu faiths, but even many Dalit and tribal peoples; and now the union government's ban on trade in cattle for slaughter anywhere in the country.

There is also continuing scare-mongering that the population of Muslims is growing faster than that of Hindus, and a day will come when Muslims will overtake Hindus in India. Apoorvanand remarks, 'Muslims are the only community in India who have to bear the indignity of their newborn being seen as a potential threat to the culture and even security of this country. After each census, even well-meaning analysts and demographers rush to assure Hindus that they will not be overtaken by Muslims. What kind of a country is this in which a Muslim birth is not celebrated, is always seen with suspicion?' There is absolutely no chance that Muslims will ever outnumber Hindus even if they maintain their current levels of fertility (which is unlikely as research shows that all households, regardless of faith and caste, tend to have smaller families as they gain in education and income). But the bigger point is – why should Indian Hindus feel threatened even if the population if Indian Muslims (and Christians) grows?

Especially during various state elections, anti-minority hatred is stoked cynically, not often by Modi directly, but by his close associates of the BJP and RSS. Never in free India has the public discourse been so poisoned by MPs and ministers of an elected ruling alliance. BJP MP Sakshi Maharaj labels madrassas as 'hubs of terror' fostering 'love jihad' and 'education of terrorism'.[35]

33 Dhruv Munjal, "Life after ghar wapsi in Agra", *Business Standard*, April 4, 2015. Available at http://www.business-standard.com/article/current-affairs/life-after-ghar-wapsi-in-agra-115040400659_1.html

34 Dhirendra K Jha, "Yogi effect: RSS men convert 43 Muslims in Uttar Pradesh", *Scroll*, 23 May 2017. Available at https://scroll.in/article/838416/yogi-effect-rss-men-convert-43-muslims-in-uttar-pradesh-to-hinduism

35 Faiz Rahman Siddiqui, "Madrassas are schools of terror: BJP's Unnao MP Sakshi Maharaj", *The Times*

He exhorts Hindu women to bear four children, declaring that in the Modi yug (era), the alleged Muslim practice of having four wives and 40 kids – a fiction of majoritarian paranoia – should be forcefully halted.[36] He further describes Nathuram Godse, Gandhi's assassin, as a 'patriot' and 'martyr'.[37] When he was BJP MP, Yogi Adityanath declares that an India without Ram cannot be imagined, and that those who allegedly torment Hindus with riots will have to pay dearly. Moreover 'for every Hindu converted, 100 Muslim girls will be converted as retaliation.'[38] Minister Sadhvi Niranjan Jyoti in a public rally staggeringly describes those who don't worship Ram as 'haramzade' or bastards.[39] A Shiv Sena MP force-feeds a Muslim canteen functionary during his roza fast.[40] Another, Sanjay Raut, calls for the disenfranchisement of Muslims.

Without even a single Muslim MP in the Lok Sabha, the ruling coalition further alienates its Muslim people when a BJP MP on the floor of Parliament asks a Muslim MP to 'go to Pakistan', as though the country belongs any less to its many minorities.[41]

These are not hate provocations by non-state fringe fanatics. These are displays of unrepentant public bigotry week after week by elected public representatives of the ruling alliance in Parliament.[42] A BJP Parliamentarian Modi's cabinet minister Mahesh Sharma participates in the funeral of a man accused of lynching a Muslim for unproved allegations of eating beef, with the body wrapped in the national flag, an honour reserved for the

of India, 15 September 2014. Available at http://timesofindia.indiatimes.com/india/Madrassas-are-schools-of-terror-BJPs-Unnao-MP-Sakshi-Maharaj/articleshow/42477118.cms

36 Mohammad Ali, "Produce 4 kids to protect Hinduism: Sakshi Maharaj", *The Hindu*, 7 January 2015. Available at http://www.thehindu.com/news/national/sakshi-stokes-another-controversy-asks-hindus-to-have-4-kids/article6763837.ece

37 "Godse was a patriot just like Mahatma Gandhi: Sakshi Maharaj", *The Hindu*, 11 December 2014. Available at http://www.thehindu.com/news/national/uproar-in-rs-over-eulogising-godse/article6682464.ece

38 "Watch: BJP's Yogi Adityanath tells Hindus to marry a 100 Muslim women", *Firstpost*, 27 August 2014. Available at http://www.firstpost.com/india/watch-bjps-yogi-adityanath-tells-hindus-to-marry-a-100-muslim-women-1684103.html

39 "India 'hate speech' minister Niranjan Jyoti keeps job", *BBC News*, 4 December 2014. Available at http://www.bbc.com/news/world-asia-india-30326774

40 "Uproar over Hindu nationalist MP 'force feeding' Muslim during Ramadan", *The Guardian*, 23 July 2014. Available at https://www.theguardian.com/world/2014/jul/23/india-hindu-nationalist-mp-force-feed-muslim-ramadan

41 "'Go to Pakistan!': BJP MP reacts to AIMIM chief's claim that Mumbai bombing convict was sentenced to death due to religious prejudice", *The Daily Mail*, 24 July 2015. Available at http://www.dailymail.co.uk/indiahome/indianews/article-3173897/Go-Pakistan-BJP-MP-reacts-AIMIM-chief-s-claim-Mumbai-bombing-convict-executed-Muslim.html

42 Some of the above was reproduced from an earlier article I wrote that was published in *Scroll*, "One year on, Modi has battered many constitutional principles – but the biggest victim is fraternity", dated 26 May 2015.

country's bravest and highest martyrs and heroes.[43] The minister also brokers state compensation for the accused man who died after illness in prison. The union home minister Rajnath Singh characterises Muslims who were rendered refugees by hate attacks in Muzaffarnagar in 2013 and who therefore took refuge in a Muslim majority town, not as victims but as people who habitually harass Hindu girls; and he roars that they will be taught which of them has 'drunk his mother's milk'.[44] Several hundred youthful protesters in Kashmir are blinded with pellet guns by security forces. The Chief Minister of Madhya Pradesh justifies the extra-judicial killing of eight Muslim men charged with terror crimes, asking whether the state should be feeding them chicken biryani in prison instead.[45] The list is endless and unrelenting.

As Muslim refugees from hate violence in Western Uttar Pradesh migrated to Muslim majority settlements, BJP MP Hukam Singh stirred a nation-wide controversy in 2016 by claiming that more than 300 Hindus had been forced to leave the Muslim majority urbanised village Kairana in Shamli district of Uttar Pradesh because of extortion, threats and violence by criminals of the Muslim community. He was forced to backtrack when investigations confirmed that many in his list were dead, or had left the village even 10 years earlier in search of better schooling or jobs.[46] It is remarkable then that the forced permanent exodus of fifty thousand Muslims from Hindu majority villages because of violence and fear attracted little public attention, even less outrage, although this represented a grave betrayal of the constitutional guarantee of fraternity; but the addition of a few hundred more displaced Muslims in Kairana town was discussed nationally as a threat to the Hindus of that town! The statutory National Human Rights Commission for the first time opened itself to grave criticism not just of inaction (for which it is often justly critiqued), but of actively contributing to a majoritarian communally charged discourse, after it took active cognisance of a complaint of a

43 "At Funeral of Dadri Murder Accused, Communal Speeches – and Ministerial Support", *The Wire*, 8 October 2016. Available at https://thewire.in/71935/dadri-lynching-bisada-ravin-sisodia/

44 Ashutosh Bhardwaj, "In divided Kairana, Rajnath Singh pitch: Dekehenge, kitna ma ka doodh piya", *The Indian Express*, 8 November 2016. Available at http://indianexpress.com/article/india/india-news-india/uttar-pradesh-elections-bjp-rajnath-singh-parivartan-yatra-kairana-hindu-exodus-4363180/

45 "Terror Suspects Fed 'Chicken Biryani': Chief Minister Chouhan on SIMI Row", *NDTV*, 2 November 2016. Available at http://www.ndtv.com/india-news/after-simi-shooting-chief-minister-chouhan-talks-of-biryani-in-jail-1620410

46 'BJP MP backtracks on 'exodus' claims', *The Hindu*, 14 June 2016. Available at http://www.thehindu.com/news/national/BJP-MP-backtracks-on-%E2%80%98exodus%E2%80%99-claims/article14422264.ece

Hindu 'exodus' from Kairana, because their homes and families had been attacked and they felt unsafe to return as Muslims had moved into the town. Despite BJP MP Hukam Singh's communally explosive charges to this effect being disproved,[47] the NHRC still felt it fit to reinvestigate the same communally motivated charges. Its team visited Kairana and concurred in its report that the rise of Muslim populations in the town 'has permanently changed the social situation in Kairana town and has led to further deterioration of law and order situation.' The NHRC report in effect reflected majoritarian prejudice by regarding these Muslim migrants not as hate-refugees deserving the defence of the NHRC but as people responsible for raising levels of crime and the harassment of women which resulted in the 'exodus' of law-abiding Hindu residents of Kairana.

The BJP waged a polarising election campaign in a bid to form its first government in Assam during the stat elections of 2017, confirmed by Reuters' reports. In campaign rallies in Assam, it 'vowed to disenfranchise millions of Muslim immigrants in Assam', and also promised to 'identify and deport younger illegal migrants, in response to rising discontent among the state's Hindus.' Himanta Biswa Sarma, the BJP's election manager, after his party's resounding victory, told Reuters that the government would bar Muslims of Bangladeshi origin who entered India between its first census in 1951 and 1971, when Bangladesh won independence, from voting. But Modi's government said it would welcome Hindu minorities from mainly Muslim Bangladesh and Pakistan.[48] The BJP election victory in Assam – the first in the state – was followed by massive official coercive action that targeted and uprooted tens of thousands of Muslims in Assam, charging them to be forest or riverine encroachers or foreigners. 'There is an openly and distinct anti-Muslim bias in all of these actions', human rights lawyer Aman Wadud tells me. People are barely given a few hours' notice before they are displaced, their homes destroyed, without any chance to show their documents. It is not unusual for some blood relations from the same family to be deemed foreigners, and others legitimate citizens. Life in foreigner detention camps, says Abdul Kalam Azad, a postgraduate researcher from TISS Guwahati, is worse than even a jail, and families sometimes have to spend years

---

47 'Uttar Pradesh: Officers say Kairana MP list has dead, 68 who left long back', *The Indian Express*, 13 June 2016. Available at http://www.thehindu.com/news/national/BJP-MP-backtracks-on-%E2%80%98exodus%E2%80%99-claims/article14422264.ece

48 Krishna N Das, "Modi's BJP vows to strip Muslim immigrants of vote in Assam", *Reuters*, 10 March 2016. Available at https://in.reuters.com/article/india-politics/modis-bjp-vows-to-strip-muslim-immigrants-of-vote-in-assam-idINKCN0WC2WR

there to prove that they are legitimate Indian citizens. 'The Border Police are supposed to conduct investigations before forwarding the Reference Cases to the tribunals. But, rarely do they investigate the cases at this point. They often file the cases against people despite [the fact] they have all valid Indian citizenship documents, because of a communal bias and also when they fail to extort the demanded bribes from the poorer victims,' Aman Wadud said. 'So, it's easy to figure out why over 95 percent of the people, who were identified as suspected citizens by border police in the past few years, have been declared Indian citizens by the tribunals. ... That the Muslims are becoming victims of a bias is clear from the fact that over 80 percent of the Reference Cases involved Muslims,' Wadud added.[49]

Through all of this of course Prime Minister Modi maintains a sage-like silence, with never a public reprimand, strategically voiceless even as his hand-picked party president, ministers, chief ministers and legislators continue to stoke divisive fires. 'Throughout repeated assaults on freedom of expression, Modi has remained stoic and stony-faced. When he does address the public, he uses banal phrases instead of taking a stance against bigotry. He cannot be held accountable for every instance of intolerance; undoubtedly, many take place out of his purview. But his typical, ostrich-like response, of saying nothing or tweeting platitudes when something serious or disturbing happens, is inadequate'.[50] When his Defence Minister Manohar Parrikar, no less, declares that he has no patience with a nuclear policy that pledges India not to resort to first-use nuclear aggression,[51] the Prime Minister just days later describes the Minister as one of the finest of the 'nine jewels' of his cabinet.[52]

❊

Fraternity, our common sisterhood and brotherhood, would if fully realized, result in a seamless oneness, or unity, amidst the almost limitless diversities of this country. This is an ideal we the people of India wrote into our constitution

49 Maaz Hussain, "Muslims claim bias in anti-illegal immigrant operation", *VOA News,* 9 September 2016. Available at https://www.voanews.com/a/india-hindus-muslims-assam-state/3500713.html
50 Shanoor Seervai, "The Rising Tide of Intolerance in Narendra Modi's India", *Kennedy School Review,* July 27, 2016. Available at http://ksr.hkspublications.org/2016/07/27/the-rising-tide-of-intolerance-in-narendra-modis-india/
51 "Sushant Singh, "Manohar Parrikar questions India's no first-use nuclear policy, adds 'my thinking'", *The Indian Express,* 11 November 2016. Available at http://indianexpress.com/article/india/india-news-india/manohar-parrikar-questions-no-first-use-nuclear-policy-adds-my-thinking-4369062/
52 "Manohar Parrikar, the brightest ratna in Cabinet: PM Narendra Modi", *The Indian Express,* 14 November 2016. Available at http://indianexpress.com/article/india/india-news-india/manohar-parrikar-the-brightest-ratna-in-cabinet-pm-narendra-modi-4373866/

and then forgot. Instead of complete unity, we articulated with the passing of the years, interim ideals of amity, harmony and peaceful co-living. These in turn required at the minimum two fundamental principles in public life – of public civility, and public fairness. Both these minimum principles for fraternal co-living have been badly battered in during Modi's stewardship of the central government.

Not just public civility. Take now public fairness. Only consider the state of Gujarat. Maya Kodnani, convicted with 28 years for leading the brutal slaughter in Naroda in 2002 of 97 Muslims, including 36 women and 35 children, is released on bail for an intestinal malady since July 2014, and has remained on bail since.[53] Another infamous organiser of the slaughter Baju Bajrangi, also serving an extended life term, is freed on bail for an eye aliment in April 2015. Caught in 2006 by Tehelka on secret camera it may be recalled that he had bragged, 'we hacked, burned, set on fire ... because these bastards don't want to be cremated ... I have just one last wish ... let me be sentenced to death ... just give me two days before my hanging and I will go and have a field day... I will finish them off ...... at least 25,000 to 50,000 should die.'[54] Senior police officer Vanzara, charged with the murder in fake encounters of teenager Ishrat Jehan, Sohrabuddin and others, was released on bail in February 2015 to a hero's welcome.[55] By contrast, courageous and brave whistle-blowing police officers Rahul Sharma, Satish Verma and Rajnish Rai face a barrage of literally scores of charges. An exhausted but unbending Sharma finally took voluntary retirement.[56] Gutsy Teesta Setelvad who pursued many battles for legal justice for survivors of the 2002 carnage, faces multiple criminal charges and escaped imminent arrest only through the intervention of the Supreme Court.[57] Human rights lawyer Indira Jaising who filed my appeal in the Mumbai High Court against the discharge of Amit Shah from grave criminal charges framed by the Central Bureau of Investigation for his role in the 'fake

---

53 "Gujarat HC grants bail to Maya Kodnani", *The Hindu*, 30 July 2014. Available at http://www.thehindu.com/news/national/gujarat-high-court-grants-bail-suspends-sentence-of-maya-kodnani/article6264567.ece

54 Ashish Khetan, "'Muslims, They Don't Deserve To Live", *Tehelka*, 43(4), 3 November 2007. Available at http://www.tehelka.com/2007/11/muslims-they-dont-deserve-to-live/

55 Rahi Gaikwad, "Vanzara walks out of jail after eight years to grand reception", *The Hindu*, 18 February 2015. Available at http://www.thehindu.com/news/national/other-states/controversial-cop-vanzara-walks-free-says-acche-din-have-arrived/article6908844.ece

56 "Gujarat: Rahul Sharma seeks voluntary retirement", *Hindustan Times*, 21 November 2014. Available at http://www.hindustantimes.com/india/gujarat-rahul-sharma-seeks-voluntary-retirement/story-4XJFgGo4yiHrWUYXJ3JMWK.html

57 David Barstow, "Longtime Critic of Modi Is Now A Target", *The New York Times*, 19 August 2015. Available at https://www.nytimes.com/2015/08/20/world/asia/teesta-setalvad-modi-india.html

encounter' killing Sohrabuddin, was submerged in a deluge of legal actions against her NGO.[58]

Dissent with the government's political and cultural agenda, economic policy or militaristic postures is savagely attacked as 'anti-national'.[59] Bludgeoning dissenters with sedition charges, as in Jawaharlal University in Delhi,[60] and left-leaning students with right-wing student violence as in Ramjas College,[61] also in Delhi, has become more common.

The Alliance for Justice and Accountability, an umbrella coalition of progressive organizations across the United States, in its report titled Minority Rights Violations in India, released on May 23, 2017, observed that 'The same forces that have perpetuated caste discrimination are also spearheading India's seemingly relentless drift away from secularism and religious pluralism, especially over the course of the last three years.' It observed that in 2016, a global index of human rights and social and religious freedoms by Pew Research Center placed India among the worst 10 of the world's 198 countries when judged for 'social hostilities'. It further stated that 'Laws curbing religious conversion, the ban on sale and possession of beef in many states and the curbs placed on NGOs represent the state's response to forced conversions, the brutal violence of 'cow protection' groups and the harassment and intimidation of human rights defenders respectively. In all cases, *the state has become an enabler of repression, often going to great lengths to defend and normalize the abuse* (my italics)'.[62]

Leading social and political commentator Pratap Bhanu Mehta says it would be churlish not to admit to the power of Modi as a politician. 'Modi is an unprecedented phenomenon in the annals of popular politics. He has reduced his competition to minions fighting over scraps. He has weathered

58 Rahul Tripathi, "FCRA licence of Indira Jaising's NGO Lawyers Collective cancelled", *The Indian Express*, 7 December 2016. Available at http://indianexpress.com/article/india/indira-jaising-ngos-fcra-licence-cancelled-4414280/

59 See Harish C Menon, "In Modi's India, there are only two sets of people: nationals and anti-nationals", *Quartz India*, 16 February 2016. Available at https://qz.com/617389/in-modis-india-there-are-only-two-sets-of-people-nationals-and-anti-nationals/. See also Supriti David, "India's Newest Scapegoat: The 'Anti-National'", *The Citizen*, 15 June 2017. Available at http://www.thecitizen.in/index.php/en/newsdetail/index/8/11005/indias-newest-scapegoat-the-anti-national

60 Krishnadev Calamur, "The Sedition Charge Against a Student Leader in India", *The Atlantic*, 12 February 2016. Available at https://www.theatlantic.com/international/archive/2016/02/india-jnu-sedition/462567/

61 See Akshit Sangomla, "ABVP Disrupts, Vandalises Literary Event at Ramjas College", *The Wire*, 22 February 2017. Available at https://thewire.in/education/abvp-disrupts-event-ramjas-college

62 "Minority Rights Violations in India: A Report by Alliance for Justice and Accountability", 23 May 2017, Washington DC, p.3. Available at http://www.indianet.nl/pdf/MinorityRightsViolationsInIndia-2017.pdf

every criticism. He has taken every risk and put himself on the line. He has defied every prediction, and written his own script of popular acclamation. No conventional wisdom of politics applies to him. Modi still manages to make other parties look like tired, corrupt, negative emblems of the past; people still repose faith in him as the energetic, clean, dynamic, hopeful repository of the future.'[63]

But Mehta too is intensely dismayed by what he sees as Modi's author-itarian suppression of dissent, an undeclared Emergency. 'Nationalism is used to stifle all thinking. The cultivation of collective narcissism to stifle all individuality, the promulgation of uncontested definitions of nationalism to pre-empt all debate over genuine national interest, the constant hunt for contrived enemies of the nation, is suffocating thought. ...The articulation of social protest is more difficult (with) use of preventive detention...The covert use of state power to keep the press, particularly television media, aligned with the government's purposes, has produced something far more insidious than censorship: It has shown how much conformity can be produced without overt censorship...The effective way in which Indian civil society's revolt against corruption has been neutralised and made invisible is astounding. Every corruption scam, from Vyapam onwards, is wiped out of public discus-sion. ... Academic institutions are threatened if students and faculty exercise their rights. He speaks of the 'unfettered use of surveillance', the 'attempts to control the judiciary', the 'arbitrary use of the state machinery of law enforcement, from police to CBI', 'the growing use of militarism and military iconography in politics', and 'clamping down on those who question govern-ment propaganda.'[64]

Salil Shetty, Secretary General of Amnesty International, also observes that India is firmly on the path to become an illiberal democracy. But he adds that this is a global phenomenon. 'I was at the G20 [summit] in Hamburg, that picture of G20 leaders' group is a rather scary one. If you take out [French Presi-dent Emmanuel] Macron, [Canadian PM Justin] Trudeau and [German Chan-cellor Angela] Merkel and the EU, which is one of the G20 members, and you look at the other 16, it is not a very encouraging picture right now. We are at that juncture in history where for a combination of reasons, we have a set of leaders

63 Pratap Bhanu Mehta, "Victor and the vanquished", *The Indian Express,* 13 March 2017. Available at http://indianexpress.com/article/opinion/columns/victor-and-the-vanquished-narendra-modi-bjp-elections-results-congress-opposition-uttar-pradesh-uttarakhand-4567245/

64 Pratap Bhanu Mehta, "There is no Emergency", The Indian Express, 5 November 2016. Available at http://indianexpress.com/article/opinion/columns/emergency-period-india-ndtv-ban-media-freedom-3737771/

who have come to power through elections. ...In practice, all of these leaders are using a similar playbook. They start with silencing the media, they crush civil society, and kick up the entire de-legitimisation discourse, and systematically emasculate the judiciary. The three pillars of a democracy are systemically dismantled.... Even in campuses (in India), academics are very nervous to speak their mind. They have to look over their shoulders. It is very easy to create this kind of a paranoia in the society, it has a kind of chilling effect.'[65]

UCLA historian Vinay Lal said in an interview to the Indian Express that he believes that 'the kind of anti-Muslim sentiment in US or parts of Western Europe has repercussions, emboldens the advocates of Hindutva. The notion is that if Muslims, particularly in the so-called modern West, can be attacked, then we can do that too, we have the licence to do that. In the US, I see many advocates of Hindutva who are now suggesting US, India and Israel form a natural alliance with one another as, in their worldview, "these democracies" are being "threatened" by forces of Islam. ...It is not just the RSS or VHP but a slightly larger strand of Indian society that has become complicit in (these attacks), exactly like in the US. There was a virulent white racism that was so pervasive that you did not need to have institutional membership in the KKK or John Birch Society, people were complicit without a formal association.'[66]

Therefore I cannot find hope in the straws in the wind of occasional progressive utterances by Modi. The enormous chasm between these stray statements and the actual practice of his government and party is not mere 'inconsistency' as characterised by Varshney, but dangerous and cynical double-speak. I worry deeply about the Prime Minister's deafening silences, as well as his demonising of opposition to his policies[67] – while his government, his party and the Sangh organisations to which he bears allegiance, continue to create wounds that may never heal. I worry about how bigots across the country persecute and attack minorities,[68] their places of worship

65 Josy Joseph, "This is a general crackdown on anybody critical of govt., says Amnesty International head", *The Hindu*, 21 July 2017. Available at http://www.thehindu.com/opinion/interview/interview-with-salil-shetty-amnesty-international-secretary-general/article19326754.ece

66 Seema Chishti, "What we see in India is the difference between formal and real citizenship: Historian Vinay Lal", *The Indian Express*, 31 July 2017. Available at http://indianexpress.com/article/india/what-we-see-in-india-is-the-difference-between-formal-and-real-citizenship-historian-vinay-lal-ucla-professor-4755247/

67 For instance, "India suffering because of Cong policies, Modi says and lists Partition and hurry over Telangana", *The Telegraph,* 7 February 2018. Available at https://www.telegraphindia.com/india/india-suffering-because-of-cong-policies-modi-says-and-lists-partition-dgtl-206814. See also Jatin Gandhi, "Modi attacks opposition for criticizing 'war on black money and corruption'", *Hindustan Times,* 25 November 2016. Available at https://www.hindustantimes.com/india-news/common-man-has-become-a-soldier-against-corruption-black-money-pm-modi/story-wI6v740pZE5cgVJhuBwNHM.html

68 See Sandipan Baksi and Aravindan Natarajan, "Mob lynchings in India: A look at data and the

and livelihoods, often with impunity. Divisive agendas, cloaked in claims of patriotism, are raised keeping communal tempers also high. One day it is love jihad, another cow slaughter, a third Pakistan's perfidy, a fourth university dissent. Muslims and Dalits have been reduced to living with fear and violence, almost like second-class citizens.

None of this still prevents world leaders from warmly embracing and endorsing him, including Obama when he was President of the United States, quickly developing an amnesia about his long record of not just minority-baiting but also the taint that one of the most cruel pogroms of massacring Muslim people occurred under his watch. Barack Obama agreed to author an article in *Time*'s annual list of the hundred most influential people in the world, where he wrote 'As a boy, Narendra Modi helped his father sell tea to support their family. Today, he's the leader of the world's largest democracy, and his life story–from poverty to prime minister–reflects the dynamism and potential of India's rise.' Modi has travelled a long way from being a global pariah, his 10 year visa ban to the United States, and boycott by the European Union and the United Kingdom for his alleged role in the brutal massacre of Muslims in Gujarat in 2002.

✺

Despite all of this, for those still inclined to give Mr Modi the benefit of the doubt, in 2017 more than half-way through his tenure, he finally threw all masks, however thin, to the winds. Prime Minister Modi and his most trusted aide Amit Shah audaciously signalled to both national and global public opinion that they feel no need for either masks or fig-leafs any longer. So many commentators in the mainstream media had wasted reams to persuade us that the emphatic vote for the BJP in the spring elections of 2017 in Uttar Pradesh represented not a hard communal consolidation of the Hindu voter against the perceived Muslim 'other'. It was instead, they argued, a cross-caste, cross-community vote for *sab ka vikas,* for development for all, and Modi was the new Indira Gandhi, the combative leader for building a better life for the poor. Journalist and Union minister MJ Akbar wrote in the *Times of India* before the UP elections results: '[T]his election was not about religion; it was about India, and the elimination of its inherited curse, poverty. It was about good governance.'[69]

story behind the numbers", *Newslaundry,* 4 July 2017. Available at https://www.newslaundry.com/2017/07/04/mob-lynchings-in-india-a-look-at-data-and-the-story-behind-the-numbers
69 MJ Akbar, "The poor have embraced Modi, and the vote-merchants still don't get it", *The Times*

Many Hindu voters evidently read the election results quite differently. They saw it just the way many voters saw the election of Donald Trump in the United States a few months earlier, as a vote for majoritarian triumphalism, a vote against Muslims and minorities, a vote that legitimised prejudice and hatred. I saw a Facebook post of a notice pasted in villages of Gorakhpur district in Uttar Pradesh. It starts with the rallying slogan of the Ram Janm Bhumi movement – Jai Shri Ram. It goes on to give notice to the Muslims of the village that they must leave the village by the end of the year. It warns them that if they do not comply, then they themselves will be responsible for the consequences. It goes on to warn them that they will be treated in the way that they are being treated in Trump's America, because a BJP government will be installed in Uttar Pradesh. Decide quickly, the notice says, because you do not deserve to live in the village.[70] It is signed by the Hindus of the village, whose *sanrakshak* or patron is said to be Yogi Adityanath, Member of Parliament from Gorakhpur. *The Times of India* reported that similar posters had come up in more than a dozen places in villages of Bareilly.[71]

By selecting one of its most belligerent anti-Muslim campaigners, given to unapologetically coarse hate speech and skirmishes, Yogi Adityanath as Chief Minister of the country's largest state Uttar Pradesh, Modi and Amit Shah gestured unambiguously and brazenly their frank and unashamed resort to hard-line Hindutva as the calling card of their party. The election speeches of Modi and Shah in the UP elections had already signalled the direction the party has chosen.[72] Yogi Adityanath's hate speeches are in-the-face and dangerously toxic. Ever since he was hand-picked by Modi and Shah as Chief Minister, the social media is full of his pronouncements.[73] His intent is unambiguous:

of India, 12 March 2017. Available at http://timesofindia.indiatimes.com/home/sunday-times/all-that-matters/the-poor-have-embraced-modi-and-the-vote-merchants-still-dont-get-it/articleshow/57597948.cms

70 "In Modi's 'Uttam Pradesh', posters asking Muslims to leave is a sign of things to come", *Daily O*, 16 March 2017. Available at http://www.dailyo.in/politics/uttar-pradesh-bareilly-muslims-leave-jiangla-hindutva/story/1/16204.html

71 Piyush Rai, "Posters in Bareilly village ask Muslims to leave", *Times of India*, 15 March 2017. Available at http://timesofindia.indiatimes.com/city/bareilly/posters-in-bareilly-village-ask-muslims-to-leave/articleshow/57655088.cms

72 Ajoy Ashirwad Mahaprashasta, "Polarisation, 'Nationalism' and Confusion: BJP's Unholy Mix of Strategies in UP", *The Wire*, 26 February 2017. Available at https://thewire.in/112037/bjp-up-election-strategies/

73 I rely here on two compilations. The first is by Meghnad Bose, "New UP CM Yogi Adityanath's Tryst With Free (Hate?) Speech", *The Quint*, 19 March 2017. Available at https://www.thequint.com/india/2017/03/19/new-up-cm-yogi-adityanath-most-controversial-quotes-hate-speech-or-free-speech – The second is "Hindutva unmasked: Yogi Adityanath, BJP's most strident face, will be its chief minister in UP", *Scroll*, 18 March 2017. Available at https://scroll.in/article/832168/hindutva-unmasked-yogi-adityanath-bjps-most-strident-face-will-be-its-chief-minister-in-up

'I will not stop till I turn UP and India into a Hindu rashtra.' He blames Muslims for communal violence: 'In places where there are 10 to 20% minorities, stray communal incidents take place. Where there are 20 to 35% of them, serious communal riots take place and where they are more than 35%, there is no place for non-Muslims.' He claims successive governments in Uttar Pradesh pursued policies of 'pseudo-secularism and appeasement' which 'speak against the majority community in the name of secularism.' A falsehood that even Prime Minister Modi was to echo was that 'Governments in UP give land for kabristans (graveyards) but not for shamshanghats (cremation grounds).' Even more sinister are his open threats to Muslims. 'Every time a Hindu visits the Vishwanath temple, the Gyanvapi mosque taunts us. If given a chance, we will install statues of Goddess Gauri, Ganesh and Nandi in every mosque.' 'If one Hindu is killed, we won't go to the police, we'll kill 10 Muslims.' And worse, 'If they take one Hindu girl, we'll take 100 Muslim girls.' The Ram Mandir is high on his agenda. 'When they could not stop karsevaks from demolishing the Babri Masjid, how will they be able to stop us from carrying out the construction of the mandir?' He cautioned Hindu parents to warn their daughters about 'love jihad', by which young Muslim men are alleged to try to trap Hindu girls in marriage only to convert them to Islam and produce dozens of Muslim babies. He also expressed fears that 'high Muslim fertility rates' could lead to a demographic imbalance. He said those 'who want to avoid Yoga and Lord Shankar can leave Hindustan.' He also declared that those opposing the surya namaskar sequence of yogic exercises should 'drown themselves in the sea'. He compared actor Shah Rukh Khan to Pakistani terrorist Hafiz Saeed and said the actor should go to that country if he did not like the atmosphere in India. He demanded that the family of Mohammad Akhlaq, who was lynched in Dadri by a mob of his neighbours who claimed he had stored beef in his refrigerator, should face charges for cow slaughter and be stripped of state assistance they had been given after his killing. Remember that Dadri falls in Uttar Pradesh.[74]

Any of these declarations amount to gravely provocative and culpable criminal hate speech. Yogi Adityanath has a number of hate crime cases lodged against him.[75] (As Chief Minister, he is now closing the criminal

---

74 See "Polarisation, 'Nationalism' and Confusion: BJP's Unholy Mix of Strategies in UP", *The Wire*, 26 February 2017. Available at https://thewire.in/112037/bjp-up-election-strategies/
75 Dhirendra K Jha, "Yogi Adityanath as Uttar Pradesh chief minister: What happens to the cases against him", *Scroll*, 21 March 2017. Available at https://scroll.in/article/832327/with-adityanath-now-chief-minister-of-uttar-pradesh-what-happens-to-the-cases-against-him

cases filed against him in brazen disregard of the obvious conflict of interest). These are not the utterances of an outrageous fringe rabble-rouser. He is the man chosen by the country's Prime Minister to lead the country's largest state, which if it was independent would be the world's fifth most populous country of over 200 million people. Among these, a fifth or around 40 million are people of Muslim faith. The fringe has become the core.

It is instructive to look at 4 private member bills that Yogi Adityanath had introduced in Parliament. Apart from the one seeking a nationwide ban on the slaughter of the 'cow and its entire progeny', another sought to amend the Indian Constitution to replace 'India, that is Bharat' with 'Bharat, that is Hindustan', presumably to underline this to be a nation of Hindus. One more sought to ban religious conversions in India, and yet another to secure a uniform civil code throughout India. Yogi Adityanath, with his agenda and history of aggressive minority-baiting, one that would teach them to submit to life as second-class citizens, was handpicked to lead a state which if independent would be the fifth largest in the world.

Pratap Bhanu Mehta expressed profound dismay after the selection of Yogi Adityanath as the Uttar Pradesh Chief Minister. 'In the moment of his political triumph', he observed sadly, 'Modi has chosen to defeat India. Hubris has set in. The BJP believes it can get away with anything – it now intends to.' He describes the elevation of Yogi Adityanath as an 'odious and ominous' development, for the BJP to pick 'the single most divisive, abusive, polarising figure in UP politics', 'the mascot of militant Hindu sectarianism, reactionary ideas, routinised conflict and thuggery in political discourse, and an eco-system where the vilest legitimations of violence are not far away.' It sends as clear a message as it is possible to send that 'the already accomplished political fact of the marginalisation of minorities in UP and elsewhere will now be translated into a programme of their cultural, social and symbolic subordination.' It signals that the politics of the BJP will now be 'shaped largely by resentment rather than hope, collective narcissism rather than an acknowledgement of plurality, hate rather than reconciliation, and violence rather than decency.'[76]

Even Varshney, in his later commentaries, worries about the emergence of Modi as what he describes as a right-wing populist. 'The world' he says, 'has begun to notice the lynching of Muslims, the BJP's preoccupation with

76 Pratap Bhanu Mehta, "In the moment of his political triumph, Modi has chosen to defeat India", *The Indian Express,* 20 March 2017. Available at http://indianexpress.com/article/opinion/columns/yogic-madness-yogi-adityanath-uttar-pradesh-bjp-narendra-modi-4576588/

cow protection, Modi's aversion to the press... his preference for leaders such as Yogi Adityanath, known for their pro-Hindu private militia, not disbanded even after ascension to power. Allowing vigilante forces is the opposite of democratic governance...(F)or him, ideology triumphs over governance, civil liberties are less important than political conformity, and enforcement of a Hindu majoritarian politics is more significant than India's economic ascendancy.'[77]

Betwa Sharma of the *Huffington Post* spent two days with the recently elevated General Secretary of the private militia, the Hindu Yuva Vahini, which Yogi Adityanath had raised in 2002. Nagendra Singh Tomar, whose day job is as a college teacher, 'was raised on Hindutva, so to speak. He was five-years-old when his father began taking him to the local Rashtriya Swayam-sevak Sangh (RSS) shakha. His mother went to jail for protesting the Emergency imposed by Indira Gandhi. Later, he joined Akhil Bharatiya Vidyarthi Parishad (ABVP) and the Bharatiya Janata Party's youth wing. He joined Adityanath's HYV in 2005.' With Sharma in tow, he addressed numerous crowded gatherings of HYV volunteers (he said they have a one-year waiting list), in which he instructed the young men in saffron that 'they were to report 'anything wrong' such as cow slaughter and 'Love Jihad' to the authorities or to their superiors if the police did not take any action.' 'The earlier governments did not listen to us', he said, 'they would turn on us. But you can trust this government.' Tomar speaking of Muslims and Christians to Sharma, 'stuck to script, touching on Love Jihad, the 'lying' missionaries who duped Hindus into converting, and Muslims who were trying to outnumber Hindus by out-procreating them.' One speaker in his rallies said that 'Muslim religious leaders were the ones who instructed their young men to have sex with Hindus. He railed, 'If you get a Brahmin girl, you will get so much. If you get a Kshatriya girl, you will get so much. If you get a Vaishya girl, you will get so much. If you get a Shudra girl, you will get so much.'' In his speech in Bulandshahr, Tomar said, 'Hindus, Muslims and Christians, we all have the same DNA. The only difference is that we are the bravehearts and they are the cowards who converted.' Hindus, he continued, no longer had to 'kill' those who threatened Hinduism, but rather defeat them by 'showing unity'.[78]

77 Ashutosh Varshney, "Is Narendra Modi a populist?", *The Indian Express*, 23 October 2017. Available at http://indianexpress.com/article/opinion/columns/india-prime-minister-narendra-modi-a-popu-list-populism-democracy-donald-trump-pro-hindu-4901786/
78 Betwa Sharma, "With Boss Yogi as CM, Hindu Yuva Vahini is Hawking A Savvier Shade of Hindutva", *Huffington Post*, 27 April 2017. Available at http://www.huffingtonpost.in/2017/04/27/with-boss-yogi-as-cm-hindu-yuva-vahini-is-hawking-a-savvier-sha_a_22057575/

It is the same Tomar who justified the raid by his brigade on house in Meerut where an adult couple were meeting on April 12, 2017. These are called anti-Romeo squads, Romeo a code-word for Muslim boys in romantic relationships with Hindu girls. The young man was Muslim, the woman Hindu. The vigilantes thrashed the man, recorded the incident and then handed him over to police. They let off the weeping woman 'with a warning'. 'We are not against love', said Tomar, 'but this guy changed his name (to a Hindu one) to mislead the girl. Let police investigate.'[79]

It is a frightening time to be a Muslim in Uttar Pradesh today. It was bad enough that the election results reflected the unification of most Hindu caste and class groups against the Muslims; that the BJP found it unnecessary to field even one Muslim candidate from a fifth of the state's population; and that the Prime Minister and even more his party chief and other candidates openly resorted to a communally charged discourse. But if some among them were still hoping that with such a large majority, there would be an advance to more responsible governance in the state, the choice of Yogi Adityanath as their chosen leader left no ambiguity to their status in the state of Uttar Pradesh. They must learn the same lesson that Muslims in Gujarat have been forced to learn so painfully since 2002. This is that they would be 'permitted' to live in the state, but only as second class citizens, if they accept the political, cultural, economic and social superiority and dominance of their Hindu neighbours. It is the further fruition of the vision for India of the RSS, less than a hundred years since the RSS was constituted in 1925.

Over tea at his home, surgeon Wijahat Kareem, 62, who describes his own political philosophy as 'Gandhian' laments to the *Guardian* that 'Gandhi is losing his sheen.' 'Politicians cannot win on the basis of Muslim votes,' he says. This has now been established. 'So we have to keep believing in the right-thinking Hindus. That's what we are all hoping for. Our staying in the mainstream of the country depends on them.' Hope, he concedes, is all Uttar Pradesh's Muslims have left to rely on.[80]

'Can you call this election?' asked Sudhir Panwar, the Samajwadi Party candidate from Thana Bhawan in West Uttar Pradesh, when he spoke to journalist Ajaz Ashraf. His analysis of the 2017 UP election voting patterns

79 Sujoy Dhar, "Attacks on India's minority Muslims by Hindu vigilantes mount", *USA Today*, 5 May 2017. Available at https://www.usatoday.com/story/news/world/2017/05/05/attacks-indias-minori-ty-muslims-hindu-vigilantes-mount/100951514/
80 Michael Safi, "Rise of Hindu 'extremist' spook Muslim minority in India's heartland", *The Guardian*, 26 March 2017. Available at https://www.theguardian.com/world/2017/mar/26/modis-man-flex-es-muscular-hinduism-shock-election

showed a near-complete polarisation of religious lines: 'It is Hindu-Muslim war through the EVM [Electronic Voting Machine].' (Panwar lost to Suresh Rana, accused in the Muzaffarnagar riots, who stood on the BJP ticket.) His counsel of despair was – 'I feel extremely sad when I say that Muslims will have to keep away from contesting elections. This seems to be the only way of ensuring that elections don't turn into a Hindu-Muslim one.' Former Rajya Sabha MP Mohammed Adeeb agrees. 'If Muslims don't wish to have the status of slaves, if they don't want India to become a Hindu rashtra, they will have to keep away from electoral politics for a while and, instead, concentrate on education.' They should refuse to contest elections. 'We Muslims chose in 1947 not to live in the Muslim rashtra of Pakistan. It is now the turn of Hindus to decide whether they want India to become a Hindu rashtra or remain secular. Muslims should understand that their very presence in the electoral fray leads to a communal polarisation. Why? A segment of Hindus hates the very sight of Muslims. Their icon is Narendra Modi. But 75% of Hindus are secular. Let them fight out over the kind of India they want. Muslim candidates have become a red rag to even secular Hindus who rally behind the Bharatiya Janata Party, turning every election into a Hindu-Muslim one.' Poet Munawwar Rana agrees. 'Muslims need to become like the Parsis or, better still, behave the way the Chinese Indians do in Kolkata. They focus on dentistry or [their] shoe business, go out to vote on polling day and return to work.'[81]

We hear this counsel of despair to abjure elections and politics from growing numbers of Muslim commentators. Mirza Yawar Baig observes after the BJP's landslide victory in Uttar Pradesh in 2017, 'More than being divided, the Muslim presence in politics and the way it was portrayed to others, resulted in the Hindu vote getting consolidated behind the BJP. Muslims have become the bogeyman of Indian politics and it appears that the mere presence of a Muslim candidate is enough to bring out the worst fantasies in the minds of others. That none of this is based on fact is not important. Legend and mythology has never needed facts to thrive.' It appears, he goes on, 'it appears that in the future, when the words of the Constitution are spoken, "We the people of India", somehow 200 million citizens will not be included in this definition. So, we should not stand for election any more at least for a five-year period. If you are not there, you can't become the bogey

---

81 Ajaz Ashraf, "The fear of Hindu Rashtra: Should Muslims keep away from electoral politics", *Scroll*, 14 March 2017. Available at https://scroll.in/article/831693/the-fear-of-hindu-rashtra-should-muslims-keep-away-from-electoral-politics

man.' These are words of anguish and despair, not bitterness. Instead, he suggests, reaching out to fellow-Hindus: 'Elections apart, we simply have to win the hearts of the person on the street, the person next door and the person sitting next to us at work. If we do that well, then the sentiment will protect us from those who seek to harm us. We need to be seen as beneficial for all people.'[82]

Modi is leading our nation into a long, blistering majoritarian summer. This has scorched the fairness of institutions of the state, the traditionally diverse political fray, as well as fraternal social relations. None but the most delusional right-wing radicals actually expect millions of people of minority faith to leave this nation. But what they aspire is that they learn to live in separate ghettoes, economically enfeebled, socially submissive, politically disenfranchised. This is their competing idea of India.

Big communal conflagrations are now unlikely, I will argue later, because they attract international condemnation and troublesome domestic activism. But these have been replaced by the outbreak of continuing small but deeply toxic communal attacks and skirmishes across the length and breadth of the land. Assaults on churches here, disputes over mosques and cemeteries there, raids on religious processions, throwing of animal carcasses in shrines, raising of communal tempers when young people choose to love or marry outside their religions, and cow slaughter, have resulted in several hundred communal clashes throughout the country, peaking in states which are due to face elections. And now the rising scourge of lynching.

I feel an intense unrest and foreboding thinking about how fundamentally the idea of India is changing, and the consequences of a leadership that so profoundly polarises and divides us. It is imperative for the majority of Indians –people of every faith and caste, students, women, farmers, workers – to defend peacefully the precious idea of India. The idea of a land where the mind is without fear, and the head is held high. Of a country that belongs equally to all. For this reason, I write this book.

'Let us put it on record', Apoorvanand says, 'that India was pushed into this (civil) war by its ruling parties, the governments that they created and fostered disaffection towards a large section of society and stoked violence against them. Let it be recorded that the finest minds of the educated youth who form our civil services and the police collaborated in this with the

---

82 Mirza Yawar Baig, "Indian Muslims: Looking Ahead", *Countercurrents*, 4 April 2017. Available at http://www.countercurrents.org/2017/04/04/indian-muslims-looking-ahead/

murderers. Let it be said that we went about our lives unperturbed when our neighbours were doubling with pain and not allowed to scream even for it would sound a sectarian cry. It would be a long war and we would come out of it one day, with stories of the banality of violence and our shame of participating in it and mutilated bodies.

'Victims are being blamed for forging victimhood; asked to free themselves of this imaginary cage. This duplicity would be noted in some distant time. We would not be there then. But let us stand witness to what is being done on our behalf and call it by its name. That much we can do at least.'[83]

---

83 Apoorvanand, "The anti-Muslim pitch", *The Tribune*, 27 March 2017. Available at http://www.tribuneindia.com/news/comment/the-anti-muslim-pitch/382700.html

CHAPTER FIVE

Less Than a Cow[1]

On a busy crossing of a national highway, an indigent dairy farmer, grey-bearded, visibly Muslim, only a few years younger than me, was lynched by a mob of young men with stones and sticks. They claimed that he was a cattle smuggler. It was 1 April 2017, on an early summer afternoon. The man, Pehlu Khan, died two days later in a private hospital. Compelled and haunted by images of his attack – captured for history in jumpy visuals on some mobile phone cameras – a few colleagues and I went to meet his bereaved family in their village Jaisinghpur in Mewat, Haryana. When we sat with them, our eyes lowered, we found it hard to find the words to convey to the bereaved, distraught and terrified family our sadness, our shame, and our rage.

The village is indistinguishable from many others in the district Nuh, earlier known as Mewat or the home of the Meo Muslim, who constitute 80 per cent of this arid and water-scarce, impoverished district. We approached their home with trepidation. We had made the journey because we felt compelled to offer solidarity in a small personal way, in the times that we live in. But we did not want to intrude in their time of grief which was already far too public.

Theirs was a small modest village brick home. A green cloth canopy had been erected outside the house, as the family could not accommodate the visitors who streamed into their nondescript village every day after Pehlu Khan's lynching hit the headlines. There had been before us some journalists, many local politicians, some religious leaders, and members of the Kisaan Sabha affiliated with the Communist Parties. The men led my women colleagues into the inner rooms, and they emerged an hour later harrowed. Pehlu Khan's mother, a wizened old woman now completely blind, his widow, and his daughters were inconsolable. Pehlu Khan was an only son. He in turn had

---

1   Some of this chapter has been reproduced from an article I wrote for *Scroll*, "A country for the cow: The chronicle of a visit to cow vigilante victim Pehlu Khan's village", 24 April 2017. Available at https://scroll.in/article/835315/a-country-for-the-cow-the-chronicle-of-a-visit-to-pehlu-khans-village

eight children. Some were married, including Irshad in his twenties. Arif in his teens was also beaten up with him at Alwar. His daughters and daughters-in-law could not make sense of why he had been killed. His youngest sons and grandchildren were too young to understand what had happened and they just looked at the commotion around their home with questioning haunted eyes.

Outside, where I sat with the men, the mood was sombre. More and more men gathered in the hours that we spent there. The elders sat on benches, the young men squatted on the ground, deferential to age. I opened the discussion by saying, 'We hesitated to come, but at the same time we could not stay away. Because we want you to know that we share in your grief, and in your anger against the injustice that has been done to you.' They accepted our awkward words with grace, and then insisted that we must first accept their hospitality and only then talk further. We protested but to no avail. 'We have been taught by our ancestors about how we should treat our guests, even at times like this.' After much persuasion, we still had to accept some sweetened soda, before we began to talk.

The story of what transpired with them was well-known by then, but as Pehlu Khan's older son Irshad and others who were part of this traumatic journey – nephews, neighbours – spoke, the horror became for us even more palpable. The family owns barely one acre of dry land, and this yields little for the family. Therefore they have always raised milch cattle – cows or buffaloes – and they sell the milk in the village or to richer landowners in the surrounding villages. They also buy milch cattle in the cattle markets in Rajasthan, and then sell the milk for a while after which they resell the cow at a slight profit of a couple of thousand rupees. This helps feed the family. The sons help out their father, and when they can, they drive a pick-up van or jeep taxi. On his last fateful journey, Pehlu Khan took with him even his younger son Arif because he wanted him to learn early the cattle trade that would in good times and bad help feed their family.

The month of Ramzan is a good one for milk sales, the best time in the year. People buy milk and curds for the pre-dawn *sehri* or the evening *iftar*. Pehlu Khan took a loan as he always does from richer neighbours, many of them Hindu Thakurs, at an interest rate of 5 per cent compound per month. They hired a pick-up van from a neighbour, loaded on it their buffalo which had stop giving milk, to sell, and with Irshad on the wheel and teenaged Arif, a nephew and some neighbours at the back, they set off for the weekly cattle market at Ramgarh Road near Jaipur.

This was a market they visited frequently over the years. The cattle traders knew Pehlu Khan well. He had initially set his heart on buying a buffalo to replace the one that he sold. If he had, he might still be alive. But he was offered a milking cow who had just recently delivered a calf at a lower price. The cattle seller milked her in his presence and she produced 12 litres of milk. It was a deal. This was the decision that was to cost him his life. Other villagers also made their purchases. Together they hired one more pick-up truck from the market. Pehlu Khan sat in the hired truck, with two cows and two calves. Irshad carried three cows in his van, and drove with a young neighbour and friend Asmat. All the cows were beautiful, healthy, with young calves and bountiful milk yields. In their villages, they describe cows after they become pregnant as *biyahi,* or married.

It was at the Jaguwas crossing in Behror, Alwar that the pick-up trucks were stopped by an ugly crowd of around fifty men. They dragged them out of the trucks, slapped and heckled them, claiming they were cow smugglers. Irshad says he showed them the receipts of the cows from the cattle market, but they tore these up. (Fortunately he was later able to get copies from the cattle market later, and he showed us these copies.) They asked the driver of the truck that they had hired in the cattle market what was his name. It was a Hindu name – they slapped him and asked him to run away. The other terrified men also tried to run away, but the crowd caught them easily. His father Pehlu Khan was the oldest among them, and received the harshest blows. He tried to pick himself up weakly, but the men rained blows on him again. They beat Asmat on his back and spine, and injured Irshad's younger brother Arif in his eye. They vandalised the trucks, twisted the bonnet, and threw rocks at the windscreen and into the engine. They snatched their wallets, watches, mobile phones and all their money. Irshad had 75,000 rupees left from the money they had taken on loan. They snatched this as well. The crowd swelled. Some more men joined the lynching, some further vandalised the trucks as though for sport, some watched, a few took videos on their mobile phone cameras, some walked past looking at the screens of their mobile phones as though nothing amiss was happening around them. No one came to their aid.

They lost track of time as the beating continued – with sticks, stones and belts – and one by one all the men fell, stretched on the road or pavements in twisted inert heaps, almost unconscious. They heard the men talk about emptying out some petrol from their motor-cycles and diesel from the truck to set them on fire. They were too weak now to flee or fight. Their lives were saved only because the police finally arrived. They confiscated their cows, and sent them to a local private gaushala.

The police admitted them to a nearby private hospital, Kailash Hospital in Behror. It is there that Pehlu died on April 3. The doctor who performed the post-mortem told The Indian Express: 'Injuries were the main cause of death. As said in our post-mortem report, the (thoracoabdominal) injuries were "sufficient cause of death". The heart attack was secondary.'

Irshad spoke to us haltingly, in a low monotone. He was still visibly traumatised, and in mourning; besides young people do not talk loudly in the presence of their elders. The older men spoke of how the families were ruined. How will they repay their loans? Will they ever get back the cows they had bought? Even if they ultimately got back their cows, who would return to them the beautiful milch cows that they had bought? They would get back some useless scrub cattle in the end, if at all. The remaining cash they had taken on loan at 5 per cent interest compound per month had been stolen from them. They would also have to pay for the vandalised pick-up truck that they had borrowed. And their father had taken all the decisions, but he was not there now to guide them any longer. He had no brothers, so there was no older man whose palm rested on their heads.

We went also to their neighbour Azmat Khan's home. The young man, father of a little infant girl, lay on a cot, wrapped in an old nylon sari converted into a sheet. He was still in a lot of pain, not recovered from his spine injury. He held my hand for a long time as I sat by his bedside. We looked at his medical papers, from the private hospital in which he was being treated. They did not look good. 'I hope he will be able to walk again', I whispered in English to my colleagues. (He did later recover enough to walk). Asmat too had taken a loan to buy a cow for selling milk in the Ramzan month of fasting and prayers.

In the strange, fraught times we live in, even I feel obliged to underline that the murdered man and his sons were innocent of any crime, that they were not cattle-smugglers but legitimate dairy farmers. As though the crime of their brutal mob killing would be any less monstrous if they had in some way broken the law. The Rajasthan Home Minister Gulab Chand Kataria blamed the victims saying, 'The problem is from both the sides (echoes of Donald Trump after Charlotteville!). People know cow-trafficking is illegal but they do it. Gau Bhakts try to stop those who indulge in such crimes.' His description of the marauders as Gau Bhakts or 'worshippers of the cow' brought back memories from my years as a District Collector in the districts in Madhya Pradesh during the Ayodhya Ramjanambhoomi movement, when rioters with naked upraised swords who terrorised, burnt and murdered their Muslim neighbours in town after town of communal frenzy were described benignly in the press and political speeches as Ram Bhakts or worshippers of Ram. The felling of Pehlu Khan on April 1 2017 on National Highway 8 near Behror, Alwar by self-styled cow vigilantes, had as little to do with the love of the cow as the annihilation of the Babri Masjid had to do with the love of Ram. The Home Minister was to repeat his charges in the Rajasthan assembly, where he claimed that the man who had been lynched to death was a criminal, a cattle smuggler who had three criminal cases filed against him.[2] His charges turned out to be false, but he has neither retracted them nor apologised.

His rationalisation for the hate-crime echoed in many television debates. The studied refusal of the Chief Ministers of Rajasthan, where the crime occurred, and Haryana which is home to the dead man, as well as the otherwise voluble Prime Minister to express any outrage or public regret for the killing reflects the same implied validation. The Rajasthan Chief Minister did briefly criticise the mob violence after more than 20 days,[3] but both the Prime Minister and the Haryana Chief Minister have persisted with their silence. No one from the Haryana state administration visited the home of Pehlu Khan. The Alwar Superintendent of Police Alwar Superintendent of Police Rahul Prakash categorically told Rediff.com's PD Zore that the 15 men from Haryana's Mewat district – including Pehlu Khan who was beaten up by a mob in Rajasthan's Alwar district on suspicion of smuggling cows – had no verified documents to prove that they were in the dairy business and not cow smugglers, and therefore '100 per cent they were cow smugglers; there is no doubt about that.' But he was reluctantly prepared to admit: 'I don't know if they (*the people who began beating*) knew for sure if they (*the people who were beaten*) were cow smugglers or not, but according to the police version they were cow smugglers.'[4]

2 See "Pehlu Khan had 3 cases of cattle smuggling: Gulab Chand Kataria", *The Times of India*, 25 April 2017. Available at http://timesofindia.indiatimes.com/city/jaipur/pehlu-khan-had-3-cases-of-cattle-smuggling-gulab-chand-kataria/articleshow/58353034.cms

3 "Pehlu Khan's lynching: Almost a month later, CM Vasundhara Raje breaks silence, says won't tolerate violence", *India Today,* 25 April 2017. Available at http://indiatoday.intoday.in/story/vasundhara-raje-pehlu-khan-alwar-lynching-rajasthan/1/938020.html

4 "Pehlu Khan, others '100% cow smugglers': Alwar SP", *Rediff,* 10 April 2017. Available at http://www.rediff.com/news/interview/pehlu-khan-others-100-cow-smugglers-alwar-sp/20170408.htm

Before any criminal cases were filed against the lynch mob, the Rajasthan police first registered a First Information Report (FIR) against Pehlu Khan and the young men with him under the Rajasthan Bovine Animal (Prohibition of Slaughter and Regulation of Temporary Migration or Export) Act 1995. I have a copy of the FIR with me. It mentions that they are charged under Section 5 of the Act. According to this section, 'No person shall export and cause to be exported any bovine animal himself or through his agent, servant or other person acting in his behalf from any place within the State to any place outside the State for the purposes of slaughter or with the knowledge that it may be or is likely to be slaughtered.' The men were transporting five milch cows who had only recently delivered with their young calves, with papers to prove their purchase from the cattle market on Ramgarh Road in Jaipur. The only cattle who are taken to slaughter are those who are too old or diseased to yield milk. Why would any person transport expensive pregnant high-milk yielding cows for a slaughter-house that would pay them a small fraction of what they would earn if they were sold as productive milch cows? The dairy farmers told us that milch cattle costs anything between forty and seventy-five thousand rupees, whereas a cow for slaughter fetches never more than about seven thousand rupees. So once the mob or the police found expensive milch cows and their calves being transported, this was evidence enough that the animals were not being moved across state borders for slaughter (which in popular officialese is now called 'cow smuggling'). And what is more, if an animal was being transported illegally for slaughter, they would do this clandestinely; why would they be taken by day in an open truck?

To transport milch cows for dairying, no papers or permission were required by the law. Therefore there was no ground for any presumption by the police (nor by the vigilante mob) that the men had transgressed any law, and even less that they were cattle smugglers. Even so, criminal cases are registered against them for crimes that could confine them behind prison walls for ten years. They were also charged under Section 9 of the Rajasthan Bovine Animal (Prohibition of Slaughter and Regulation of Temporary Migration or Export) Act 1995, which makes it illegal to cause bodily pain, disease or infirmity to a bovine animal. The claim was that the cow was being treated cruelly because two or three were packed with their claves in the back of a pick-up van. I wondered in the policepersons had ever travelled in an unreserved train compartment, a state transport bus, or seen casual workers transported at the back of trucks.

By contrast, police registered cases against six men named in the FIR, and 200 others only after the men who had been lynched were charged. Their attackers were charged under relatively mild sections of the Indian Penal Code – Sections 147 (rioting), 143 (unlawful assembly), 323 (voluntarily causing hurt), 341 (wrongful restraint), 308 (culpable homicide), and 379 (theft). On April 3, section 308 was changed to that of murder (section 302) after Pehlu Khan died in hospital around 7.30 pm. Many days and nationwide protests passed, but none of the men mentioned in the FIR and in Pehlu Khan's dying declaration were arrested. Saddam Hussain, president of Mewat Yuva Sanghtan, alleged to the Hindustan Times that the police were unwilling to arrest the named accused because of their affiliations with right-wing Hindu organizations, the RSS, the Hindu Dharma Jagran and the Akhil Bhartiya Vidyarthi Parishad (ABVP). 'Either there is pressure from the government to not arrest them or police are not trying hard enough,' he said.[5] These are echoes here from the earlier case of lynching to death of Mohamed Akhlaq in Dadri by his neighbours on the rumour that he stored beef in his refrigerator, which also stirred the national public conscience. Despite country-wide outrage, criminal cases are registered against Akhlaq's family, whereas a man charged with his murder who died of an illness in prison was cremated with his body was wrapped in the national flag, in the presence of a union minister. Any Muslim or Dalit victim of mob lynching is somehow criminally guilty, and the killers are nationalist Hindus understandably outraged because they believe that the sacred cow is in danger.

Virtually outside every house in the village in Nuh is tied a cow or two, or a buffalo. 'Our children rarely can drink milk. We have to sell every drop to repay our loans and bring food home.' But now they are terrified about what the future would hold for all of them. Anyone can come into our houses and claim that we are raising the cows for slaughter. They have very few options. The land is dry and infertile, and the rains fickle. Education levels are low. Thousands of young men are drivers. But getting a driving license for heavy vehicles was notoriously difficult from the corrupt district transport office. Young men over the years got licenses from far corner of the country, probably because they had to pay smaller bribes. But in the last two years these licenses have been suddenly derecognised by the district transport authorities.

---

5   Rakesh Goswami and Devendra Bhardwaj, "Alwar lynching: Police yet to make arrests despite 6 named in FIR", *Hindustan Times,* 16 April 2017. Available at http://www.hindustantimes.com/india-news/ kid-glove-treatment-for-six-in-alwar-lynching-fir-cops-look-for-complicity/story-AjYwC9EFu5mcRfx-qLaejKK.html

Ramzan Chaudhary alleges this was done to spite them in this overwhelmingly Muslim district, rendering an estimated seventy five thousand drivers out of work. A few thousand men opened biryani stalls on the highways, but in 2016 raids by policepersons checking if the meat that they used was of cows or buffaloes caused them to shut these down – today you see a much smaller number, and they hasten to tell you that the biryani they sell is chicken and not beef. And now even dairy farming has become a dangerous vocation. They do not know what the future now holds, how they will feed their children. We asked them how they will manage. *Bardashth karenge, aur kya?* they replied dully. We will bear it, what else? *Bhuke marenge* – we will die of hunger – said others even more dismally. But some said they planned an unusual and desperate act of civic resistance. They planned to take their cows to the office of the District Collector, tie them to his gate, and hand them over to the government to do what it will with them. 'You do not trust us with the cow, and we are no longer safe in tending them. Let then the government take them over!' But even this revolt fizzled out.

As we sat with a large group of men under the makeshift canopy outside the house of Pehlu Khan, the talk would return over and over again to their anguish about the new climate of hate and suspicion against Muslims that they found surrounded them. "It has never been like this before", they said. Hindus and Muslims have always lived together like brothers and sisters. Just in the last two or three years everything has changed. 'We are *watanparasth,* true nationalists. Our ancestors made so many sacrifices for our country. They fought against Babur's army on the side of Rana Sangha.' I wanted to stop them – please, please, you don't have to say this – why must you feel you must prove your love for your country? But the words got stuck in my throats, as they went on insistently. And they would also ask – who loves the cow more than us Meo Muslims? Go to any Meo village home, and see how much they love their cows, like a member of the family. Any evening, see how lovingly they bathe their cows. And yet we are being called cow-murderers.

In a dharna in Jaipur some days later, I spoke to the crowd of women and men who had gathered to protest Pehlu Khan's lynching outside the Rajasthan legislative assembly. I said to them – I am pained by the Prime Minister's silence, and by the silence of the Chief Ministers. I am outraged by the rationalisations of the Home Minister and the partisan action of the police against the victims. I am enraged by the crowd of men who attacked innocent people and killed an old man. But more than all of these, I am dismayed by you and I. That a man is lynched on an afternoon on a busy highway in which hundreds of people pass by, but not one person finds it fit to come to the man's defence. We can fight all the others. But most of all, we need to fight ourselves.

By strange coincidence, the driver of the taxi we had hired from Delhi to travel to Nuh, a young Dalit Sikh, turned out to be a man who loved cows. He stopped our taxi as we were travelling on way to the village, still early morning, and took out rotis from the car and fed them to stray cows. He said that he had worked as a driver to the owner of a gaushala, and at that time had come to adore cows. When he is off-duty from driving even today, he volunteers to tend stray cows in gaushalas. Returning from Pehlu Khan's village Jaisinghpur, our souls weighed down by all we had seen and heard, we gave him our left-over sandwiches to feed the cows. On an impulse, I joined him in feeding them. As the cows nuzzled on my fingers, I realized afresh that what had transpired on the highway at Behror had nothing at all to do with the love of this gentle animal. Nothing at all.

The words of the villagers in Nuh echoed in our ears. What is our place in this country, they asked us over and over again – a country in which our life has less value than that of a cow?

※

My visit to commiserate with Pehlu Khan's family after his lynching was not the first time I had visited Mewat in Haryana. I had gone there a year earlier, when news came in of widespread fear unleashed among the residents of the district after policepersons in uniform raised street biryani stall to check if the meat they used was of cows or buffaloes. As a result, the traditional cheer of Eid ul Zuha in 2016 was dimmed and muted, overcast by clouds of fear.[6]

Four out of five residents of the district are Muslim. Outside Jammu and Kashmir, Mewat (now renamed Nuh) has the highest ratio of Muslim residents except Dhubri in Assam. The Meo Muslims practice Islam but also retain many Hindu names and practices. Nuh is one of the poorest districts of Haryana. In earlier years, impoverished Meos of the district would sometimes combine together for the annual Eid sacrifice, seven households joining to sacrifice one animal. This celebration, to honour the willingness of Ibrahim to sacrifice his beloved son at the command of God, is one of the two holiest festivals for Muslims. On this day, tradition prescribes the ritual sacrifice of

---

6 Some of this reproduces what I have written earlier for *The Hindustan Times* in an article titled "The Mewat biryani raids have permanently damaged livelihoods of poor Muslims", 29 September 2016. Available at http://www.hindustantimes.com/columns/the-mewat-biryani-raids-have-permanently-damaged-livelihoods-of-poor-muslims/story-9iIDje0po0GSf3RNceoqMI.html

animals and the sharing of their meat in three equal parts: one for the family, one for friends and relatives, and a third for the poor. But in 2016, for the first time in their lives, most Muslim households did not sacrifice any animal. It was too dangerous, they said to me when I visited the district.

The dread of Muslim residents mounted after raiding teams of the Haryana state police of the BJP government, supported by non-state cow vigilantes, collected samples of biryani sold by locals on the highways to Alwar and Gurgaon, to test whether these were cow meat. This was about a week before the Eid festival. No official reports were made public about the findings of the tests, but cow vigilante leaders loudly claimed that five of the seven samples tested 'positive' for cow meat.

Memories were also fresh and painful among Muslim residents of the lynching in village Dadri of Mohammed Akhlaq less than a year earlier, based on the rumour that he had killed a cow and eaten its meat during Eid. People in Mewat feared that mobs could attack any of them claiming that the meat that they were eating and distributing was cow meat, and they could be killed in the way Akhlaq was. In fact, 'Akhlaq' had become a verb in people's conversations: 'people may Akhlaq us', they said, meaning that they could be lynched for the rumour that they had killed a cow.

It has become extremely risky to transport cows, they told me. If a truck is found to carry cows, then 'gau rakshaks' or protectors of the cow stop the truck, thrash the driver, often vandalise or burn the vehicle, and then drag the driver if still alive to the police. These 'rakshaks', both young and older men, derive a great sense of social power from this role. But even if the transported animals are not cows –buffaloes, or even camels – the transporters remain equally vulnerable to attack. 'The vigilantes simply change their flag', the residents say. 'Instead of gau rakshaks they pose to be animal rights activists', often claiming allegiance to union minister and leading animal rights activist Maneka Gandhi. And they still attack the transporters even though they are not ferrying cows. It is tragic that a gentle animal like the cow, beloved to many ordinary Indian peasants; and ethically robust movements for the rights of animals; have both become instruments in a venomous battle of hate and division.

Apart from the long shadows that the Haryana police biryani raids cast on Eid festivities, the even more permanent damage they inflicted was to the livelihoods of thousands of impoverished Muslim households of the district. Along highways in every direction from Nuh, and within all major villages and small towns, extended lines of young men would sell on portable wooden carts steaming biryani to truck-drivers and working class people. They would mainly use buffalo meat, which was economical and conformed to local tastes. A plate would sell for 15 to 20 rupees, more than sufficient even for an able-bodied grown man to fill his stomach. It offered a source of inexpensive and sanitary nutrition, and had become a major part of the contemporary culture of the region. But more than this, the biryani stalls were a source of decent livelihood to approximately fifteen thousand people. It is estimated that around 3000 such stalls operated across the district. Each offered employment to at least five people, for a range of tasks from the rearing and sale of the meat and rice, collecting firewood, cooking which began typically before dawn inside thousands of Mewat homes, transportation and sale.

However after the raids by the police, almost all of these shut down overnight: the sellers were in mortal fear of the arbitrary and unaccountable violence of vigilantes, as much as of police action charging them of selling cow meat instead of the flesh of buffaloes. In an impoverished district with low literacy, there were already few jobs for residents who owned little land. Many worked in stone quarries but these were recently shut down. Tens of thousands drove trucks, but more than fifty thousand of their driving licenses were recently cancelled when they submitted these for renewal. On the back of so much livelihood distress, the abrupt closure of the entire biryani trade in terror of official action has resulted in enormous suffering and helpless anger.

Cow slaughter was legally prohibited in Haryana since the mid-1950s, under the Punjab Prohibition of Cow Slaughter Act (1955), but lawyer Ramzan Chaudhary tells me that mostly this statute was lightly enforced. This changed with the election of a BJP government in both Delhi and Haryana in 2014. The socially conservative Haryana Chief Minister Khattar, a member for four decades of the RSS, led the passage of a far more stringent Haryana Gauvansh Sanrakshan and Gau Samvardhan Act 2015. This first expanded the prohibition to include slaughter of any 'gau vanshaj' –including bulls, oxen, heifers and calves, even when these animals are disabled, diseased or barren. It made possession even of tinned and imported beef a crime. It prescribed high penalties including rigorous imprisonment of three to ten years. The earlier law made no provision for testing or sampling meat samples, but this statute provided for establishing laboratories for such testing. The Haryana government constituted a police Cow Protection Task Force, led by a DIG Bharti Arora, who spoke to newspapers about her missionary zeal to protect cows.

It was policepersons of this task force who conducted the Mewat biryani raids, sending samples to the Lala Lajpat Rai University of Veterinary and

Animal Sciences, Hisar. The Tribune reports that all that the forensic investigation could conclude was that the meat was 'cattle meat', not whether or not it was cow meat. It stated that the laboratories are not equipped to conduct any such tests that would stand legal scrutiny in a court of law.

All of this makes the official motive for the police raids on the biryani stalls even more troubling. Lacking the expertise and equipment to actually test whether the meat samples were of cows or buffaloes, what the raids by uniformed policepersons timed a week before the Eid festival accomplished was only to create a climate of dread that crushed both the festival and one major livelihood source of thousands of poor Muslim residents. The greater tragedy is that this seems to have been precisely what the government, openly hostile to this segment of its citizens based on their religious identity, actually wanted to accomplish.

✳

Reporter Niha Masih visited the village Bisada nearly two years after 55-year-old Mohammad Akhlaq was lynched by angry villagers because of an announcement from the village temple that he had killed a cow. 'He was first assaulted with fists, sticks and bricks, had his daughter's sewing machine smashed on his head and then dragged through narrow lanes onto the main road. He did not survive the attack. His 20-year-old son, Danish, was also severely injured and spent 10 days in coma.'

Mahesh Sharma, union minister and BJP MP who represents the area called the lynching an 'accident'; he was present when the body of the accused who died in jail was wrapped in the national flag. Nawab Singh Nagar, former BJP MLA from the area, blamed Akhlaq's family.

Masih found a striking absence of remorse among Hindus of the village: 'generations of harmony between Hindus and Muslims in this Uttar Pradesh village swallowed by hatred and prejudice.' The bravado of the tumultuous September night, she says, has returned as families of the accused justify and valorise the hate crime. The mother of Ravi, an accused man who died in jail said, 'Our son died for gau raksha, not for theft or (any other) crime. He is a martyr. It was right to kill Akhlaq as he had slaughtered a cow,'

The brother of Arun Sisodia, an accused out on bail, shouted that Hindus can no longer follow Mahatma Gandhi's dictum of offering the other cheek to those who want to destroy the country – an apparent swipe at the Muslim community. 'Why don't our Muslim brothers eat pig?' he taunted Muslims for who pig meat is unclean. 'What is so special about the cow? Pigs

are cheaper,' Arun says to Masih. He was Akhlaq's neighbour. He adds, 'Feel-
ings were incited. Does the Quran say anywhere that cow should be eaten?'

Akhlaq's family tells Masih that they can never return to Bisada. His wife,
Ikraman, daughter Shaista and son Danish live in Delhi with the eldest son,
Sartaj a corporal in the air force. "Mara bhi hum ko aur case bhi hum par. Yeh
kahan ka insaaf hai?" (They killed my father and yet the case is filed against us.
What sort of justice is that?), Shaista asks Masih disconsolately.[7]

It is important to underline that a tiny fraction of incidents of lynching and
mob attacks make it to even the newspapers. Even among these, even fewer like
Akhlaq, Pehlu Khan and Junaid burned their way into the public conscience.

My colleagues and I did a very quick scan of the newspapers for just one
and a half years before the time I was writing. On May 30, 2015 in Birloka
in Khimsar tehsil of Rajasthan's Nagaur district, 60 year old Abdul Ghaffar
Qureshi, 60 was killed after rumours spread that he had killed 200 cows for a
feast. Pictures of carcasses were spread on social media. Young men gathered
in the thousands in the fields of Kumhari village and brutally murdered him.[8]
On August 29, 2015, this time in Chilla village, near east Delhi's Mayur Vihar,
just adjacent to the country's capital, residents clashed with four truck drivers
who were reportedly transferring buffaloes to a slaughter house in Ghazipur.[9]
Then on Sept 28, 2015, the Dadri mob lynching episode, when Mohammad
Akhlaq was killed occurred on the charge that he had beef in his refrigerator. On October 2015, in Karhal, villagers held protests when news spread
that a cow had disappeared from a field near the village and was taken away
for slaughter.[10] An angry mob beat up two youths (55-year-old Mohammad
Shafiq and 27-year-old Mohammad Kalam, were stripped and beaten) who
were alleged to have stolen the cow, however, other reports indicate that the
cow died of natural causes and was sold to the two men by the owner.[11] MLA,

7 Niha Masih, "Hate in the hearts in Bisada: Ikhlaq's murder over cow exposes fault line", *Hindustan Times*, 25 July 2017. Available at http://www.hindustantimes.com/india-news/let-s-talk-about-hate-dadri-villagers-live-in-suspicion-faultlines-deepen-after-lynching-of-mohammad-ikhlaq/story-ER-944FgQacbVHLYrmO3N4K.html
8 See "Trail of blood: complete timeline of cow vigilante violence in the last 2 years", *Catch News,* 7 April 2017. http://www.catchnews.com/yahoo/politics-news/trail-of-blood-complete-timeline-of-cow-vig-ilante-violence-in-last-2-years-57084.html
9 Ibid.
10 After Dadri, cow slaughter rumor sparks Mulayam's Mainpuri", *India TV News*, 10 October 2015. Available at http://www.indiatvnews.com/news/india/violence-in-mainpuri-village-over-cow-slaugh-ter-allegation-55165.html
11 Priyanka Mogul, "India beef controversy: Fresh violence in Uttar Pradesh over rumours of cow slaughter", *IB Times*, 9 October 2015. Available at http://www.ibtimes.co.uk/india-beef-controversy-

Engineer Sheikh Abdul Rashid was assaulted when he walked into the Legislative Assembly House in Jammu for allegedly hosting a beef party in October
2015.[12] The same month, on October 6, 2015, in Karnataka, a cattle trader
had a narrow escape after Bajrang Dal activists attacked him with metal rods
on a rumour about a stolen cow.[13] On October 9, 2015, in Udhampur, in
Jammu and Kashmir, Zahid Ahmad a truck driver was killed in a petroleum
bomb episode on Oct 9, 2015, after communal tensions brewed in the J&K
after independent MLA Engineer Rashid's 'beef party' at the MLA Hostel
in Srinagar ten days earlier, and subsequent rumours of cow slaughter from
different parts of the state.[14] On October 17, 2015 a 20-year-old from Saharanpur was allegedly killed in Sarahan by villagers who believed he was involved
in smuggling of cattle, police said. Four others, alleged to be part of the same
smuggling gang, were beaten up.[15] On January 15, 2016, in Harda, Madhya
Pradesh, two couples were attacked by members of a Gauraksha Samiti for
allegedly carrying beef.[16] On March 18, 2016, in Latehar, Jharkhand, two
Muslim cattle traders were lynched by allegedly cattle-protection vigilantes
in Balumath forests. The attackers killed 32 years old Mazlum Ansari and 15
years old Imteyaz Khan who were found hanging from a tree.[17] Then on April
2, 2016 in Haryana, the mutilated body of one Mustain Abbas, was found in
a drain near Masana village in Kurukshetra, Haryana. The vehicle in which
Mustain, a father of four, was travelling back home, after buying bulls from
Sharif Garh in Haryana, was stopped and fired upon by alleged Gau Raksha
Dal members.[18]

fresh-violence-uttar-pradesh-over-rumours-cow-slaughter-1523320

12 Mir Ehsan, "J&K: Assaulted MLA Sheikh Abdul Rashid detained," *The Indian Express*, 10 October
    2015. Available at http://indianexpress.com/article/india/india-others/jk-mla-engineer-rashids-sup-
    porters-detained-during-march-to-assembly/

13 Sudipto Mondal, "Bajrang Dal attacks K'taka cattle trader", *Hindustan Times*, 9 October 2015. Avail-
    able at https://www.pressreader.com/india/hindustan-times-delhi/20151009/281904477006081

14 "Trucker injured in petrol bomb attack dies; violence erupts in Valley", *The Tribune*, 18 October 2015.
    Available at http://www.tribuneindia.com/news/jammu-kashmir/trucker-injured-in-petrol-bomb-
    attack-dies-violence-erupts-in-valley/147507.html

15 Ashwani Sharma, "20-year-old from Saharanpur killed in Himachal village for 'smuggling cattle'", *The
    Indian Express*, 17 October 2015. Available at http://indianexpress.com/article/india/india-news-
    india/saharanpur-youth-allegedly-involved-in-cattle-smuggling-lynched-in-himachal/

16 "Another beef row: Cow protection group attacks couple in Madhya Pradesh", *Firstpost*, 15 January
    2016. Available at http://www.firstpost.com/india/another-beef-row-cow-protection-group-attacks-
    couple-in-madhya-pradesh-2585562.html

17 Bobins Abraham, "Two Muslim Cattle Traders Hanged to Death In Jharkhand By Suspected 'Cow
    Protection Vigilantes'", *India Times*, 19 March 2016. Available at http://www.indiatimes.com/news/
    india/two-muslim-cattle-traders-hanged-to-death-in-jharkhand-by-suspected-cattle-protection-vigi-
    lantes-252255.html

18 "Uttar Pradesh cattle transporter's murder is family's mystery", *The Indian Express*, 24 May 2016.
    Available at http://indianexpress.com/article/india/india-news-india/kurukshetra-cattle-transport-

On June 2, 2016, in Rajasthan, four individuals were apprehended by policepersons for allegedly transferring beef illegally. They attempted an escape, but two of them were caught by the mob and one was stripped naked and beaten badly.[19] Then in Gir Somnath (Una), Gujarat, four Dalits were stripped and beaten by Shiv Sena members for skinning dead cows, on 12 June 2016.[20] On July 26, 2016, in Mandsaur, MP, two Muslim women were slapped, kicked and abused over beef rumours by a mob led by cow vigilantes at a railway station in BJP-ruled Madhya Pradesh near Mandsaur Railway Station.[21] NDTV aired a report which shows a group of organization members forcibly stopping a truck on the outskirts of Pune, Maharashtra, on July 31, 2016, yanking the driver out, snatching his phone, and pushing his truck to a police station. The report stated – 'They together work as extortionists, forcing the poor cattle traders to part with their money. An even bigger fact is that most of the cows that they capture are not seen in the goshalas. They sell it outside and make money out of it. So, the aim of these gaurakshas senas is not really cow protection.'[22] On August 5, 2016, in Lucknow, two Dalits were thrashed for refusing to remove cow carcasses. The Dalit workers were on protest against the growing attacks on the community since the Una attack.[23] On August 10, 2016, in Amalpuram, East Godavari District of Andhra Pradesh, two Dalits were thrashed on the charges of killing their cows by the so called 'cow vigilantes'. It was later found that the cows were safe, and the victims were removing the skin of a dead cow given away by its owner. Hindu Jagarana Vedike activists intercepted and attacked two men with sharp weapons in Hebri, Udupi district on August 18, 2016, alleging they were transporting calves to an abattoir, a senior police official said. Praveen Poojary (29) succumbed to injuries at a hospital in

er-murder-cbi-2816094/

19 Rohit Parihar, "Seven calf smugglers, one of their assaulters arrested in Rajasthan", *India Today*, 2 June 2016. Available at http://indiatoday.intoday.in/story/calf-smuggler-assaulted-arrested-rajas-than-pratapgarh/1/683354.html

20 "4 Dalits stripped, beaten up for skinning dead cow", *The Times of India*, 13 July 2016. Available at http://timesofindia.indiatimes.com/city/rajkot/4-Dalits-stripped-beaten-up-for-skinning-dead-cow/articleshow/53184266.cms

21 "First Beef Attack on Women: Mob Assaults Muslim Women Over Beef Rumour in MP", *The Citizen*, 27 July 2016. Available at http://www.thecitizen.in/index.php/NewsDetail/index/1/8314/First-Beef-Attack-On-Women-Mob-Assaults-Muslim-Women-Over-Beef-Rumour-In-MP

22 "Exposing Cow Terrorism NDTV", (video excerpt of NDTV show) posted by Beef Janata Party, Facebook, 31 July 2016. Available at https://www.facebook.com/beefjanataparty/videos/1176096285786593/

23 See "Trail of blood: complete timeline of cow vigilante violence in the last 2 years", *Catch News*, 7 April 2017. http://www.catchnews.com/yahoo/politics-news/trail-of-blood-complete-timeline-of-cow-vigilante-violence-in-last-2-years-57084.html

Bramhavar, where his friend Akshay Devadiga (22) has also been admitted but he is out of danger.[24] On August 20, 2016 in Ahmedabad, a 15-year-old Dalit boy was allegedly beaten up by two men in Bhavda village of Daskroi taluka in Ahmedabad district ostensibly because his father refused to dispose off cattle carcasses in the village, according to the police. Two persons were arrested after the boy's father, Dinesh Parmar, lodged an FIR against them.[25] On August 24, 2016, in Mewat, Haryana, 10 alleged Gau Rakshaks killed a Muslim couple in their 30s – Rasheedan and Ibrahim. Two other members of their family, Ayesha and Jafruddin, were seriously injured, a 21-year-old woman and 16-year-old girl from the family were gang-raped for allegedly eating beef.[26] On September 13, 2016, again in Ahmedabad, a 29 year old, Mohammad Ayyub Mev was admitted to V S Hospital after he was beaten up by unidentified persons on S G Highway on the night of September 13, after his vehicle met with an accident. A calf which he was allegedly carrying in the car died in the mishap. Ayyub's brother Imran alleged that he was beaten up on the suspicion that he was transporting cows for slaughter.[27] On September 25, 2016 in Banaskantha in Gujarat, a five-month pregnant Dalit woman and her husband were assaulted by half a dozen upper caste men for refusing to clear a cow carcass at Karja village.[28] On 20 January 2017 on the Jaipur Gurgaon highway, a group of 'gaurakshaks' stopped four trucks carrying buffaloes on the Jaipur-Gurgaon expressway on Wednesday night and beat up the transporters, sending one of them to hospital with injuries. The transporter was booked by the police for allegedly cruel conditions in which the cattle was packed in the truck but no case was registered against the 'gau-rakshaks'. [29]

24 "BJP worker killed by cow vigilantes", *India Today,* 18 August 2016. Available at http://indiatoday. intoday.in/story/bjp-worker-killed-by-cow-vigilantes/1/743516.html
25 "Dalit boy beaten up in Gujarat after his father refused to remove carcass", *The Hindustan Times,* 20 August 2016. Available at http://www.hindustantimes.com/india-news/dalit-boy-beaten-up-in-gujarat-after-his-father-refused-to-remove-carcass/story-LY1n4fUH3M4WyYDXOrp05M.html
26 Jahnavi Sen, "After Double Murder and Gangrape, Haryana Authorities Allegedly Seek to Protect Accused", *The Wire,* 7 September 2016. Available at https://thewire.in/64719/dingerheri-gan-grape-murder/
27 "Man thrashed by suspected cow vigilantes in Ahmedabad dies", *The Hindustan Times,* 16 September 2016. Available at http://www.hindustantimes.com/india-news/man-thrashed-by-suspected-cow-vig-ilantes-in-ahmedabad-dies/story-wAZpkTyA3K1RPosRvDC5wJ.html
28 "Pregnant Dalit woman attacked for refusing to remove cow carcass", *The Times of India,* 25 September 2016. Available at http://timesofindia.indiatimes.com/india/Pregnant-Dalit-woman-attacked-for-refusing-to-remove-cow-carcass/articleshow/54503995.cms
29 "'Gau Rakshaks' Strike Again! Cattle Trucks Attacked, Man Thrashed On Jaipur-Gurgaon Expressway", *India Times,* 20 January 2017. Available at http://www.indiatimes.com/news/india/gau-rakshaks-strike-again-cattle-trucks-attacked-man-thrashed-on-jaipur-gurgaon-ex-pressway-269875.html

I have devoted three pages of my book to this mind-numbing litany of mob assaults in the name of the cow to illustrate that lynching by empowered Hindutva mobs are not statistically trivial stray events, as claimed by supporters of the Modi administration, but are threatening to become a national contagion. The BJP still continues to be in denial. 'There has been an attempt by rival parties and sections of the media to stoke a persecution complex among minorities based on rare, isolated events,' said BJP spokesperson Narasimha Rao.[30] 'Propaganda by vested interests has miserably failed because it is unreal, fabricated and fictional.' We may have missed many incidents from the newspapers. For every incident reported, there may be ten, maybe hundred, that are never reported. People are attacked also for other reasons, particularly if Muslim men are said to be intimate with Hindu women.

India Spend did a quick survey of cow-related hate attacks since 2010 reported in the English language press. Its findings are revealing. 97 percent of such attacks occurred after Modi came to power, and more than half were in BJP ruled states. More than half the attacks were against Muslims, but 86 percent of those killed by lynching mobs were Muslim. This suggests that if one was found transporting cattle by a vigilante mob, if they discovered that your identity was Muslim, there was a much greater chance that you would be killed than otherwise. 8 percent of those killed were Dalit. Of the remaining 6 percent, some were of unknown identity, so the proportion of Muslims and Dalits killed by cow vigilante lynch mobs could be even higher.[31]

❋

These hate-lynchings raise troubling questions. On what terms can Muslim minorities live in India today? Must they subordinate themselves to what Hindu nationalists propound to be majority Hindu sentiment as the condition for being accepted as Indian? Or are they free to live in the ways they choose – in worship, dress, diet and language – and still qualify in every way as fully Indian?

The Constituent Assembly debates about cow slaughter are instructive about ways that Hindu majoritarian sentiment was negotiated by tall

30 Sujoy Dhar, "Attacks on India's minority Muslims by Hindu vigilantes mount", *USA Today*, 5 May 2017. Available at https://www.usatoday.com/story/news/world/2017/05/05/attacks-indias-minority-muslims-hindu-vigilantes-mount/100951514/
31 Delna Abraham and Ojaswi Rao, '84% Dead in Cow-Related Violence Since 2010 Are Muslim, 97% Attacks After 2014', *IndiaSpend*, 28 June 2017. Available at http://www.indiaspend.com/cover-story/86-dead-in-cow-related-violence-since-2010-are-muslim-97-attacks-after-2014-2014.

leaders of the freedom struggle. Some members passionately demanded that cow slaughter prohibition be included as a Fundamental Right. But both Ambedkar and Nehru insisted on a compromise of including cow protection instead as a non-binding Directive Principle, with carefully-crafted language. Article 48 of the Constitution reads, 'The State shall endeavour to organise agriculture and animal husbandry on modern and scientific lines and shall in particular, take steps for preserving and improving the breeds, and prohibiting the slaughter, of cows and other milch and draught cattle.' There is some dubious 'science' inherent in this formulation, because culling rather than preservation of cows may be required for scientific management of animal husbandry. But that is not the point. The reference to scientific animal husbandry rather than Hindu sentiment about cow slaughter was a salutary enunciation of the principle that the state in India must not privilege the religious or cultural sentiments of one section of people over any other. It is this fundamental secular principle that today's ruling alliance is turning dangerously on its head.

Since the RSS is the ideological lodestar of Prime Minister Modi, its opinion carries great weight with his government.[32] Days after Pehlu Khan's lynching, the powerful RSS chief Mohan Bhagwat called for a nationwide ban on cow slaughter, describing this as a 'sacred duty', adding that in states where the RSS has dedicated swayamsewaks in power, strong laws are already in place.[33]

The national government responded, less than two months of Pehlu Khan's lynching with an order that would nationwide render even more vulnerable to both official and vigilante attacks, cattle farming and trading. This notification sought to make it illegal for any cow, bull or buffalo, of any age, to be bought or sold in any cattle market for slaughter anywhere in the country. To prove that the animal was traded for dairying or farming and not slaughter would require official certification each time there is a transaction.[34] This will trap even more every cattle farmer and trader into the perpetual nightmare of being beholden to local often-corrupt officials and

---

32 Adapted from an article I authored for the *Hindustan Times,* titled "BJP must not invoke Gandhi to seek death for those who kill a cow", *Hindustan Times,* 31 May 2017. Available at https://www. hindustantimes.com/columns/bjp-must-not-invoke-gandhi-to-seek-death-for-those-who-kill-a-cow/story-MgNXrnddamvchA8tUGw14O.html

33 "RSS chief Mohan Bhagwat calls for nationwide ban on slaughter of cows", *The Indian Express,* 10 April 2017. Available at http://indianexpress.com/article/india/rss-chief-mohan-bhagwat-calls-for-nationwide-ban-on-slaughter-of-cows-4606910/

34 "New restrictions on cow slaughter", *The Hindu,* 26 May 2017. Available at http://www.thehindu.com/news/national/government-bans-sale-purchase-of-cattle-from-animal-markets-for-slaughter/article18585018.ece

in dread of inspectors and empowered vigilantes in order to struggle to earn a living. The notification was stayed by the courts at the time of writing, but the government is reportedly searching for legal avenues to push its passage.

In 1954, when Congress MP Seth Govind Das moved a resolution in the Lok Sabha for a total ban on cow slaughter, Prime Minister Jawaharlal Nehru reacted then with acerbic firmness – as he did against all forms of religious fundamentalism – declaring 'I would rather resign than accept this *nonsensical* demand (my italics)'.[35] He warded off similar demands from the President of India Rajendra Prasad, dubbing banning cow slaughter 'unimportant and reactionary'. We have such travelled a very long way as a nation since then.

However it must be admitted that the rot had set in much earlier. Congress Chief Minister Sampurnanand of Uttar Pradesh in 1955 introduced a law to ban cow slaughter in open defiance of Nehru's explicit wishes. Nehru censured it as a 'wrong step', but the law was possible because cow slaughter prohibition was included under the Directive Principles of an otherwise progressive Constitution.

Many other towering leaders sought popular Hindu support by pandering to orthodox Hindu sentiment supporting bans on cow slaughter. Socialist leader Jayaprakash Narayan in 1966 wrote to Prime Minister Indira Gandhi seeking a ban on cow slaughter, declaring 'I cannot understand why, in a Hindu majority country like India, where rightly or wrongly, there is such a strong feeling about cow-slaughter, there cannot be a legal ban.' Prime Minister Indira Gandhi refused to pass any legal ban then, resisting firmly a nation-wide agitation by many Hindu organisations. But in 1982, sobered by her 1977 electoral rout, and in line with many steps she took in that phase of her career to appease Hindu religious sentiment, she wrote to 14 Chief Ministers urging that the cow-slaughter ban be enforced in letter and spirit, and not allowed to be circumvented deviously. Prime Minister Morarji Desai had earlier admitted a move to bring a national cow-slaughter ban into the legislative competence of the central government, but his government fell before this could be accomplished.

Today most states have passed laws that prohibit cow slaughter, except Arunachal Pradesh, Meghalaya, Mizoram, Nagaland, Tripura and Lakshadweep; Assam and West Bengal permit the slaughter of cows over ages of 10 and 14 years respectively. *India Spend* estimates that 99.38 percent of the

---

35 Some of this section is excerpted from an earlier article I authored in the *Hindustan Times*, "Don't use the cow to create schisms", 2 May 2017. Available here: https://www.pressreader.com/india/hindu-stan-times-amritsar/20170502/282071981802686

country's population is covered by cow slaughter laws.[36] Laws banning cow slaughter in nearly half of these states are roughly 50 years old, enacted during the tenure of the Congress. In 24 states and union territories, the offence is cognisable, and in more than half of these, it is non-bailable. It is noteworthy that cognisable offences are serious crimes such as murder, rape, dowry deaths and kidnapping. In such cases, the police can make an arrest without a warrant and start investigation without a magistrate's permission.

Election speeches are today often laced with innuendos linking cow slaughter to minorities and to governments allegedly sympathetic to them (we noted Narendra Modi attacking the 'pink revolution' of an alleged surge of beef exports under Congress-led regimes). The BJP government in Haryana has even created a uniformed police force unit for cow protection.[37] The Gujarat legislature in 2017 approved life imprisonment for the killing cows.[38] The Chief Minister of Chhatisgarh, another BJP state, spoke nonchalantly of hanging those who slaughter cows.[39] A judge of the Rajasthan High Court Justice Mahesh Chand Sharma appealed to the Centre to declare the cow as a national animal and life imprisonment for its slaughter. It is worrying the Hindutva ethos has perculated even India's higher judiciary.[40]

The influential and pugnacious BJP MP Subramaniam Swamy intro-duced a bill in Parliament seeking the death penalty for those convicted for cow slaughter[41]. It is particularly unfortunate that Subramanyam Swamy invoked Mahatma Gandhi while seeking capital punishment for those who kill a cow in this proposed law. There is no doubt that Gandhi was deeply devoted to the cow. Gandhi said he would 'defend its worship against the whole world', that cow worship is central to Hinduism, and even that she

---

36 Alison Saldanha, "99.38% Indians Now Live In Areas Under Cow Protection Laws", *India Spend*, 14 April 2017. Available at http://www.indiaspend.com/cover-story/99-38-indians-now-live-in-areas-under-cow-protection-laws-42787

37 "Haryana considering formation of Cow Protection Task Force", *The Indian Express*, 6 July 2016. Available at http://indianexpress.com/article/india/india-news-india/haryana-considering-forma-tion-of-cow-protection-task-force-2897827/

38 "Gujarat: India state approves life term for killing cows", *BBC*, 31 March 2017. Available at http://www.bbc.com/news/world-asia-india-39454607

39 "Cow-Killers Will Hang, Says Chhattisgarh Chief Minister, But Admits His State Has None", *The Wire*, 2 April 2017. Available at https://thewire.in/120672/chhattisgarh-chief-minister-will-hang-cow-killers/

40 Sachin Saini, "Rajasthan HC judge wants cow as national animal, life term for slaughter", *Hindustan Times*, 19 June 2017. Available at http://www.hindustantimes.com/india-news/rajasthan-high-court-wants-cow-as-national-animal-suggests-life-term-for-slaughter/story-RtsiNP2QYrSFaz1Ltv2FML.html

41 Shubhajit Roy, "Subramanian Swamy bill seeks death penalty for cow slaughter", *The Indian Express*, 25 March 2017. Available at http://indianexpress.com/article/india/subramanian-swamy-bill-seeks-death-penalty-for-cow-slaughter-4584486/

is superior to our biological mothers. 'Our mother, when she dies, means expenses of burial or cremation. Mother cow is as useful dead as when she is alive. We can make use of every part of her body – her flesh, her bones, her intestines, her horns and her skin.'[42]

But still the Mahatma stoutly opposed a legal ban on cow slaughter. 'I have been long pledged to serve the cow but how can my religion also be the religion of the rest of the Indians? It will mean coercion against those Indians who are not Hindus. We have been shouting from the house-tops that there will be no coercion in the matter of religion.'[43] To therefore appeal to Gandhiji while advocating a nationwide ban on cow slaughter with death for those who defy the ban is disingenuous and unjust. He was very clear that to impose such a ban on non-Hindu Indians would amount to bullying by the majority which would run counter to the spirit and the promises of the freedom struggle, that India would belong equally to all regardless of their faith, caste, gender and language.

✻

A PUDR investigation into the operation and impact of cow slaughter restrictions in Haryana found that the legal ban has 'empowered the self-styled cow vigilante groups resulting in growing incidents of violent attack on minority community, transporters of cattle in general and ordinary sale and purchase of cattle.' Gau-rakshaks act with impunity as the 'eye and ear' of the administration and also as 'enforcers of law and dispensers of "lynch justice"'. It observes that the police and the administration are ambivalent to lynch-justice, claiming on the one hand that gau-rakshaks are independent volunteers and mildly criticizing them for taking law into their hands; but at the same time using them as informers and tending to play down the illegal activities carried out by them. 'The police administration exhibits lack of clarity on the provisions of the law and unable to deal with everyday skirmishes related to episodes of cow vigilantism.' It has also encouraged extortion rackets, as a "tax' of sorts is imposed as ageing and non-milching cows now require to be sent to gaushalas with a 'donation".[44]

---

42 Originally written in Harijan, reproduced here: http://www.mkgandhi.org/momgandhi/chap81.htm
43 See "What Mahatma Gandhi Said to Those Who Wanted Beef Banned in India", *The Wire,* 2 April 2017. Available at https://thewire.in/12170/what-mahatma-gandhi-said-to-those-who-wanted-beef-banned-in-india/. Extracted from the Collected Works of Mahatma Gandhi, Volume 88.
44 People's Union for Democratic Rights, "Cow Tale: Haryana Gauvansh Sanrakshan and Gausam-vardhan Act in Karnal, and its economic and administrative fallouts", August 2017. Available at http://pudr.org/sites/default/files/pdfs/karnal_english.pdf

UP Chief Minister Yogi Aditynath who had as an MP introduced a private members bill in Parliament seeking a nation-wide ban on cow slaughter, made his first major drive in office to close numerous abattoirs, casually imperilling the livelihoods of tens of thousands. Within hours of his becoming Chief Minister in Uttar Pradesh in the summer of 2017, police raided and closed hundreds of abattoirs and retail meat-shops, on grounds that these were unlicensed.[45] The conundrum was that ever since Yogi Adityanath had in 2002 constituted his belligerent Hindu youth militia, they violently protested the issue of licenses to anyone in the meat business, claiming that they illicitly sold cow meat. Weak-kneed successive governments buckled under their coercion, and did not issue licenses, but still informally allowed them to continue their trade. His BJP government in Lucknow was on technically legal ground to claim that all these small businesses lacked licenses. What they deliberately ignored was that these meat-sellers and butchers did not choose to work outside the law. They were given no option.

Thousands are suddenly without work. It is estimated that 2.5 million people depend on the meat export industry in UP, which accounts for half India's total meat exports. India is the second largest beef exporter and fifth largest beef consuming country in the world. This ban therefore ironically will hit poor Hindus as well, most of them of the lowest castes who alone would be willing to work in this profession. 'Except butchers, who are specialised in 'halal' (Islamic) slaughter, the rest of the workers in almost all abattoirs are Hindus,' said an office-bearer of the All India Meat and Livestock Exporters' Association to *Hindustan Times*.[46] Uttar Pradesh is establishing the template for the entire country. Rajasthan and Haryana, both ruled by the BJP, are also closing down thousands of meat-shops. Some are being gutted by vigilante mobs.[47] The central government – with questionable legal powers – has banned to sale and purchase of any bovine animal for slaughter, even buffaloes. The ban will also hit Christians, lower-caste Hindus and tribal peoples who consume cattle meat – a cheap source of protein for most.[48]

---

45 "Adityanath orders closure of illegal slaughterhouses, ban on cow smuggling", *The Hindustan Times*, 30 April 2017. Available at http://www.hindustantimes.com/adityanath-orders-closure-of-illegal-slaughterhouses-ban-on-cow-smuggling/story-G7mzsYvN4MTpMW3ZWn5f9O.html

46 Gulam Jeelani, "Job loss fear looms over UP's biggest slaughterhouse where Hindus outnumber Muslims", *The Hindustan Times*, 3 April 2017. Available at http://www.hindustantimes.com/india-news/job-loss-fear-looms-over-up-s-biggest-slaughterhouse-where-hindus-outnumber-muslims/story-wodpKHLYmScJsJdsZZnjyO.html

47 Teesta Setalvad, "Muslims Are Facing Violent Crackdowns in India", *Alternet*, 12 April 2017. Available at http://www.alternet.org/world/indian-streets-let-loose-blood-and-gore

48 Sandhya Gupta, "India's Concerning 'Saffron' Tide", Tony Blair Institute for Global Change, 7 April

Many commentators have argued that cow slaughter restrictions would be disastrous to India's livestock economy (among the biggest in the world) and would deal a further death-blow to India's dying agrarian economy. This would hit poor and middle peasants of every faith. Vikas Rawal, for instance points out that 'a ban on cow slaughter would either result in more and more unproductive animals being killed in most unscientific and cruel ways or would entail such a high cost for maintaining unproductive animals that cattle rearing would cease to be a profitable enterprise for farm households.' Restrictions being imposed on cow slaughter and the actions of the cow vigilantes would deal a serious blow to the agrarian economy and in particular to the livelihoods of the poor and middle peasants in rural India.

He says that in 2012, in comparison with about 21 crore milch cattle heads in India, there were only about 8.4 crore male cattle heads. That is, male cattle heads were only about 39 per cent of female cattle heads. The 'missing male bullock' results from these being sold for slaughter in abattoirs, abandoned in urban settlements, or even more commonly, simply made to die, such as by starving a young calf or expose it to biting cold on a winter night. With tractors, bullocks are no longer useful for cultivation. Fodder is limited and land holdings small, so the cost of feeding animals is high.

He also observes that indigenous milch cows have very low milk yields. But milch animals produce calves, that have to be fed, and hay is limited. Therefore progeny of the milch animals have to be periodically disposed of. The cattle and the calves also provide some insurance against economic shocks as farm households can sell them when there is a drought. Further he explains that for rural farm households, just abandoning unwanted cattle is not an option as these would destroy standing crops. They sell their aged milch animals to traders, who sell them to abattoirs. Modern abattoirs therefore, he explains, are essential for the bovine economy.

He estimates that about 3.4 crore male cow calves are born every year in India. If no male cow calves are allowed to be slaughtered, this will result in five times the current living population of male bullocks. In addition, no cow slaughter would mean that there would be about 6 crore unproductive old female cows to maintain. Where would we keep them and what would we feed them, he asks? He calculates that building cattle shelters for unproductive cows and bullocks would require 5 lakh acres of land and a capital expenditure of about Rs. 10,00,000 crores towards construction of cattle shelters.

2015. Available at https://institute.global/insight/co-existence/indias-concerning-saffron-tide

The annual additional cost of fodder and veterinary care would be about Rs. 5,40,000 crores. This, he says, is about 1.5 times India's total defence budget and about 35 times what centre and all State governments together spend on animal husbandry and dairy at present. It would require 70 thousand crore tonnes of fodder, but India simply does not have enough land for this. Even if each animal drinks one bucket of water a day, you would need more water for drinking by these animals than all the water humans drink. He concludes that if cow slaughter is banned, 'if a farm household that has a cow has to feed it, and all its male calves, till they all die a natural death, no farm household would dream of acquiring a cow. Restrictions on cow slaughter, legally or because of fear of cow vigilantes, would make cattle rearing uneconomical. In all likelihood, restrictions on cattle trade and cattle slaughter would result in unproductive animals being simply killed in the cattle sheds....(I)f slaughter of cows in abattoirs was not allowed: unproductive cattle would be poisoned, starved or left to die in cold. This would be the perverse outcome of restrictions on cattle trade and operation of proper abattoirs.'[49]

Brinda Karat points further that the strident campaign against cow slaughter would adversely impact also the leather industry, which employs close to 2.5 million people, mostly Dalits. 'Although the general campaign against cow slaughter targets Muslims', she observes, 'it is Hindus who will be most adversely affected if the Hindutva brigade has its way with a total ban on cattle slaughter.' This will include an estimated eight lakh Dalits who live through flaying the skin of dead cattle. This activity is within the law. Vigilantes have instilled fear among flayers, contractors, truck drivers, traders and others connected with the industry. She quotes a tannery owner in Kanpur, 'Now flaying or handling a cow hide is like having a tiger skin, which is totally illegal. Nobody wants to touch the skin of a dead cow; they are too scared.' She says that in one the biggest hide markets, the Pesh Bagh Chamra Mandi in Kanpur, the daily traffic of around 150 trucks of cattle hide has fallen to just three to four trucks a day. Tanneries and small-and medium-sized leather manufacturing units, which again employ mainly Dalits, are laying off workers because of the crunch in supplies.[50]

49 Vikas Rawal, "On Economic Implications of Restrictions on Cow Slaughter", *People's Democracy*, Vol 61, No 45, 5 November 2017. Available at http://peoplesdemocracy.in/2017/0716_pd/economic-implications-restrictions-cow-slaughter
50 Brinda Karat, "The economics of cow slaughter", *The Hindu*, 16 November 2015. Available at http://www.thehindu.com/opinion/op-ed/the-economics-of-cow-slaughter/article7880807.ece

The placid cow is no doubt beloved to millions of Indians. But the campaign today that claims to defend her has nothing to do with love of any kind. The cow is just recruited as another highly emotive symbol to beat down India's minorities into submission and fear. Other symbols are a grand Ram temple to replace a medieval mosque, charges that Muslim men are sexual pillagers and reproductively irresponsible, scare-mongering of a Muslim population explosion, allegations of their sympathy for terror, demands for curtailments in Muslim personal law, and claims of runaway Christian evangelism.

Organisations of the Sangh Parivar use the issue of cow slaughter not only to underline difference, but to actively promote hate against Muslims for political benefits to the BJP. In my travels to UP, I found that two issues were most effectively utilised to demonise Muslims. One was love jihad, or the fanciful idea that Muslim boys are trained to sexually attract Hindu girls and trap them into marriage, conversion and producing Muslim progeny. The second was the belief that Muslims continue to kill cows, trade in cow meat, and eat beef, in disregard, defiance or to outrage Hindu sentiment. Together these two ideas transform their Muslim neighbours into hateful and hated 'others'.

It was these same twin strategies that I found deployed in full throttle the last decade in coastal Karnataka, where Muslim boys seen with Hindu girls in public places are assaulted and dragged to police stations, and Muslims allegedly transporting cattle for slaughter are brutally attacked. In Gujarat, young men in the Bajrang Dal described to me their ambition to protect cows as their major motivation to join this militant Hindu ultra-nationalist formation. The sceptre of cow slaughter and alleged beef exports to Bangladesh is raised in West Bengal and Assam to drum up political opposition to the Muslims.

Indifferent to its potentially disastrous implications both for harmonious social relations and livelihoods of millions of India's poor and socially oppressed peoples, cow protection has always been an essential part also of Modi's armoury for raising communal temperatures. Addressing a function to celebrate Maharana Pratap's birth anniversary in 2012, for instance, Modi claimed (with dubious history) that Maharana Pratap had fought against Mughal sultanate on the issue of cow protection. He lamented that unfortunately even the present generation has to fight for cow protection against the government at the Centre of that time.[51] When Modi derided in his

51 "Maharana Pratap denied right place in history: Narendra Modi", *The Times of India*, 25 May 2012. Available at https://timesofindia.indiatimes.com/city/jaipur/Maharana-Pratap-denied-right-place-in-history-Narendra-Modi/articleshow/13461002.cms

2014 election speeches the 'pink revolution'[52] or the alleged support of the erstwhile UPA regime to rising beef exports, or when his minister Mukhtar Abbas asks Muslims who wish to eat beef to go to Pakistan,[53] what they are ultimately doing is to use cow slaughter to define both difference and what constitutes Hindu, and therefore legitimate Indian, sentiment, and dub political parties that were not tough on cow-slaughter bans as being 'pro-minority' which in their lexicon has always meant 'anti-Hindu'). They conflate sections of upper-caste Hindu religious beliefs with 'Indian' culture, and challenge the rights of Muslims who live in India (and indeed Dalits, tribal people and Christians) to act in ways that differ from practices and beliefs and sentiments of upper-caste Hindus.

If this alternate social contract between diverse people living in India that privileges cow protection over constitutional rights of equality and freedom is accepted, this would accomplish two objectives of Hindu nationalists. First, it would effectively reduce non-Hindus, Dalits and tribal people to second class citizens, who would be 'allowed' by the Hindu majority community to live in India only on the condition that they respect the legitimate domination of what are claimed to be Hindu (upper-caste and militant) religious and cultural beliefs. And second it would corrode the secular idea of India. India's secular idea rests on the foundational principle that India belongs equally to people of diverse faiths and belief systems, cultures and languages. It prohibits the religious, cultural, legal or moral dominance of any one religion or culture over any other. Unlike many European countries that require residents from distinct cultures and faith-systems to absorb and adapt themselves to the dominant language, culture and practices of the country, the essential secular idea of India does not require any kind of conformity of faith, culture, diet, dress or language to qualify as a fully-equal Indian citizen.

It is this uniquely Indian secular idea that Hindu nationalists challenge, by demanding that non-Hindus conform to what they claim to be the majority faith. There is no doubt that many Hindus revere the cow. Munshi Premchand's great novel 'Godaan' endearingly recreates the life-long yearning of peasants Hori and Dhania to own a cow that they can lovingly rear and gift away when they die to earn spiritual merit. But as I said before, campaigns

52 K. Balchand, "Modi fears a 'pink revolution'", *The Hindu*, 3 April 2014. Available at http://www.thehindu.com/news/national/other-states/modi-fears-a-pink-revolution/article5864109.ece
53 "Those who want to eat beef should go to Pak: Mukhtar Abbas Naqvi", *The Hindustan Times*, 22 May 2015. Available at http://www.hindustantimes.com/india/those-who-want-to-eat-beef-should-go-to-pak-mukhtar-abbas-naqvi/story-kTyciMp58MrUhrWJfp5kFK.html

against cow slaughter that we witness are not about love for the cow, but hate for fellow Indians.

Historian Mukul Kesavan dismisses as 'grotesque' the defence of apologists of the RSS BJP combine that the RSS campaign against cow slaughter on the one hand, and the lynching of Muslims involved in the cattle trade on the other, are 'separable projects'. He argues that it was Modi's campaign against the so-called 'pink revolution' during the 2014 general election, and the amplifying of this rhetoric by Yogi Adityanath and his vigilante army that 'convinced the current crop of freelance cow gundas that they had a licence to kill.' The closing of abattoirs, the curtailment of the killing of cows for meat or hides, the disruption of the transport trade in cattle are attractive, he says, because these policies are seen to hurt Muslims materially, which serves well the ideology of the BJP. (They wilfully ignore, as we noted earlier, that Hindus will ultimately be hit in even larger numbers by the cow slaughter ban). 'More importantly', he adds, 'the anti-cow-slaughter campaign has become for the BJP and its vision of Bharat what the anti-blasphemy law used to be for Zia-ul-Haq and his vision of Pakistan: an occasion for the public enactment of the supremacy of a religious majority and, correspondingly, the subordination of religious minorities.'

A majoritarian nationalism exists, he says, 'to assert that a nation state must be made in the image of its religious or racial majority and, further, that religious or racial minorities must acquiesce in their own subordination. In this context, images of minority citizens begging for their lives, or being casually murdered in full public view in a railway compartment, or being dragged out of their homes and lynched on the suspicion of beef eating, are images of violent subordination that perfectly fit the *sangh parivar*'s supremacist project. These lynchings then, are lecture-demonstrations, a way of graphically illustrating dominance.'[54]

In this environment permissive of hate speech and violence, both the Muslim and the Dalit have been demonized as the cow-killing 'other', and vigilante attacks and extortion targeting have become commonplace across the land. With bigotry sanctioned from the top, this mild pastoral animal is being used today to pit one Indian against another. Too much blood has flowed already.

✳

54 Mukul Kesavan, "Parsing murder – vigilantes and apologists", *The Telegraph*, 9 July 2017. Available at https://www.telegraphindia.com/1170709/jsp/opinion/story_160863.jsp

In the summer of 2016, on 11 July, four young Dalit men learnt that a cow had been killed, possibly by a lion, in Mota Samadhiyala village near Una in Gir Somnath district of Gujarat. They rushed to the village before the carcass decayed, and began to skin the dead animal.[55] It was socially humiliating work, but the skinning of cows for leather tanning was the occupation in which they were trapped, because of their birth in a Dalit caste.

As they were skinning the animal, upper-caste men who claimed to be member of cow protection group arrived in two cars and accused them of killing cows. Dalits tried to convince them that they had not killed the cow; they were only skinning a cow that was already dead. The men refused to believe them. To publicly punish them for killing the cow, they tied Dalits to the car and beat with sticks and iron pipes. Proud of their violence and assured of their impunity, they filmed the lashing of the young men and uploaded the video on the internet. They then drove the men to Una town, thrashed them publicly again, and later handed them in at the Una police station.

The videos of public lashing of the emaciated young men stripped to their waists went viral on internet and stirred the public conscience, even as it incensed Dalits across India. Protests and demonstrations erupted across the country. In the Saurashtra region of Gujarat, twelve Dalit youth attempted suicide in protest, and one of them died. A ten-day protest march was organised along the 350 kilometre route from Ahmedabad to Una, in which thousands of Dalits, Muslims and their supporters joined.[56] The march culminated on Independence Day at Una, where Radhika Vemula, mother of doctoral scholar Rohith Vemula who had taken his life earlier in the year because of institutional discrimination that he encountered in his university, unfurled the national flag. Thousands of Dalits gathered there pledged to liberate themselves from their caste occupation of lifting dead animal carcasses and skinning these, and demanded land instead. Kanhaiya Kumar, JNU student leader who had been arrested on sedition charges earlier that year, said to a wildly cheering crowd:

'You have exposed the Gujarat model of development.'

55 'Protests continue in Gujarat over thrashing of Dalits near Una', *The Hindu*, 21 July 2016. Available at http://www.thehindu.com/news/national/Protests-continue-in-Gujarat-over-thrashing-of-Dalits-near-Una/article14501552.ece

56 'In Dalit flogging, Una police fudged facts, looked other way: Chargesheet', *The Indian Express*, 8 September 2016. Available at http://indianexpress.com/article/india/india-news-india/una-dalit-flogging-cow-skinning-police-arrested-gujarat-probe-lion-killed-beef-ban-3019541/

CHAPTER SIX

'Encounter' Killings, Terror, Innocents and the Wages of Official Prejudice

News came in from the lake city of Bhopal of the extraordinarily murky alleged jailbreak, the murder of one jail guard, on the night of 31 October 2016, and the killing by policemen of eight alleged members of the banned organisation SIMI the morning after.[1]

I travelled to Bhopal two days after the killings, and felt as though I was caught in a time-warp, swept back a dozen years in time to the city of Ahmedabad. There too we had been witness to a series of extra-judicial killings of 'dreaded terrorists' (never even 'alleged' terrorists, although their crimes were never established in a court of law before their lives were taken). Those killed by the police in Gujarat in those years included a young nineteen year-old woman, a petty criminal and his wife, and the only surviving witness to their custodial killing. The stories of these 'encounter deaths' as divulged by the police seemed from the start to have big holes, but those who raised doubts about the truth of these official killings were quickly dubbed anti-national sympathisers of terrorists who almost by definition had to be covertly sympathetic to Islamist ideologies or cynical purveyors of 'vote-bank' politics.

The collective impact of these repeated killings of alleged Islamist terrorists helped consolidate and widen further the already profound divide between religious communities in Gujarat, and also promote a public image of siege of those political leaders especially Chief Minister Narendra Modi who positioned themselves as the only leaders with the courage to fight the Muslim – the fifth columnist 'enemy within'. This strategy manifestly paid rich political dividends in Gujarat, and later nationally. It appears today that this element of the 'Gujarat model' is also being extended to new territories

---

1 Portions of this chapter are excerpted from an article I authored for *Scroll*, "What the Bhopal jailbreak, killings teach us: Patriotism isn't blind obedience to the government", 12 December 2016. Available at https://scroll.in/article/823226/what-the-bhopal-jailbreak-killings-teach-us-to-be-a-patriot-not-just-obedient-to-the-government

administered by the BJP, now to Madhya Pradesh. Chief Minister Shivraj Chauhan combatively described the eliminated men eliminated by his police force as 'dreaded terrorists who could have wreaked devastation'[2] although none of this is proved, either that they were terrorists or that they were about to wreak terror violence. He jeered that they enjoyed chicken biryani during their long incarceration, again an emotive and deliberate falsehood by the head of the state administration.[3] His suggestion was that the delayed trials of terror-accused are not unconscionable injustices but signs of state softness, and only the muscular state would respond fittingly – by killing them.

Chief Minister Modi in feverish speeches in Gujarat had asked audiences what he should do with Sohrabuddin, who had been killed in what was alleged to be a fake 'encounter' with his police force, and who his government alleged was a terrorist determined to assassinate Modi. The crowd responded feverishly to his question with the call, 'Kill him! Kill him!'[4] Chief Minister Chauhan asked an audience a similar rhetorical question in Bhopal and got the same bloodthirsty answer from the gathering. This is why I feel caught in a time-warp in Bhopal, swept back to a dangerously and deliberately divided Ahmedabad a dozen years earlier.

In Ahmedabad then, as in Bhopal (and indeed much of the nation) now, raising questions about whether these killings of alleged terrorists were actually acts of self-defence by the police or cold-blooded murder, were and are demonised by those in authority or sympathetic to their world-view as disloyal and unpatriotic acts against the nation. Some suggest that such scepticism reeks of sympathy with terrorists and their ideologies. This stigmatisation has resulted in the suppression of a great part of public interrogation and scrutiny. But in Gujarat, heroes emerged from outside but also within the criminal justice system, and ensured that colleagues in uniform, and ultimately even Home Minister Amit Shah were sent behind bars. The official versions of the Sohrabuddin, Kausar Bi, Ishrat Jahan and Tulsiram Prajapati encounter killings were riddled with huge holes that were exposed through

---

2 "CM Shivraj Singh Chouhan slams dirty politics over killing of SIMI terror suspects", *The Times of India*, 1 November 2016. Available at http://timesofindia.indiatimes.com/home-page-sections/ CM-Shivraj-Singh-Chouhan-slams-dirty-politics-over-killing-of-SIMI-terror-suspects/articleshow/ 55178729.cms

3 "Terror Suspects Fed 'Chicken Biryani': Chief Minister Chouhan on SIMI Row", *NDTV*, 2 November 2016. Available at http://www.ndtv.com/india-news/after-simi-shooting-chief-minister-chouhan-talks-of-biryani-in-jail-1620410

4 "What Narendra Modi said in his election speech at Mangrol on December 4", *The Hindu*, 13 December 2007. Available at http://www.thehindu.com/todays-paper/What-Narendra-Modi-said-in-his-election-speech-at-Mangrol-on-December-4/article14894083.ece

public vigilance and diligent officials. But the story of the Bhopal jailbreak and subsequent killings are even more audacious in their improbability. There are not just wide holes in the story: the story is entirely one wide hole!

Challenging our credulity to its limits, the Madhya Pradesh home minister wishes that we believe that highest-security jail locks were broken by keys fashioned out of tooth brushes and knives out of spoons, and tall walls were crossed by tying together bed-sheets which are never issued to prisoners. Commentators ask pertinently how the prisoners managed to make ten separate keys (eight for the individual cells they were locked in and one each for the two wards) out of toothbrushes in the prison. And even if they did it, where did they get tools and equipment to do this? Once out of their cells, according to the official version, they brutally killed one of the prison guards patrolling the courtyard with a knife fashioned out of their steel plates! They then scaled the twenty-five feet wall and the final prison wall of thirty-five feet by constructing a ladder out of 35 bed-sheets issued to the jail residents, and they used wooden planks as rungs for this cloth ladder crafted from the prison bed-sheets. No one explained how the prisoners had access to not eight bed-sheets (one for each) but 35, when prison regulations strictly bar issue of bed-sheets to especially high-security prisoners for fear that they may use these to commit suicide. The state government further claims that just on that night all the numerous 360 degree cameras inside the prison including in the terror cells were not working or disabled and the prison was shockingly understaffed.

A group of nine young concerned people, many of them alumni of the Tata Institute of Social Sciences visited Bhopal and released on 30 November, 2016, a month after the killings, a highly damning detailed fact-finding report that further illuminates the utter improbability of the claims of the state government.[5]

The young fact-finders were unsurprisingly not allowed access inside the prison, but instead they interviewed a jail under-trial Kabir (name changed) who had been released on bail a week earlier. He was housed in the same B Wing of the prison where all the eight men who were killed had been detained. He testified that each of the eight slain men was housed in separate solitary rooms in the most highly secured terror cell. The terror-cell is most secure because it is in the centre with three layers of boundary walls – like a box in a box in a box – most closely monitored by cameras and security officers mounted across the prison.

5 The report is downloadable here: http://thecompanion.in/wp-content/uploads/2016/12/Bhopal-FFC.pdf

Kabir testified that 'in order to have escaped from the prison, each of the inmates would have had to unlock their own individual cell, then unlock the door of their ward, then overpower the six *jaagiyas* (guards assigned to keep an eye all night on the terror wards) watching the wards as well as the two guards patrolling the terror cell, evade being detected by anyone from the headquarter office which is right opposite the terror cell.' This, he declared, is next to impossible because with slightest noise the entire system of guards, alarms and other security measures would get activated. 'Even if they break the terror cell, kill all *jaagiyas* and two security guards, they would have to then scale the 25 foot long wall of the B wing. It is not possible to cross it with clothes or blankets. Now, even if they cross that wall, they would land right in the centre of B-ward prison compound facing the medical ward inmates, guards, etc., leaving no possibility of remaining undetected. After this if they reach the compound wall without being seen by any guards or prison officials, they would have to then climb the 35 foot long wall of the Bhopal Central prison. After this they would have to cross the third wall, which is external wall, again undetected by any officials. Kabir said to the Fact Finding Team that, 'I can challenge, that if all security, surveillance is removed and an Olympian is asked to cross the wall, he would still fail. The Jail can't be broken.'[6]

I visited the hilltop that was the site of the 'encounter' and was shocked first to find that it had not even been cordoned off by the police. No police personnel were visible anywhere. Journalists and curious villagers were walking over the smudges of blood on the rocks and the police chalk-markings of where the corpses lay. It was evident that the state actually wished for the destruction of all evidence. The large rock where the men were killed by the police ended in a cliff-edge so steep that if the men had been surrounded by the police, they would have had nowhere to run except to their death.

The amateur videos and audios that have surfaced suggest that they wanted to surrender, that they were deliberately killed at close range, and the forensic reports that most wounds were above their waists add to the apprehension that the police killed them instead of capturing them alive. The ATS Chief admits now that the slain men had no firearms, therefore there is no basis to believe that they were killed in self-defence by a force that was left with no options. The Fact Finding Team describes the two videos (taken from different angles) which show policemen 'shooting an already collapsed body of one of the accused victim. In one video the firing has been done from

6   Ibid, p 7-8.

a very close range, to an already dead (or half dead) body. Voices can be clearly heard saying 'hit him in the chest. Finish him, $%&# (abusive words) etc..' In another video of same incident, we see more than one bullet (at least two) being fired at the already collapsed body. Bodies of other deceased are lying very close to each other. Earlier in the video, one policeman is shown recovering a shining sharp weapon resembling a chopper knife from the waist of one of the deceased. The deceased (all eight) are lying very close to each other, wearing clean clothes (almost brand-new) fitting perfectly body sizes of the deceased, their faces (all eight) are clean shaved.' The dead men 'are wearing watches, belts and very clean shoes.' In another video five men standing atop the cliff can be seen raising their hands. The video is shot from a point very close to where the police personnel are standing in the valley. They can be heard saying loudly on the walkie talkie 'We can see five people, they want to talk. Three are running, one is leaping.'[7]

The videos raise many disturbing questions, elaborated carefully in the Fact Finding Committee report. Where did the accused men acquire the clean clothes, watches, shoes that they were wearing, which under-trials are not issued or allowed to wear? If there were handlers who provided them with all of this, who were these handlers and why has there been no efforts to get hold of them? If they could organise clothes, shoes and watches for the escaped men, why wouldn't the handlers arrange vehicles for them to escape as well? Why did the men stay together after escaping, instead of dispersing into ones and twos in different directions, by which stratagem finding them could possibly have become as difficult as searching for needles in a haystack? The village near where they were shot dead is a well-populated, and to reach it from the Bhopal Central Jail the fugitives would have had to cross three highways. Why would those fleeing the law choose to cross three highways, and then climb a cliff thereby make themselves visible to the entire village?

The team also points to the fact that the dead bodies lying so close to each other. If all the accused were standing next to each other, the greater possibility is of that they offered to surrender, rather than being locked in a bloody gun-battle as claimed by the police (one in which no policemen were injured). The videos of dead bodies shot by the family members of the dead men was seen by the Fact Finding Team; they showed more than 25 bullets shots on their bodies. There were hardly one or two bullet wounds in the lower parts of the bodies, mostly the shooting was systematically focussed

---

7 Ibid, p.10.

above their waist. Few bullets mark were found on back of the skull. Bullets seemed to have pierced through the body leaving big holes suggesting firing from close range.

There can therefore be little doubt that intention of the police force was to kill the men, not to capture them alive. Nothing justifies cold-blooded killings, legally or morally, even if the men were terrorists, or they had escaped from the jail and killed a guard. They should have been captured and faced the majesty of the law. The policemen who killed the eight men have committed brazen cold-blooded murder in uniform. The law demands that they should be arrested and forced to face trial. But this is highly unlikely to happen. Instead the 21 SIMI accused who are still in prison have complained to the court as well as to the NHRC that they are being continuously harassed, humiliated and physically assaulted ever since this 'encounter', and they believe that their lives are also in danger.[8]

The Union Minister of State for Home Kiren Rijiju declared that 'we should stop this habit of raising doubts and questioning the authorities and police. This is not a good culture.'[9] Chief Minister Chauhan agreed, pronouncing that 'government and the public and the nation are foremost.' He appealed 'to stop playing dirty politics' declaring 'Patriotism is important.'[10]

۞

Along with extra-judicial killings of mostly Muslim, Dalit and Adivasi men, the abduction, arrest, and detention for many years of Muslim men on charges that they were terrorists has been for many years the centre-piece of the 'war on terror' of the Indian state.[11] It matters little that ten, fourteen, sometime twenty-four years later, the courts acquit them of all charges, and they walk free, men broken after many years of their lives have been embezzled from

---

8 "NHRC orders probe into 'harassment' of SIMI members lodged in Bhopal jail", *The Hindustan Times*, 26 May 2017. Available at http://www.hindustantimes.com/india-news/nhrc-orders-probe-into-harassment-of-simi-members-lodged-in-bhopal-jail/story-t0M3O9C5YVbgZGFKMShYFK.html

9 Stop habit of questioning authorities, police: Rijiju on killing of SIMI men", *The Hindustan Times*, 1 November 2016. Available at http://www.hindustantimes.com/india-news/stop-habit-of-questioning-authorities-police-rijiju-on-killing-of-simi-men/story-7kgPmLZ38g7Jmw5zo4d5fJ.html

10 "CM Shivraj Singh Chouhan slams dirty politics over killing of SIMI terror suspects", *The Times of India*, 1 November 2016. Available at http://timesofindia.indiatimes.com/home-page-sections/CM-Shivraj-Singh-Chouhan-slams-dirty-politics-over-killing-of-SIMI-terror-suspects/articleshow/55178729.cms

11 Portions of this section are excerpted from an article I authored that appeared in the *Economic and Political Weekly*, "Terror, Innocence, and the Wages of Official Prejudice", 52 (16), 22 April 2017.

them. There are several communally charged assumptions that underlie these astounding state injustices – that all acts of terror are by Muslims, that the burden of proof must shift to the Muslim accused if the state charges them with terror crimes, and that they deserve no rights and protections that other accused persons have. To be fair, these have been standard practice of governments in India long before Modi took the reins of office. But in his government, what is dramatic is that all people of Hindutva ideologies who were charged credibly with terror crimes are being systematically freed of all guilt.

Imagine being wrongfully charged and jailed after torture for 14 years, never knowing if you will ever walk free. This is Mohammed Aamir Khan's harrowing story, of unspeakable injustice that stole the best years of his youth from him. But his story is, at the same time, one of exceptional endurance, love, and hope. In the three years I have known him, I found him a remarkably gentle person, free of bitterness and anger, and convinced about justice, democracy, and secular values.

In a deeply affecting book he has written with Nandita Haksar, *Framed as a Terrorist: My 14-year Struggle to Prove My Innocence*,[12] he describes how when he was 20, one late winter evening in February 1998 on a by-lane of Old Delhi close to his small home, he was picked up by policemen in plain clothes, and driven to a torture chamber. He recounts his days and nights of torture–stripped naked, his legs stretched to extremes, boxed, kicked, subject to electric shocks, anti-Muslim abuse, and threats to frame his parents. He finally succumbs, and agrees to sign numerous blank sheets and diaries. As a result, he was charged in 19 cases of terror crimes, and accused of planting bombs in Delhi, Rohtak, Sonipat, and Ghaziabad.

From here began a nightmare that lasted nearly 14 years. Housed often in solitary confinement in jails in Tihar and Ghaziabad, his only encounter with the world outside was his innumerable court hearings. No judge asks him about his torture, nor do doctors record his torture wounds. He is acquitted in one terror case, only for another to begin. What he endured would break the spirit of most men. There are times when he is close to despair. Even more than his confinement, isolation, dehumanised conditions, and the hopelessness of the proceedings, what grieves him most is helplessly watching his parents suffer outside.

But it was also their love and faith in his innocence that sustained him through bleak, long years of suffering. He describes how his father Hashim Khan was present at every hearing:

12 (2016), New Delhi: Speaking Tiger Books.

Abbu arrived before the courts opened. He went straight to the typists
who sit in rows outside the lawyers chambers. ... He came early so he
could get his applications typed ... for permission to meet me in the lock
up ... to give me home-made food ... Armed with his application Abbu
made his way through the crowds to the court where my case would
come up ... to catch a glimpse of me.[13]

The police continued to harass his parents, money for lawyers ran out, and none came forward to help, as they were stigmatised as parents of a terrorist.

His father died in 2001, satisfied that by then he had been acquitted in 11 of the 19 cases. The burden then fell on his mother, who negotiated the unfamiliar and male-dominated worlds of courts, jails, and lawyers' chambers for 11 years. She would now attend court proceedings and carry messages she barely understood to the lawyers. There was no money for fees, and he was now represented by legal aid lawyers. Sometimes he was acquitted in trial courts, sometimes in high courts.

One day, without warning, on a winter evening in January 2012, he was told that he was free to walk out of prison. Some of the most poignant passages in the book are those where Aamir describes how much the world changed during the 14 years of his incarceration. He learned about the internet – how you could instantly send messages and gather knowledge from across the world. He learnt about mobile phones. He was amazed how many channels television had; he only knew Doordarshan. People had begun to shop in tall buildings called malls.

But by the time he was freed, his mother was confined to her bed, with a stroke. She could not speak to him. He often tells me how fortunate he feels that Allah allowed him to take care of his mother in her last years. His childhood love, Alia, had waited for him these 14 years. They have a daughter now, the centre of their lives.

※

Aamir's story is sadly not exceptional. There are many things that should weigh unbearably on our collective public conscience. Yet many of these – remarkably and culpably – do not. One such is the confinement behind prison walls of innocent men (and very occasionally women), often for many years (sometimes even decades), on charges of bloody terror crimes that are ultimately proved to be false. Several years of their lives are stolen from them by criminally slipshod,

13 Ibid, p.134-35.

malicious, and prejudiced police investigations and the complicity of courts. Even while we welcome such acquittals, it remains incontrovertible that those years spent behind prison walls by innocent persons can never be restored, or compensated for. The stigma and suffering can also never be erased.

No official data is available on the number of persons acquitted after being charged with terror crimes. This lack of information is probably not an unintentional official lapse, but by design, to escape scrutiny and accountability. In 2014, Minister of State for Home Kiren Rijiju informed the Rajya Sabha that the central government did not have any data on whether a large number of Muslim youth arrested on the charge of terrorism had been 'honourably exonerated' by various courts after the cases were found to be false.[14] The National Crime Records Bureau maintains extensive and detailed records on numerous aspects of crime and punishment. Its unwillingness, therefore, to compile and publish data about those acquitted after being charged with terror crimes is not a chance lapse. It is a deliberate attempt to hide from public knowledge the enormity of continuing state injustice and profiling, and to avoid public accountability and redress for these state actions.

However, groups of human rights defenders have developed dossiers of some of these cases, and each is a deeply troubling record of dishonourable, deliberate, and recurring state injustice. The Jamia Teachers' Solidarity Association (JTSA) in 2012 published a chilling report, *Framed, Damned and Acquitted: Dossiers of a Very Special Cell*, detailing 16 cases involving more than 40 Muslim men who spent long and painful years in jail before being acquitted.[15] More recently, the Innocence Network organised its first Peoples' Tribunal on Acquitted Innocents on 2 October 2016 in Delhi, chaired by Justice A P Shah. In this were the recorded statements of men who had spent between three and 23 years in prison before being acquitted. The jury noted,

Testimonies were uniformly distressing and did not fail to move anyone who heard those stories of lives destroyed by years of wrongful incarceration. In testimony after testimony, we heard of illegal and wrongful detention, torture in police custody, forced confessions extracted under duress, long incarceration, repeated denial of bail, to be acquitted finally years after their arrest.[16]

14 "Many Terror Accused Acquitted due to Lack of Evidence," *Business Standard*, 16 July 2014. Available at http://www.business-standard.com/article/pti-stories/many-terror-accused-acquitted-due-to-lack-of-evidence-114071600682_1.html
15 Full report available here: http://www.jamiajournal.com/wp-content/uploads/2012/09/JTSA-Report-Framed-Damned-and-Acquitted-Dossiers-of-a-Very-Special-Cell.pdf
16 "Report of the Jury of the 1st Peoples' Tribunal on Innocent Acquitted, Towards a Framework for Compensation and Rehabilitation for Victims of Wrongful Prosecution/Conviction," (2016)

Over the past many years, in the course of my work, I have met several such men, released after years in prison, struggling to piece together the pieces of their broken lives. Some, like Aamir, I have come to know closely, and in other cases, members of their families. On 27 February 2002, after the fire in a train compartment in Godhra killed 58 Hindus, this tragedy was used to set aflame many bloody weeks of communal violence in most of Gujarat. We recall how Narendra Modi, who was then chief minister, publicly alleged that the train was burnt as part of a pre-planned terrorist attack (a charge that has not been backed by the courts). Hours after the train burning, several Muslim youth were arrested on the charge that they were part of a terrorist conspiracy executed with cross-border support. Among these were three brothers, Shamsher, Sultan, and Sadiq, who lived in an impoverished house-hold in a slum called Signal Falia close to the station. They spent nine years in prison before they were released. Their father died halfway through this of cancer, their mother Bibi Khatoon was reduced to begging to keep the wives and children of her imprisoned sons alive. The youngest son, who was unmarried, suffered from a grave mental illness while in prison.

I also got to closely know Ibrahim Junaid, a young medical student of 25 years, who was arrested after the terror attack on the historical Mecca Masjid in Hyderabad on 18 May 2007. Although the attack was on a mosque during Friday prayers, the investigating authorities immediately assumed that the bombs must have been planted by Islamist organisations. A number of Muslim youth were held, tortured, and jailed. Junaid's parents, along with the families of 20 other young men who had been similarly abducted and detained, filed habeas corpus petitions in the High Court of Andhra Pradesh, petitioned national and state human rights and minorities commissions, and convened high-profile protest meets and press conferences. It took two years for them to be acquitted and released. With Junaid, the other youth, local activist Lateef Khan, and Teesta Setlavad, I was part of a petition to the high court for compensation to be awarded to the men who had been wrongly charged and jailed. This petition has still to be decided.

Eight men wept in a courtroom in Mumbai when, on 25 April 2016, the judge pronounced them innocent of terror crimes in Malegaon a decade earlier.[17] This brought an end to their 10-year nightmare, during which time

---

Innocence Network India.

17 This section is adapted from an article that I wrote for *The Indian Express*, titled "The ghost of Malegaon", 9 June 2016. Available at http://indianexpress.com/article/opinion/columns/malega-on-blast-case-mumbai-hemnat-karkare-islamist-terror-hindutva-terror-2841902/

they endured arrest, torture, incarceration, and charges for crimes they never committed. They spent more than half these years in prison; the remainder fighting a protracted court battle to prove their innocence. One of the nine accused men died before his innocence was confirmed. I spoke to Noor-ul-Huda, a power-loom worker who was the first to be arrested. He said the 10 years had destroyed his health, his dignity, his reputation, and his family. 'Who can return these years to me?' he asked me. Maulana Azhari declared to a reporter, 'The charges were not against the nine men, but the entire Muslim community. We stand vindicated.'

Ten years had passed by since 6 September 2006, when in Malegaon, 300 kilometres from Mumbai, two bombs planted on bicycles exploded near a mosque where crowds had gathered for prayers for the festival of Shab-e-Baraat. The blast left 37 people dead and more than 100 injured, all Muslim. And, yet again, the police took little time to declare that the blasts must have been engineered by international Islamist terror groups such as Lashkar-e-Toiba, Jaish-e-Mohammed and Harkat-ul-Jihad-al-Islami, with Indian collaborators from the banned Students Islamic Movement of India (SIMI). All the accused men, devout practising Muslims, were tortured after their arrest in 2006. Two years later, in September 2008, explosives concealed in a motorcycle parked outside a transport company in Malegaon detonated once again, this time killing eight people and injuring 80. Once more, five Muslim men said to be belonging to Lashkar-e-Toiba and SIMI were initially held guilty.

However, investigations led by Hemant Karkare, an exceptionally courageous police officer with a rare sense of fairness, blew the lid off a form of terror that investigating agencies and the popular imagination had failed to acknowledge till then. This was terror attacks by persons inspired by Hindutva ideologies. The initial breakthrough was achieved by tracing the ownership of the motorcycle to Sadhvi Pragya Singh Thakur, a former Akhil Bharatiya Vidyarthi Parishad (ABVP) activist. Even more sensational was the alleged role of a serving army officer, Lt Col Shrikant Purohit, and a retired Major, Ramesh Upadhyay, in the conspiracy, the first such case against a serving army officer in the country. Others indicted were sadhus and mahants, as well as some associated with Sangh affiliates and a shadowy organisation called Abhinav Bharat, named after the terror-based formation established by Vinayak Savarkar in 1904.

These arrests and investigations led to an uncovering of the roles of Abhinav Bharat and Hindutva organisations in several other terror attacks, including the

Malegaon blasts of 2006 and 2007, explosions in the Samjhauta Express to Pakistan, in the Hyderabad Mecca Masjid, and in Ajmer Sharif Dargah on the eve of the last Friday of Ramadan. Bajrang Dal activists were found manufacturing bombs in makeshift factories in Nanded, Kanpur, Bhopal, and Goa. Such findings by, for instance, the Secular Citizens' Forum and the People's Union of Civil Liberties, were corroborated by K P Raghuvanshi, head of Maharashtra's Anti-Terrorism Squad. In an interview to *Communalism Combat*,[18] he described it as "terrorist act" by "Hindus," "manufactured for unlawful ends to wreak violence through terror." Besides their targets–and a similar culture and history of communal polarisation–what was common in most of these cases was the use of fake beards and skullcaps.

What lay exposed was a deeply worrying communal mindset in India's police and security establishment. In all these episodes, despite the blasts clearly targeting Muslims, investigators assumed in each case that the perpetrators were Islamist militants. In Hyderabad, for instance, police claimed that the blasts were set off by a cell phone in Bangladesh, involving the Harkat-ul-Jihad-al-Islami (HUJI), and arrested several young Muslim men such as Junaid, who were tortured and forced to confess. The same pattern was followed in all the other cases. Clear leads pointing to Hindutva terror groups were ignored. Instead, transborder Islamist groups were blamed and Indian Muslim men arrested under terror laws, tortured, and forced to sign 'confessions.'

Official bias does not end here. In cases where Islamist organisations are responsible for terror attacks, such as the Bombay blasts of 1993 and the 26/11 attack, the police, prosecution, the judiciary at all levels, the government and public opinion, all combined to ensure the highest punishment for those charged with even abetment of these crimes. By contrast, after Karkare was tragically killed during the Mumbai terror attack on 26 November 2008, almost no further evidence against Abhinav Bharat and Hindutva terror groups was collected by his successors, or by the Central Bureau of Investigation (CBI), or by the National Investigation Agency (NIA) constituted after 26/11 to investigate terror cases.

These biases were aggravated by a Bharatiya Janata Party (BJP)-led government coming to power at the centre. Rohini Salian, a law officer appointed special public prosecutor in the Malegaon matter at the insistence of Karkare, made sensational revelations in a 2015 interview to the *Indian Express*. She

---

18 Cited by Praful Bidwai, "A Litmus Test of Impartiality," *TNI*, 23 September 2006. Available at https://www.tni.org/es/node/13414

said that officers of the NIA were pressuring her to 'go slow' on the accused of radical Hindutva organisations in the 2008 Malegaon case to facilitate their eventual discharge.[19] Witnesses turned 'hostile' one by one. Now, the NIA claims that Karkare's investigations were dubious and that he 'planted' fake evidence, and that Sadhvi Pragya is innocent though she owned the motorcycle. The case is rapidly crumbling. On April 25, 2017, the Bombay High Court granted her bail, observing 'If reports of Anti-Terrorist Squad (ATS) and NIA are considered conjointly, it cannot be said that there are reasonable grounds for believing that accusation made against her are prima facie true. The benefit of bail cannot be withheld, even if the offences alleged against her by ATS are grave and serious one.'[20] The court relied upon statements of witnesses to show that Sadhvi was not in possession of the said motorcycle used for the blasts much before the incident. 'Even assuming that the said motorcycle was found at the place of the incident, the fact that she was the registered owner of it, by itself cannot be sufficient in the light of material placed on record,' the court stated. It went on, 'Though there is some material on record that she was present at the Bhopal meeting, it, however, shows that apart from her, several other persons were also present at the said meeting. In our view, the same cannot be considered as circumstance against her alone, excluding the other participants, especially, now in the absence of any objectionable and incriminating material attributed to her.'[21]

Since earlier investigations pointed to her being the fulcrum of the conspiracy, the investigative agency alleging her innocence weakens the case against all other accused. The Court at that time dismissed Lt. Col. Purohit's appeal. But the Supreme Court approved bail after nine years in prison for Lt Col Purohit in August 2017. Col Purohit had been chargesheeted both by the Maharashtra ATS in 2009 and by the National Investigation Agency (NIA) in May 2016. The Indian Express reports that in its chargesheet, which absolved Sadhvi Pragya for lack of evidence, the NIA said, 'Purohit had proposed theory for a separate constitution for Hindu Rashtra with separate flag (Bhagwa flag) the constitution of Abhinav Bharat, and discussed about the formation of Central Hindu Government (Aryawart) against the Indian

19 "Since this new govt came, I have been told to go soft on accused (Hindu extremists): Special Public Prosecutor Rohini Salian", *The Indian Express*, 25 June 2015. Available at http://indianexpress.com/article/india/india-others/since-this-new-govt-came-i-have-been-told-to-go-soft-on-accused-hindu-extremists-special-public-prosecutor/
20 Sonam Saigal "Sadhvi Pragya gets bail in Malegaon blast case", *The Hindu*, 25 April 2017. http://www.thehindu.com/news/national/sadhvi-pragya-gets-bail-in-malegaon-blast-case/article18204488.ece
21 Ibid.

government and put forth concept of forming this government in exile in Israel and Thailand.' An inquiry conducted by the Directorate General of Military Intelligence had concluded that 'the officer is highly indoctrinated, deals with illegal proliferation of weapons and hiding facts.' The inquiry report also said that his wife, Aparna Purohit, 'revealed that her husband has deep hatred for Islam and he may be involved in activities directed against them'.[22] After his release, Col Purohit has been given security on par with that of the highest serving army officials.

Contrast this with the determination at the highest levels of the executive and judiciary to refuse even a day's parole, let alone bail, and to hang persons accused of terror crimes – on far thinner evidence – if they are Muslim.

᠅

One of the most moving and inspiring of the growing litany of stories of 'terror innocents' is that of Shahid Azmi. Shahid was just 15 when he watched Mumbai burn for weeks in 1992-93 after the razing of the Babri Masjid. He was briefly radicalised by what he saw during the Mumbai riots, and crossed the country's borders as a young teenager to join a terrorist formation. But he was quickly disillusioned and returned home within months. However, these few months changed the course of his short life permanently. Police detained and tortured him, and charged him with terror crimes. The persecution stopped only when he was acquitted of all charges by the Supreme Court after seven years of incarceration.

Refusing either to lose hope or become embittered, he persisted with his college education during his years in prison, and emerged with a postgraduate degree. Despite his family's strained means, he resolved, after his discharge, to study law. His legal practice was mainly devoted to defending Muslim youth unjustly charged with terror crimes, subjected – just as he had been – to torture and long, hopeless years of imprisonment. He was undeterred by many of the death threats he was subjected to because he defended men charged with terror crimes. Ultimately, he was gunned down by four assailants in his office at the tragically young age of 32. 'Shahid was in love with the idea of justice,' his friend Monica Sakhrani recalls. 'Fighting against injustice was the driving force of his life. This is what cost him his life.'[23]

22 Deeptiman Tiwary, "Lt Col Shrikant Prasad Purohit claims he kept Army in loop, Army blew his cover", *The Indian Express*, 24 August 2017. Available at http://indianexpress.com/article/india/colonel-shrikant-purohit-claims-he-kept-army-in-loop-army-blew-his-cover-4810786/
23 Harsh Mander (2015), *Looking Away: Inequality, Prejudice and Indifference in New India*. New Delhi: Speaking Tiger Books.

The latest in this soul-numbing catalogue of state-imposed injustice and suffering include Mohammad Rafiq Shah and Mohammad Hussain Fazili, charged for the Delhi blasts in 2005 that killed 80 people and injured 225. They were released after more than 11 years on 16 February 2017 after Additional Sessions Judge Reetesh Singh dropped all charges against them. As the *Indian Express* reported, Fazili could not even recognise his mother. Rafiq's mother had suffered a stroke, and his family could not visit him in jail for many years as they were too poor.[24]

Around the same time, the same judge acquitted Irshad Ali and Mourif Qamar, who also spent 11 years in jail on terror charges. Earlier day labourers, they were recruited as police informers, but the Special Cell charged them with terror crimes in 2006. Their nightmare should have ended in 2008 when the Delhi High Court ordered the CBI to investigate. The CBI in its report of 11 November 2008 confirmed Ali's version that the Special Cell had concealed that Ali and Nawab were its informers and had implicated them in a fictitious case. The CBI recommended their discharge and action against erring officials. Ali told the *Indian Express* in 2016:

> *I thought we would be free now. But that didn't happen. Instead of taking action against its officers, the Delhi Police and government started defending them ... Our lives, our destroyed families didn't matter ... An entire system was up against two poor nobodies.*[25]

It took nine years before they could walk free.

❀

Although these many stories happened to different men at the hands of different policepersons and courts at various geographies, there is a chilling and instructive commonality to most of these stories. As observed by the JSTA:

> *It is when you place all the cases side by side that you notice how remarkably similar the script is in all the cases. The terror modules are busted in precisely the same manner ... the accused are apprehended by identical means ... even the procedural lapses in the course of the investigation and operation are similar!*[26]

24 Mir Ehsan and Bashaarat Masood, "2005 Delhi blast acquittals: The Lost Years", *The Indian Express,* 26 February 2017. Available at http://indianexpress.com/article/india/2005-delhi-blasts-case-hussain-fazili-rafiq-shah-the-lost-years-4543842/
25 Muzamil Jaleel, "'CBI said charges false, I thought there would be an outcry... But we won't even get a sorry", *The Indian Express,* 28 December 2016. Available at http://indianexpress.com/article/india/irshad-ali-inder-enclave-cbi-said-charges-false-4445036/
26 See report available here: http://www.jamiajournal.com/wp-content/uploads/2012/09/JTSA-Re-

The institutional injustices begin in most cases with the security establishment, political leaders, and a mostly obedient media declaring that a terror attack is the handiwork of specified Islamist groups, usually with cross-border linkages to Pakistan or Bangladesh. This is followed by the rounding up of Muslim men, some who have been police informers, others who are overtly religious, and others with petty criminal records. Most testimonies speak of their being picked up in civilian, usually unmarked, vehicles by men in civilian clothes and their transportation to civilian locations. These are not formal arrests, and, as Aamir put it, they are more in the nature of abductions or kidnappings by security personnel. These are followed by remarkably similar accounts of torture, including being stripped naked; electric shocks administered to genitals, ears, lips, nipples, temple, and joints until victims pass out; reviving them and starting again; beating them on the soles with rubber belts; pulling legs wide apart, climbing on shoulders and pounding; all of this interspersed with communal taunts.

The men are ultimately presented to a magistrate several days later, showing their arrest to have occurred just a day earlier. The magistrate does not pay attention to the signs of torture on their bodies, nor does he or she confirm that they were actually arrested a day earlier. The torture continues now in the police lock-up. If this does not break their spirit, then members of their families, especially women and old parents are called to police stations every day and made to wait late. In the end, the men agree to sign blank papers, which constitute their 'confessions.'

These 'confessions' become the fulcrum on which the police case against them is constructed. Normal law does not admit confessions made to policepersons as evidence, but these become admissible under various 'special laws' designed to address terror. As observed by Farasat et al,[27] the human rights of the accused are diluted or erased in the context of terror charges. The rights that anti-terror laws typically compromise are the protections against forced confessions, providing reasons for arrest, communicating the charges and the evidence against them, prompt presentation before a judicial authority, the right to bail and fair trial in a reasonable period of time, and the presumption of innocence until guilt is proved. The abridging of their rights under special laws designed to fight terror are done using ethically flawed utilitarian arguments. The argument is that because the public at large is threatened by terror violence, possible injustice to a few is justified because compromising the good of a few is required to ensure the good of the majority. The result of this kind of reasoning is that, in the words of the Innocence Network People's Tribunal, these 'laws have a decided lawless character, and have resulted in the false implication of scores of youth on charges of terrorism.'[28]

The cases against the men tend again to have many similarities, as noted by the JTSA report. The police discover their terror links because of 'secret information' that cannot be revealed. They are often shown to be arrested in public places, but independent public witnesses are rarely presented. Private vehicles are used in the operations so that their logs cannot be subsequently verified. Seizures are shown to be made from them, from their bodies, their computer hard discs, or their rooms of incriminating documents, usually alleged Islamist literature and films. But seizure memos are often not made on the spot but later in police stations, in the same ink and handwriting as the first information report (FIR).[29]

The investigation is typically and deliberately clumsy, leaving large holes. To take just one recent example, the *Indian Express* report on the order passed by Additional Sessions Judge Reetesh Singh of the Delhi Sessions Court points to several discrepancies in the probe carried out by the Special Cell in the Irshad Ali and Mourif Qamar case. The Special Cell had maintained that the two men were arrested with arms and ammunition on 29 February 2006 from Mukarba Chowk in Delhi, minutes after they got off a bus from Jammu. It observed that 'private vehicles were used in the raid' and 'No logbook of use of private vehicles has been maintained. None of them could recall the registration numbers of these private vehicles.' Also, "no crime team was called to the spot' and 'no efforts' were made by the Special Cell 'to lift any fingerprints from the ammunition' that police claims was seized from the accused. The Special Cell's 'site plan' of the place from where the duo was apprehended 'does not contain full material particulars.' 'No written order of any senior police official regarding assignment of investigation' was produced by the prosecution. Further, the *Indian Express* reported that the court said that 'no credible effort' was made by the police to find public witnesses, despite there being a bus depot and a police post nearby.[30]

28 "Report of the Jury of the 1st Peoples' Tribunal on Innocent Acquitted, Towards a Framework for Compensation and Rehabilitation for Victims of Wrongful Prosecution/Conviction," *Innocence Network India*.
29 Full report available here: http://www.jamiajournal.com/wp-content/uploads/2012/09/JTSA-Report-Framed-Damned-and-Acquitted-Dossiers-of-a-Very-Special-Cell.pdf
30 Kaunain Sheriff M, "2 acquitted after 11-year trial in terror case: No logs, no fingerprints, Delhi court

These mala fide arrests and investigations are followed by prolonged trials lasting for several years during which the accused are almost never granted bail or even parole. The first People's Tribunal headed by Justice Shah observes,

Almost all those who testified in the tribunal had suffered long periods of incarceration in the course of their trials. The nature of charges in terror cases, the public sentiment whipped up by the media, and the legal provisions in anti-terror laws, all work to ensure that (a) even if deserving, the accused's applications for discharge are not entertained; and (b) bail applications are rejected as a matter of routine. Many of the accused also suffer on account of poor legal representation. Some of those who presented their cases before the Tribunal had been convicted by lower courts.[31]

Delays are compounded manifold because the police typically foist a number of terror charges on each of the accused, so even though the accused may get discharged in one, other cases continue, thereby building a web from which the person believes there is no escape.

What is important to understand is that each of these cases represents a double whammy. One, innocent persons are charged and jailed for long traumatic years. Two, the victims of terror violence are deprived of justice because the shabby and mala fide investigations enable the real perpetrators of the terror acts to walk free.

※

There is something else that characterises every one of these cases. We have not come across a single case in which a police officer has been even charged with criminal proceedings, let alone punished, for creating false evidence against innocent men, resulting in long years of unjust incarceration and suffering and stigma to their families. Court judgments often make adverse observations against police officers, but their strictures and censures do not come in the way of medals, awards, and promotions. For instance, in the Dhaula Kuan fake encounter case, the court held that 'there cannot be any more serious or grave crime than a police officer framing an innocent citizen in a false criminal case. Such a tendency ... needs to be curbed with a firm hand.'[32] But these remain empty words.

---

points to lapses in police probe", *The Indian Express*, 22 January 2017. http://indianexpress.com/article/india/irshad-ali-maurif-qamar-acquitted-after-11-year-trial-in-terror-case-no-logs-no-finger-prints-delhi-court-points-to-lapses-in-police-probe-4485672/

31 See "Report of the Jury of the 1st Peoples' Tribunal on Innocent Acquitted, Towards a Framework for Compensation and Rehabilitation for Victims of Wrongful Prosecution/Conviction," *Innocence Network India*, p 5.

32 Full report available here: http://www.jamiajournal.com/wp-content/uploads/2012/09/JTSA-Report-Framed-Damned-and-Acquitted-Dossiers-of-a-Very-Special-Cell.pdf, page 6.

Police officers culpable of framing innocent persons are spurred most often by communal bias against persons of particular identities. And if one is looking for the reason why such crimes can be committed with impunity, then one is forced to acknowledge that they are not exceptions or aberrations by a few 'bad eggs,' but a systemic pattern. The People's Tribunal observes,

The rampant discourse on 'war on terror' legitimates the arrests of Muslim youth and grants impunity to investigators. In every single testimony, we heard sordid tales of torture, narco analysis, and manipulated evidence. The Jury recognises that this is not a case of 'some bad officers' but points to a widespread institutional crisis, where violence against suspects has become entrenched, where false arrests are condoned, where investigators guilty of framing innocents are not punished–but rather decorated and feted.[33]

Indian law makes no provision for paying monetary compensation to persons who are wrongfully charged, imprisoned, and prosecuted in this way. This despite that it is bound by the obligations of the International Convention on Civil and Political Rights. But while signing this, India stated that its legal system does not recognise the right to compensation for victims of unlawful arrest and detention. Yet, the Supreme Court on more than one occasion has endorsed the right of such persons or their families to such remedies, relying for this on expanding the fundamental right to life under Article 21 of the Constitution.

It ordered the state of Bihar to pay Rudul Sah,[34] who had been illegally detained for 14 years after his acquittal, a compensation of ₹35,000. The Supreme Court in the Nilabati Behera case[35] maintained that the award of compensation by high courts and the Supreme Court is 'a remedy available in public law; based on strict liability for the contravention of fundamental rights to which the principle of sovereign immunity does not apply.' In accordance with these principles, in December 2015, the National Human Rights Commission issued a show cause notice to the Delhi government asking why monetary relief of ₹5 lakh should not be paid to Aamir. It described him as a 'victim' whose youth was destroyed due to 'wrongful confinement for 14 years as a terrorist'; he 'lost his parents, his career, his hopes, dreams and

33 See "Report of the Jury of the 1st Peoples' Tribunal on Innocent Acquitted, Towards a Framework for Compensation and Rehabilitation for Victims of Wrongful Prosecution/Conviction," *Innocence Network India*, p. 6.
34 *Rudul Sah v State of Bihar*, 1983, 4 SCC 141.
35 *Nilabati Behera v State of Orissa*, 1993, AIR 1960.

everything.' In January 2017, it directed the Delhi government to pay him the compensation in six weeks.[36]

But I wonder if anything, anything at all can indeed compensate Aamir for all that he has lost. He said that the money does not mean much to him, beyond an acknowledgment that he suffered injustice at the hands of the state. He said that what he would most appreciate a government job, one that allows him to help other people. This, he said, would heal his wounds and wipe out the stigma of being a terrorist.[37]

I believe that monetary compensation is just one of many things the state must do to offer any meaningful recompense to those whose lives it destroyed due to profiling and prejudice, and by criminally creating false evidence. The first of these is a public acknowledgement that a wrong has been done, accompanied by a public apology. Denial or grudging acknowledgement and lack of remorse of the kind reflected in Minister of State for Home Kiren Rijiju's statement in 2014 in Parliament is just not enough. He said that although acquittals by court are the outcome of free and fair trials, acquittal cannot be taken to prove that innocent civilians were being wrongly framed in every case. 'The acquittal by the courts may also be because of lack of sufficient evidence which could establish/prove charges beyond all reasonable doubt,' he said neglecting to mention that in the majority of these cases, the courts have found the evidence to have been maliciously created by the police.[38]

Beyond this, reparation cannot be restricted to a single monetary transfer. The state owes assistance to the innocent person whose life was destroyed through mala fide state action. It should resolve to assist the person and his family to be restored as far as is possible to a situation better than what they would have enjoyed if the person had not been so targeted. A compassionate state would bring in counsellors and develop a plan with the released person, involving elements of psychosocial healing, education, and livelihood support. And the final element of atonement by the state should involve justice, ensuring that a fair enquiry is conducted into whether the person was deliberately framed, and if this is found to be the case, then criminal proceedings be launched against the officials responsible.

36 "NHRC Issues Fresh Directive to Delhi Government for Paying ₹5 Lakh to Terror- Exoneree Aamir Khan," *Siasat Daily*, 12 January 2017. Available at http://www.siasat.com/news/nhrc-issues-fresh-directive-delhi-govt-paying-rs-5-lakh-terror-exoneree-aamir-khan-1107196/
37 "Many Terror Accused Acquitted due to Lack of Evidence," *Business Standard*, 16 July 2014. Available at http://www.business-standard.com/article/pti-stories/many-terror-accused-acquitted-due-to-lack-of-evidence-114071600682_1.html
38 Ibid.

In both popular social common sense and the ways law is designed, interpreted, and enforced in India, there is an implied steep hierarchy of crimes. The gravest crimes are seen to be those connected with terror violence, meriting harsh laws, criminal procedures that severely curtail the human rights of the accused, and stricter penalties, including death. Even interrogating the justice of court decisions in such crimes is today deemed criminally anti-national. Crimes of communal violence, on the face of it, are closely akin to terror crimes because these are also driven by hate ideologies and target innocent populations with death and destruction. However, it is noteworthy that these do not carry nearly the same censure and disgrace as terror crimes, both in popular morality and the law.

Yakub Memon, convicted for complicity in the 1993 Bombay terror blasts, spent 21 years in prison *without a single day's parole* before his hanging. By contrast, Maya Kodnani, convicted and awarded life imprisonment for being what the trial court described as the 'kingpin' in the 2002 massacre in Naroda Patiya of 97 people, including 35 women and 36 children, was granted three months bail in November 2013 for medical treatment. The Gujarat High Court confirmed her bail for ill health from July 2014, which continues until the time of writing.

This hierarchy of crimes was implicit even in the turmoil in Indian universities in 2016. Granting interim bail to Jawaharlal Nehru University (JNU) student leader Kanhaiya Kumar, Justice Pratibha Rani deemed 'anti-national' students who 'raised slogans on the death anniversary of Afzal Guru, who was convicted for attack on our Parliament.'[39] Remarkably, not just Kanhaiya Kumar, Umar Khalid, and Anirban Bhattacharya but also Rohith Vemula was judged by union ministers, police, university administrations, and sections of both the judiciary and media as anti-national for questioning the justice of the capital penalty awarded to Yakub Memon and Afzal Guru, convicted of terror crimes. Even more remarkably, Rohith's other alleged unpatriotic act was to demand justice for those reeling under the communal violence in Muzaffarnagar. In the first case, demanding justice for the perpetrators of mass crimes (of terror) was seen as anti-national. In the second case, seeking justice against the perpetrators of mass crimes (of communal violence) was seen as acts against the nation.

39 Aneesha Mathur, "JNU row: Kanhaiya Kumar gets bail and a lesson on thoughts that 'infect... (like) gangrene'", *The Indian Express*, 3 March 2016. Available at http://indianexpress.com/article/india/india-news-india/kanhaiya-kumar-bail-jnu-delhi-high-court/

This implied hierarchy of crimes was even accepted by the Law Commission, chaired by the otherwise impeccably progressive Justice AP Shah, that which recommended abolition of capital punishment in all crimes, except terror-related ones and waging war against the state.[40] This same idea–that crimes of terror fall into a different category from other crimes, including mass crimes that target people for their religious identity and caste–is the rationale for special terror laws in India (as in many parts of the world). These laws, as we have observed, dilute accepted standards of human rights protection of accused persons. The human consequences of these special laws are incalculable.

We must reject the argument that these human costs are regrettable but inevitable when the country battles ever-looming perils of terror attacks, and that the cost of possible injustice to a small number are morally acceptable to protect the majority. This is an ethically problematic position because justice is indivisible, and injustice to some cannot result in authentic justice for the many. However, even in a practical sense, officially sanctioned and effected injustice can only breed fear and discontent that ultimately further imperils the social order.

What I find striking is how these same arguments are not applied to communal hate crimes. I have studied with colleagues in the Centre for Equity Studies many major communal massacres from independence on, and what binds all of them without exception is that few, if any, are punished for these mass crimes.[41] This results from communal bias or apathy in all arms of the criminal justice system, the police, prosecution, and courts; and the political, social, and economic powerlessness of the victims of communal crimes. Except among survivors of these mass crimes – many of who fight lifelong epic, brave, and ultimately hopeless battles for justice like the widows of the 1984 Sikh massacre or the survivors of the 2002 Gujarat massacre – there is little popular outrage that these crimes go unpunished. Unlike for terror crimes, there is no popular demand for special laws and procedures to ensure different standards of evidence, bail, and punishment for those who commit mass hate crimes against persons of particular targeted religions and castes. We wish to see those responsible for the 1993 Bombay blasts hang; but we

40 "Law Commission recommends abolition of death penalty, except in terror cases", *The Hindu*, 31 August 2015. Available at http://www.thehindu.com/news/national/law-commission-recommends-abolition-of-death-penalty-except-in-terror-cases/article10344061.ece

41 See Prita Jha and Warisha Farasat (eds.), *Splintered Justice* (2016), Gurgaon: Three Essays Collective and Surabhi Chopra and Prita Jha (eds.), "On Their Watch: Mass Violence and State Apathy in India" (2014), Gurgaon: Three Essays Collective.

are indifferent when those named by the judicial commission as guilty for the Bombay communal killings in 1992–93 continue to walk free.

I am emphatically not making the case here for death penalty for perpetrators of communal violence, nor for the dilution of their basic human rights. What I am arguing is that both popular stigma and the imperative of law should apply equally to those who are alleged to participate in terror crimes as those who are charged with hate crimes targeting persons for their religious or caste identity. The stark selectivity in popular outrage and the application of the majesty of the legal system reveal a very troubling majoritarian bias in society and law. The majority of those charged with communal crimes are from the majority Hindu community, whereas most of the victims are from religious minorities. Here popular opinion and the criminal justice system seems to work to protect the rights of the accused much more than those of the victim, therefore impunity is the norm. By contrast, in the popular as well as institutional imagination, in terror crimes the victims are assumed to be mainly Hindu and the accused Muslim, then everything turns on its head. The effort now is to protect the victim, even if the cost is the denial of rights and even years of unjust incarceration without even parole or bail for the accused. And if on occasion, the accused turns out to be Hindu and not Muslim, then the system again somersaults to protect the accused.

If law and social outrage apply so differently when the minority is charged with committing hate crimes and from when they are the paramount victims of mass hate crimes, then the promises of our secular constitution – of equal treatment of all before the law – stand irreparably damaged.

CHAPTER SEVEN

'Loving' By Hating

A question bitterly contested in the India of today – what does it take to love your country? How do you nurture this love? And is love for your country obligatory, is it a kind of national, even constitutional duty? How do you demonstrate it? Must you demonstrate it? Who will decide if you make the grade of 'nationalism'? And what should be your fate if you do not qualify?

This question is posed pointedly, accusingly, to the country's religious minorities and liberal dissenters. Earlier pages of this book have pointed to the many answers to these questions that are influentially and forcefully propagated by the currently triumphalist Hindutva nationalists. For them, nationalism first requires acceptance of India's Hindu identity. And since Hinduism is an intensely heterodox and pluralist faith system, this entails that a true nationalist accepts the version of Hinduism – belligerent, militant and intolerant – that the RSS and its associate organisations subscribe to. This requires, for instance, the violent defence of the cow; restraint on assertive and independent women who cut their hair, wear western clothes, drink liquor and mix freely with partners they choose with and without marriage; acceptance of caste as the principal organising principal of social relations; prohibitions on same-sex love; and reverence to the primal deity of Ram. And that too a warrior Ram (as portrayed in most posters of Sangh organisations with bow and arrow), not the gentle Ram who ate the berries offered by an old tribal woman Shabri after she bit into each of them first to confirm that they were sweet. I recount a friend asking, 'Which Ram do we speak of? The Ram whose name was on Mahatma Gandhi's lips when Nathuram Godse took his life, or the Ram in whose name Nathuram Godse killed him?'

Hindutva nationalism mandates that every Indian must accept and willingly submit to the cultural, social and indeed political dominance of the Hindu faith *as interpreted by the Sangh*. It matters little if the Sangh's idea of Hinduism is pugnacious, exclusionary, patriarchal, upper- caste, north-Indian and anti-reason. If the Sangh declares that it is their belief that Ram was born precisely at the spot that lies under the central dome of the Babri Masjid in Ayodhya, then without protest Muslims must consent to the 'removal' of their mosque to give way to a Ram temple. If they pronounce that Hinduism bars the eating of cow-meat, ignoring the reality of history and geography – that Brahmins ate beef in the past,[1] and that today Dalits, Adivasis, India's north-eastern communities, as well as Hindus in several regions eat beef[2] – then all Indians of every faith and cultural system must willingly abjure eating beef. Hindutva nationalism entails no reciprocal respect or tolerance for the myriad other religious belief systems and cultural arrangements that proliferate in this most diverse of all countries.

Sagarika Ghosh makes a ringing call to the liberal Hindu to resist.[3] 'Liberal Hindus', she says, 'you don't recognise this new angry, religion. Why should you?...You've sung qawaalis, bhajans and Christmas carols, enjoyed your kababs without guilt. You've never been ruled by a religious police or been asked to prove your Hinduness through political loyalty. But suddenly you're being ironed into a vegetarian, Muslim-hating, puritanical uniformity. You're being asked to hate when your religion teaches love. You're being asked not to question when your traditions are full of vaad, vivaad, samvaad (debate). You're being asked to be perpetually angry when your gods have always been playful and genial.' 'The attempt to create a homogeneous religious loyalty to only one set of deities', she goes on, 'the insistence on a single form of worship, a single set of dietary preferences, a single racial type, a single language, a single temple is a repudiation of the faith of your ancestors who lived in ease with dizzying diversities. Liberal Hindus, it's time for you to show there's more to Hinduism than lynchings and police complaints and abusive language on social media. Haven't generations of Hindus heard the muezzin's call without feeling remotely threatened?'

The late Prabhash Joshi, a doyen of Hindi journalism and a proudly practising Hindu, told me that he felt compelled to fight Hindutva in order to save Hinduism. His close associate Apoorvanand writes in similar tenor,

---

1 A key text on this is Dwijendra Narayan Jha's *Holy Cow: Beef in Indian Dietary Traditions* (2001). Pondicherry: Navayana Books. Another important essay on the subject is by BR Ambedkar, excerpted in "Read what Ambedkar wrote on why Brahmins started worshipping the cow and gave up beef", in *Scroll*, 2 August 2016. Available at https://scroll.in/article/812645/read-what-ambedkar-wrote-on-why-brahmins-started-worshipping-the-cow-and-gave-up-eating-beef

2 See Anirvan Ghosh, "How Different States in India Treat Beef Eating", *Huffington Post*, 3 March 2016. Available at https://www.huffingtonpost.in/2015/03/03/beef-ban-maharashtra_n_6790006.html

3 Sagarika Ghosh, "Manifesto for a liberal Hindu", *The Times of India,* 26 April 2017. Available at http://blogs.timesofindia.indiatimes.com/bloody-mary/manifesto-for-a-liberal-hindu-its-time-for-secular-hindus-to-say-garv-se-kaho-hum-liberal-hain/

'Hindus need to worry. Not about Muslims being beaten up or killed on the pretext of cow smuggling or slaughter, or Christians being attacked on the pretext of conversion. Hindus need to stir out of slumber because Hinduism is in peril... there is a clear threat now of Hinduism being taken over by an organisation called the Rashtriya Swayamsevak Sangh. Hinduism, a religion that is a way of life, as its adherents like it to be known, is now in the hands of organisations and people who want to transform it into an ideology of dominance over populations, which are seen, feared and abhorred as 'others'... We used to take pride in the chaotic diversity that made Hinduism a riddle for many. It was not a monolith, it did not need a central book, was not chaired by only one God-figure... Now, all of them (Krihsna, Shiva, Ram) have started resembling each other. All of them now look as if they have been afflicted with a new-found nationalist aggression. (This) spell(s) the end of Hinduism as we have known it for millennia... deployed in an anti-Muslim and anti-outsider campaign.'[4]

And all of this is being done in the name of love – love for the cow, love for Ram, love for the Hindu faith, love for the nation. 'Let us record', Apoorvanand urges, 'that the educated and the media reported and exalted the pious and hard lives of the hate-mongers and murderers, that they weaved stories of their love for the animals with a singular aim to humanise and legitimise their hatred of Muslims. Why do Muslims fail to find place in such kind hearts? The fault must lie in them.'[5]

꙰

This brand of nationalism brooks no dissent with the leader if he (and it must be *he*) is chosen from their ranks. There is a seamless convergence between the supreme leader, the government he leads, the party to which he belongs, and the (version of the) Hindu faith to which he owes allegiance. Any deviance from these 'Hindu' beliefs, as much as dissent from the government's ideology and policies are acts against the nation.

Many new battle-lines have been drawn in Modi's India even as old battle-lines have become more entrenched. And one of the most bitter sites of contestation of different ideas of India are the university. Not all universities – only those that from which dissenting voices arise.

---

4 Apoorvanand, "Hinduism at risk from RSS", *The Tribune,* 10 April 2017. Available at http://www.tribuneindia.com/news/comment/hinduism-at-risk-from-rss/389461.html
5 Apoorvanand, "The anti-Muslim pitch", *The Tribune,* 27 March 2017. Available at http://www.tribuneindia.com/news/comment/the-anti-muslim-pitch/382700.html

The charging of progressive university students in the country's premier Jawaharlal Nehru University with sedition further refurbishes Modi's ideological world-view in which all left and liberal dissent against the economic and social policies of the government are unpatriotic, because the Hindu nationalist ruling party, the government, its leader and the nation all converge into one seamless whole. When an idealistic young doctoral student – who described himself as a Marxist Ambedkarite – Rohith Vemula in the Central University in Hyderabad tried to organise film-screening protesting communal violence, and debate the justice of the death penalty to Yakub Memon convicted for the 1993 Bombay blasts, he was tainted as anti-national by two Ministers of Modi's cabinet.[6] This led to his suspension from the university and ultimately his tragic suicide. When leftist students in JNU again organised a meeting to interrogate the justice of the death penalty to Afzal Guru, hung for alleged complicity in the attack on India's Parliament, they were charged with the grave crime of sedition, for which they could be jailed for life.

Elected BJP leaders dubbed all those who protested this action, including senior leaders of the Left parties and the Congress, as anti-national. Idealistic activists fighting human rights abuses in Chhatisgarh were hounded as Maoists.[7] Through all the nation-wide debates, when voices were raised against police action targeting dissenting university students, here once again Modi maintained his trademark selective silence.[8] In his public addresses, however, he regularly decried the political opposition, anti-national students, and also NGOs supported by foreign funds (he taunted these as five-star NGOs).[9] He suggests that they were unreconciled to his assumption of the country's high office because of his humble birth and this is why they tirelessly attack him. Once again opposition to his leadership and the ideology of his government are conflated with petty elitism on the one hand, and betrayal of the nation on the other.

6 See Peter Ronald deSouza, 'Rohith and the real anti-nationals', 2 February 2017. Available at http://www.thehindu.com/opinion/lead/on-rohith-vemulas-suicide-and-the-govts-response/article8179928.ece

7 Ushinor Majumdar, "Hounded in Bastarville", *Outlook,* 9 January 2017. Available at https://www.outlookindia.com/magazine/story/hounded-in-bastarville/298311

8 'Rohit Vemula suicide: Silent PM, botch colleague, insincere handling vitiate BJP stand', *ABP Live,* 22 January 2016. Available at http://www.abplive.in/india-news/rohith-vemula-suicide-silent-prime-minister-glib-colleagues-botch-reaction-278726

9 Dhananjay Mahapatral, "Don't fear 5-star activists, be fearless in giving judgments, PM tells judges", *The Times of India,* 6 April 2015. Available at https://timesofindia.indiatimes.com/india/Dont-fear-5-star-activists-be-fearless-in-giving-judgments-PM-tells-judges/articleshow/46817635.cms

I wrote to the union Home Minister Rajnath Singh and the Commissioner of Police, Delhi BS Bassi, an open letter in which I said that if Kanhaiya Kumar is charged with sedition, it was my demand that I am tried and jailed for the same crime.[10] I wrote:

Mahatma Gandhi taught us how to respond when confronted with an unjust law. You must publicly disobey the unjust law, and demand that the state either withdraws the unjust law or punishes you under this law. The state in these circumstances does not have the option of persisting with the upholding the law, and refusing to apply it against persons who publicly disobey the law because they regard it to be unjust.

I am deeply convinced that the law related to sedition under Section 124A of the Indian Penal Code is a profoundly unjust law, the incongruous continuance of a colonial law that had been created precisely to criminalise freedom fighters who are publicly opposed to the colonial regime. I am even more outraged by the gross misuse of this law in our democratic republic against student leader Kanhaiya Kumar. Kumar's public positions passionately and vigorously supporting the values of the Constitution, social and economic equality, democracy and secularism, qualify him in my eyes to be a young Indian who is a role model for all of us, of all ages. The application of the law to him seems to have been done with the mala-fide purpose of curbing his democratic right to dissent with the policies and programmes of the central government...

By all credible accounts, the meeting of February 9, 2016 in Jawaharlal Nehru University, Delhi, was organised to protest against the principle of the death penalty awarded to Afzal Guru, and not to uphold separatist politics (even though anti-national slogans were allegedly raised by some persons during this meeting). I recall my own writings at the time Afzal Guru was marched to the gallows. I wrote then in the Hindu: 'The hanging of Afzal Guru on 9 February, 2013 raises a thicket of debates – ethical, legal and political – about justice, law, democracy, capital punishment, and a strong state. What is the quality of true justice? It is it enough for it to be lawful, fair and

---

10 See Harsh Mander, "If Kanhaiya Kumar is to be Prosecuted, then Charge Me With Sedition Too", *The Wire*, 17 February 2016. Available at https://thewire.in/21822/if-kanhaiya-kumar-is-to-be-prosecuted-then-charge-me-with-sedition-too/

dispassionate, or must it also be tempered with mercy?' I went on to say that the High Court's reference in its 2003 judgment to 'the collective conscience of the society' being satisfied by awarding the death penalty to Guru caused me great unease, because the only legitimate reason for a court to award any punishment should be the fair application of the law to the evidence placed before it, not the appeasement of alleged majoritarian public opinion. I also expressed my anguish at the distressing failure of official compassion and public decency in denying Afzal Guru's wife and teenaged son the chance to meet him for the last time before his execution. This was done by the UPA government and I wrote my criticisms about the actions of the government of that time. My point was then, as it is today, that no government has the right to destroy constitutional norms of public decency and morality. The haste and secrecy of the execution also unconscionably denied him his last available legal resource, affirmed by the Supreme Court in the Kartar Singh case, to seek judicial review of the rejection of his mercy petition. I had concluded my article with these words: 'Many believe that the belated execution signalled a strong and decisive state, especially to the "neighbouring country". One glance at the daily reality of this neighbouring country will reflect the brutalising wages of years of "decisive" politics of militarism and public vengeance. It is not a weak, but a stable, mature and confident democracy which can display compassion even to those we may believe have most wronged the country.'

Unsurprisingly, I was attacked savagely on social media by trolls of a particular political persuasion, casting me to be 'anti-national' for months and longer. But I was not booked by the police for sedition. It worries me deeply that today this same debate – that raises most fundamental questions of public ethics and law – initiated by students in a university, instead of being welcomed, is treated as criminal sedition, for which the principal organiser is at the time of writing under police remand...

The legal position has been clarified by many legal experts, that even if the said slogans against the Indian nation were raised during the meeting in the university on February 9, 2016, it still does not constitute the crime of sedition. A Constitution bench of the Supreme Court has clarified that allegedly seditious speech and expression may be punished only if the speech is an 'incitement' to 'violence', or 'public disorder'. It has also drawn a clear distinction between 'advocacy' and 'incitement', stating that only the latter could be punished. The said slogans cannot be said to amount to inciting violence.

However it is important to add that even if there were some Kashmiri students who did raise slogans expressing disagreement with the policies of the Government and in support of independence for Kashmir, the fitting response to this would only have been open public debate in which students and teachers heard their views and challenged these, not to charge these students with the grave colonial crime of sedition that could result in their imprisonment for life. Universities are places where young people must feel free to challenge the received wisdom of the times they we live in. Their minds and hearts must be freed of the fetters of fear and the obligation to conform to powerful or dominant opinion. It is in universities that students the world over have fought colonialism, unjust wars, tyranny, hate and unequal social orders. Governments and indeed majority opinion may be pitted powerfully against their views, but a democracy requires the stout defence of their right to profess and debate these ideas, even by those who are opposed to these ideas. Universities in a democracy cannot be allowed to become places where the university leadership allows the police to walk in and arrest students at will, and where dissent by students or indeed teachers is demonised and criminalised.

From the lessons of civil disobedience that I have learnt from Mahatma Gandhi, I feel compelled to demand that because despite all the evidence and legal opinion to the contrary Kumar is being charged with the grave crime of sedition for the opinions he has publicly espoused, then since I have publicly espoused similar opinions, I must be charged with the same offence. The Government of India and the Delhi police that reports to it, have only two legal options. It either absolves Kanhaiya Kumar of all charges of sedition. Or, if it persists in its belief that he committed the crime of sedition, then it must charge me also with criminal sedition, and arrest me, and subject me to the same investigation to which Kanhaiya Kumar is being subjected. This is because I have, in writing, taken similar positions on the issues for which his conduct is criminalised.

I received no reply from either the Home Minister or the Delhi Police Commissioner. After countrywide protests, the three students were meanwhile finally released on bail, but not before a mob of lawyers beat up student union president Kanhaiya on the court campus. In sharp contrast to the criminal action against the students which could, if proved, result in their imprisonment for life, there was belated, reluctant and perfunctory criminal action initiated against the violent lawyers, and none so far against those responsible for doctoring the videos to inflame and polarise public opinion.

The students returned to their campus, their spirits defiant and upbeat. Thousands of students gathered to hear their fiery speeches in defence of their freedom to protest and dissent, their fervent opposition to the communal politics of the RSS, Prime Minister Modi and his government, and the advancement of social and economic equality. Their speeches were first circulated widely on social media and then on live television, and captured the imagination and hearts of people across the country.

Eighty six years earlier, on 23 March 1931, Bhagat Singh had walked bravely, proudly to the gallows, his two young colleagues Rajguru and Sukhdev by his side. His lustre continues undimmed as an icon for succeeding generations, so that it is easy to forget he was only 23 years old when he was hung from the gallows. Subhash Bose spoke then of Bhagat Singh as a 'symbol of the new awakening among youth.' Nehru saw in him 'a spark that became a flame in a short time and spread from one end of the country to another dispelling the prevailing darkness everywhere.' His popularity rivalled that of Mahatma Gandhi.

In the decades after his passing, in times of public ferment, despair, confusion and anger, successive generations in India have found their own inheritors of young Bhagat Singh's mantle, men and women embodying defiant youthful idealism and dissent, young people battling for social and economic equality, for true freedom, sparks that once again set aflame a beleaguered wearied country battling the darkness of the times.

I believe that our generation in India today – in young people like Rohith Vemula, Kanhaiya Kumar, Umar Khalid, Anirban Bhattacharya, Shehla Rashid and Chintu Kumari – has found its own youthful heroes, with courage to speak truth to power, to sacrifice, to fight and dream of equality, freedom and solidarity. All in their twenties or early thirties, in many ways they are this generation's heirs and progenies of Bhagat Singh –uncompromising, unflinching in their audacious love for the country and its oppressed people that Bhagat Singh lit in his tragically brief life. These youthful warriors fight today another kind of freedom struggle from that of Bhagat Singh and his comrades, but it is a struggle for freedom nonetheless.

Bhagat Singh underlined the centrality of dissent if the world has to change. 'Every man', he declared, and indeed this must include every woman, 'who stands for progress has to criticise, disbelieve and challenge every item of the old faith.' Note the words 'has to...' For him, dissent was not just a right but a duty, an obligation, for all who seek a more just world. It is this duty to dissent that has thrown all these young people today into trouble with their governments. For Bhagat Singh and his comrades, dissent ultimately led to the scaffolds. For today's young freedom fighters, their rebellion had different consequences. It resulted in the suspension from his university of one young man for 'anti-national activities', an expulsion that pushed him down a slippery slope into an abyss of so much despair that he took his life. For the others, criminal charges of sedition, or acts against the nation, were slapped, subjecting them to long hours of police interrogation, and for three of them jail.

Bhagat Singh was deeply anguished by the communal violence that erupted in the mid-1920s, when he was still a teenager, and often warned that communalism was as big a threat as colonialism. Each of the young people charged with 'anti-national' acts today also see communal ideologies of the RSS as the biggest threat of the times. Both Umar and Anirban wonder poignantly if they would have received the same nation-wide solidarity if they were charged with sedition as practising, skull-capped Muslims from Azamgarh, and call for collective resistance to communal profiling by the state as much as communal hate-mongering by the Sangh.

What also bind together these youthful freedom fighters across the generations is a craving for equality, and a passionate solidarity with the oppressed and suffering of their world. Bhagat Singh declares: 'I am a man and all that affects mankind affects me.' Generations later, Rohith Vemula says that every human being is 'a glorious thing made up of star dust. In every field, in studies, in streets, in politics, and in dying and living.' But he mourns that the 'value of a man was reduced to his immediate identity and nearest possibility. To a vote. To a number. To a thing.'

But none of these young people, then and now, allow themselves to be reduced to their immediate identity. Theirs is a much larger solidarity with all oppressed people. Bhagat Singh was only 20 years old when he issued a searing statement in 1928 about 'labourers and producers' who 'are victims of exploitation and have been denied basic human rights...Farmers, who produce, die of hunger. The weaver who weaves clothes for others cannot do so for his own family and children...Masons, carpenters, ironsmiths who build huge palaces die living in huts and slums.' Nearly nine decades later, Anirban Bhattacharya, when released from prison on bail, raged in similar vein: 'What is the boiling point for your blood?' When Muslims, Dalits, Adivasis are killed, does your blood not boil? When more than 70 per cent people are forced to live on 20 rupees a day, when security forces rape women in Kunan Poshpora in Kashmir, when women in Manipur strip themselves naked protesting rapes by the army, when rationalists like Pansare and Dabholkar are killed, when women are told to stay at home by the RSS, does your blood not boil?' In the same vein, he spoke of half the countryside reeling under drought, school meals being closed in drought-hit Bundelkhand, farmers pushed to suicide, a Muslim constable stripped naked, Christian nuns raped, Rohith Vemula driven to suicide, a couple killed in broad daylight because they had married out of their caste. Is this nationalism, he asked. If so, he was proud to be 'anti-national'.[11]

Umar's teacher Sangeeta Dasgupta writes affectionately of his passionate engagement with Adivasi history and politics. She recalls that he tried to understand conflicts and struggles of the Adivasis in the past, in order to help him understand the injustice of Adivasi societies today. The country's political and security establishment, as well as mainstream media saw him only as a Muslim, and could not comprehend his wider solidarities. That he was an atheist and communist committed to Adivasi justice was irrelevant to them. He was reduced, as Rohith put it, to his 'immediate identity', to the 'accident of his birth'. When he was accused of being a Jaish-e-Mohammed terrorist, his family and friends joked sadly that he would first have to be a follower of Mohammed before he could be a follower of Jaish-e-Mohammed! He was treated throughout his incarceration in ways different from those of his two fellow student dissenters, Anirban and Kanhaiya, only because if his religious identity.[12]

All these young people, then and now, were deemed by governments as persons pitted against the nation – traitors and seditionists. But Bhagat Singh spoke luminously of his love for his country. 'May the sun in his course', he wrote, 'visit no land more free, more happy, more lovely than our own country.' I think today of Kanhaiya Kumar's resounding call for freedom in India, not from India, freedom from hunger, poverty, exploitation and fear.

✷

11 See "'What is the boiling point of your blood?' Watch Anirban Bhattacharya's speech after his release on bail", *Scroll*, 19 March 2016. Available at https://video.scroll.in/805365/what-is-the-boiling-point-of-your-blood-watch-anirban-bhattacharyas-speech-after-his-release-on-bail

12 Sangeeta Dasgupta, "Umar Khalid, My Student", *The Indian Express*, 22 February 2017. Available at http://indianexpress.com/article/opinion/columns/jnu-protest-sedition-umar-khalid-anirban-my-student/

The trademark of hyper-nationalism of the Hindu Right also importantly mandates absolute reverence for the soldier. The Ministry of Human Resource Development has launched a Vidya, Veerta Abhiyan (Education, Valour Campaign) to encourage universities to install a 'Wall of Heroes' with portraits of soldiers who were awarded India's highest gallantry awards, the Param Veer Chakra. This was originally the brainchild of the JNU Vice Chancellor M Jagadesh Kumar, who felt that portraits not just of these men who demonstrated extraordinary courage to defend their motherland, but also of tanks used in war, would instil 'nationalism' and 'patriotism' among students (who presumably display too little of these sterling qualities with their protests and rebellions). The Ministry had earlier prescribed with the same objectives that every university must install the national flag in a prominent location at the height of 207 feet (why precisely this height remains a mystery), and illuminated at night, so that it remains always in the students' line of vision as they traverse their classrooms, hostels, library and canteens.

Respect for the soldier is demanded every time citizens protest any other policy that causes civic distress. In queues that formed outside ATMs across the country after the government's shock-and-awe note ban in November 2016, if anyone grumbled, chances are that someone would be there in the line to remind them sternly of the sacrifices made by India's soldiers guarding India's border in the snow-bound glaciers of Siachen. 'If they are sacrificing so much for the nation, can you not even stand cheerfully in a queue for the good of your country?' If you went on to argue that the note-ban ultimately yielded on none of its promises, but instead caused unprecedented suffering to people in informal employment and outside the formal banking system, this too was dismissed as unpatriotic because it questioned the wisdom of the supreme leader. The narrative of the soldier cheerfully guarding our frontiers cracked briefly when one soldier uploaded a post about how bad was the food the soldiers got, alleging corruption and callousness of his superiors (he was later dismissed from service); and other copy-cat videos followed. One cartoonist portrayed a young soldier being scolded by his superior, 'Look at you grumbling about food, when civilians are standing in lines outside banks across India for the good of the country'!

The soldier is supposed to define the essence of patriotism. I have no doubt that many soldiers love their country. My father joined the army when he was 18, and loved his years of service in it until he was handpicked to join the Indian Frontier Administrative Service in the difficult terrains of NEFA (now Arunachal), under the direct tutelage of Nehru and Verrier Elwin. He

loved his country when he served it as an army man – he recalls picking up
bodies from the streets of Calcutta during the bloody riots around Partition,
and service in a turbulent Nepal – and he loved it when he served in NEFA
in mountainous regions where he had to trek for four days to reach his head-
quarters, and among the tribal people of the Andaman and Nicobar Islands.
My father-in-law was a doctor in the armed forces. He wore the uniform of all
three forces, and was loved by the soldiers he led.

I have met many soldiers who looked upon their work as a calling. But
there are several others for who this is a job. When more than 3000 youth
turned up at a Kashmir army recruitment centre, it cannot be assumed that
they were all burning with love for the Indian nation. And there is nothing
dishonourable about looking to the armed forces as an avenue for honest,
reasonably remunerated and secure employment. If you are not a pacifist,
then why not? There was no reason to troll Nivedita Menon when she made
this point.

There are indeed many decent men and women in the armed forces.
But as in any walk of life, there are disreputable people also in their ranks,
people who dabble in corruption, grand and petty, and people who commit
sexual and other crimes. There are many soldiers who have firmly hold India's
constitutional secularism as their creed, and accord equal respect to every
faith; this is why we rely on the army as the last resort to act fairly and deci-
sively in dousing large communal conflagrations. But I have met too many
senior defence personnel who are fervently and unapologetically communal
and anti-Muslim, and who dismiss human rights.

The point is that there are many honourable soldiers, attempting to do
a difficult job honestly, often in testing terrains, far away from their families,
sometimes risking their lives. I may, and do, disagree with a muscular military approach in many cases, including of internal conflict, in Maoist regions,
Kashmir and India's north-east; I also favour friendship and peace with our
neighbours and much lower investments in defence. These can be debated.
But I do not hold the soldier responsible for these policies, which emerge (as
they should) from the country's civilian political leadership. And so I grieve
when soldiers are killed, in bloody Maoist attacks in Chhatisgarh as much as
in militant raids in Kashmir, or on the border (any border), as much as I do
when civilians are killed.

My problem is when we are told that we must revere the soldier above
all – that they epitomise patriotism in the way that no other profession does
– because they defend India's freedom. Perhaps some of them do. But it is

important to recognise that there women and men in many other vocations who also defend India's freedom – and its constitutional values of justice, equality and fraternity – again often at great personal cost and sacrifice, sometimes also risking or losing their lives. It is only a militarist and illiberal kind of nationalism that celebrates the army alone as the pinnacle of public service and patriotism, and excludes those who fight injustice, suffering, want and hate, sometimes only with the weapons of compassion and courage, and mostly unknown and unsung. The numbers of people I know who have fought hate and caste violence, hunger, illiteracy, disease, the exploitation of workers, human rights abuses, violence against women and children, the neglect of children on the streets, the denials endured by child workers, unjust displacement and the ravaging of the environment, could fill many books.

Our soldiers love their country. I will not take that away from them. But I fight against a hierarchy of 'patriotism' that privileges the soldier in an olive green uniform above all others. I can wear a khaki uniform of a policeperson instead, or the white coat of a doctor or a nurse, or the black robes of a lawyer, or the proverbial *jhola* of the activist, or I can wear no uniform at all. I can be a student who rousingly calls for true equality and *azadi* for all, I can be a woman who fights violence inside my home and outside it, I can be a man who travels hundreds of kilometres every year in search of back-breaking work so that my children can eat and study, spared the life to which I was condemned. All of these and a million others love, and love their country in their own ways. Who can tell them that the only true – or at least the purest – way to love your country is to wear a green uniform and pick up a gun?

※

The valorisation of the soldier carries within it the valorisation of war, marginalising voices on both sides of India's border who insist that peace is both possible and in the best interest of the people of both India and Pakistan.

I recall during the Kargil War, it was routine for television reporters to hold out a mike to the parents or spouses of soldiers who lost their lives in the war, and asked them how they felt. Most responded that they were proud that their loved one had been martyred for the country. But I recall a mother from Kerala who had lost her son. She did not reply at first. But when an importunate reporter persisted, she replied finally, 'Every boy who died in Kargil – Indian or Pakistani – was my son.'

I thought of her when Gurmehar Kaur, a twenty year old college student – whose father Mandeep Singh had been killed when a Rashtriya Rifles camp was attacked in 1999 after hostilities in in the India-Pakistan Kargil war by Kashmiri militants – posted a video on social media that moved many people. 'Pakistan did not kill my Dad', her placard read, 'War killed him'.[13] In the uproar that followed, her mother explained that she wanted to say 'that war always brings destruction. I never wanted her to look at people of Pakistan or any other country with hatred.'[14]

But hyper-nationalist outrage lunged into her – especially on social media most of which is noisily colonised by such opinion – and she was mercilessly trolled and attacked. Popular cricketer Virender Sehwag uploaded a sarcastic message, holding up placards like she did except that his read, 'I didn't score triple centuries. My bat did.'[15] Union Home Minister Kiren Rijuju deplored those leftists who apparently had poisoned the girl's mind! He said her father's soul 'must be weeping' because of her misguided daughter. Later he admitted to NDTV that he had not even seen Gurmehar's post before tweeting about her.[16]

The television studio has become the latest theatre of war-mongering, with television anchors with star following baying for blood each evening, as though they were in a reality game show or playing a new kind of video-game. After the mutilated body of an Indian soldier was found around India's LOC with Pakistan, the television anchor who has established himself the unchallenged master of high-decibel television provocation, walked up to his Pakistani guests in the studio and declared that the hands and legs of the Pakistanis must be broken! Another became hysterical when a commentator spoke of the Indian soldier being killed, rather than being martyred.

The valorisation of war in the hyper-nationalist clamour and rousing of our times, includes not just war against those other countries that our politicians teach us are our enemies. Increasingly we see the celebration even of war against our own unruly people. I was in a television debate after the Maoist attack on paramilitary soldiers in Sukma in Bastar in April 2017 in which 25

13 "Pakistan didn't kill my father, war did: Kargil martyr's daughter", *Rediff*, 2 May 2016. Available at http://www.rediff.com/news/report/pakistan-didnt-kill-my-father-war-did-kargil-martyrs-daughter/20160502.htm

14 "Gurmehar Kaur's mother to India Today: It pains when she's called anti-national, proud of what she did", *India Today*, 1 March 2017. Available at http://indiatoday.intoday.in/story/gurmehar-kaur-mother-rajvinder-kaur-ramjas-college-delhi-university/1/894254.html

15 Rohan Venkataramakrishnan, "Virender Sehwag and Randeep Hooda mock daughter of soldier who died in Kargil. Minister defends them", *Scroll*, 27 February 2017. Available at https://scroll.in/article/830380/virendra-sehwag-and-randeep-hood-mock-daughter-of-soldier-who-died-in-kargil-minister-defends-them

16 Ibid.

soldiers were brutally killed. Voices rose feverishly in the studio demanding a 'surgical strike' by the army against the Maoists, unmindful of the hundreds, even thousands, of civilian tribal men, women and children who would inevitably die in any such attack. I asked – are we at war with our own people, indeed the most impoverished and dispossessed people in our land?

It is even more worrying to see serving army officers participate in programmes with openly communal iconography. Lt General Sarath Chand, army vice-chief, Rear Admiral Kishan K. Pandey and Air Marshal H.N. Bhagwat, participated in a programme to revere Bharat Mata at the launch of the Vidya Veerta Abhiyan. The picture of Bharat Mata was the RSS version, displaying a woman seated on a lion and holding a saffron flag against the backdrop of a map of 'Akhand' or Unbroken India which includes Pakistan, Bangladesh and other neighbours. In the programme, after paying obedience to this image, Vande Mataram was sung in full, including the references to the goddess Durga, even though only the first two stanzas of the poem have been adopted as the country's national song and these contain no references to any Hindu god or goddess. A retired general chided the serving officers for participating in an event that promoted 'a particular ideology', and another former officer for government compromising secularism at an official function. This 'particular ideology' is uncompromisingly hostile to the country's Muslims and Christians.[17]

Nowhere is the sense that we are at war with our own people more in evidence than in the BJP-led government's ever-hardening line in Kashmir. On April 9 2017, a 26 year-old shawl weaver was one of the few who challenged the militant call for election boycott and turned to vote in the by-election for the Srinagar-Budgam parliamentary constituency. Later that morning, Dar was riding his bike to attend a condolence meeting when he was picked up by the army. He told *The Wire* that he was stopped by the forces a few kilometres before Gampora village, where some women were protesting against the elections. 'They damaged my bike, thrashed me severely with gun butts and wooden sticks and in an almost unconscious state tied me to the front of the jeep and paraded me through 10 to 20 villages.' A video shows him tied to the bonnet of the moving army jeep followed by an anti-mine vehicle and a bus with soldiers. 'There was no stone pelting going on in the area when the army men picked me up and neither did any stone pelting take place on the

---

17 Basant Kumar Mohanty, "Military at Bharat Mata feet", *The Telegraph*, 3 May 2017. Available at https://www.telegraphindia.com/1170503/jsp/nation/story_149524.jsp

[army] vehicles when I was being paraded,' Dar told *The Wire*, adding 'I have never ever in my life hurled stones on forces. But I am not able to understand why I was beaten ruthlessly and then tied to the vehicle. What was my crime?' 'I thought all my bones have been broken as my entire body was in pain due to ruthless beating. I was in shock, not able to understand what do to as the forces kept threatening me in case I speak to anybody moving on the road. I was pleading with them to leave me but they wouldn't listen. He was first taken to a CRPF camp and to a local army unit.[18]

In deploying an unarmed citizen, the Indian Army crossed a red line, resorting to a strategy that even the Israeli army avoids. Indian Express reports that the Supreme Court in Israel has banned the use of human shields. Despite widespread criticism, the Chief of Army Staff General Bipin Rawat conspicuously awarded Major Leetul Gogoi, the officer who tied Dar to the bonnet of his jeep during recent protests in Kashmir, with a Chief of Army Staff Commendation Card for 'sustained efforts in Counter-insurgency operations'. The BJP spokesperson Rao defended this: 'Everyone talks about the human rights of terrorists, separatists and disruptive elements. It is high time everyone realize that the security forces, fighting in tough conditions braving all odds, are also humans and have human rights. They have been highly professional and restrained even in some highly provocative situations.'[19] Paresh Rawal BJP MP tweeted that he wished to see writer and outspoken critic of the government's human rights record in Kashmir Arundhati Roy used as a human shield in Kashmir.[20] He later complained that the Twitter management had bullied him into withdrawing his tweet. Shivam Vij observed 'So Rawal thinks it's patriotic to invite such violence against people. This is the new normal in an India where lynching is as common as outrage on Twitter.' 'The question nobody will ask', he goes on, 'is why India needs the army, and the army needs to use human shields, against what it calls its own people?'[21]

18 Mudasir Ahmad, "He Voted, Never Hurled Stones, 'What Was My Crime', Asks Army's 'Human Shield' in Kashmir", 15 April 2017. Available at https://thewire.in/124465/kashmir-farooq-ahmad-dar-army/

19 Sujoy Dhar, "Attacks on India's minority Muslims by Hindu vigilantes mount", *USA Today*, 5 May 2017. Available at https://www.usatoday.com/story/news/world/2017/05/05/attacks-indias-minority-muslims-hindu-vigilantes-mount/100951514/

20 Praveen Swami and Liz Mathew, "Army officer major Gogoi, who tied youth to jeep gets award; Paresh Rawal says do this to Arundhati Roy", *The Indian Express*, 23 May 2017. Available at http://indianexpress.com/article/india/officer-who-tied-kashmiri-man-to-jeep-gets-award-bjp-mp-paresh-rawal-says-do-this-to-arundhati-roy-4669043/

21 Shivam Vij, "Actor Paresh Rawal Has Scored A Spectacular Self-Goal Suggesting Writer Arundhati Roy Be Used As A Human Shield", *Huffington Post*, 22 May 2017. Available at http://www.huffington-

Earlier, India's army chief, General Bipin Rawat chose to hold out dire public warnings of 'tough action' against stone-pelting young people of Kashmir.[22] He declared that government is prepared to give those who support terror activities an opportunity to join the 'national mainstream', but warned if they continued their actions, security forces would respond with 'harsher measures.' He also gave notice that those pelting stones at security forces during anti-militancy operations would be considered anti-national overground workers of militants. 'They may survive today but we will get them tomorrow. Our relentless operations will continue.'[23] He added that the army would go 'helter-skelter' against local boys who pick up arms or aid besieged militants. Close on the heels of these ominous warnings, the Director General of the Central Reserve Police Force K Durga Prasad announced the government's resolve to continue to use pellet guns against protesting civilians in the valley, although with some modifications to reduce injuries to the face and eyes.[24]

The bloody months of stone-throwing mass agitations in the Kashmir valley in 2016 left in their wake what has come to be known as the 'epidemic of dead eyes'.[25] Despite widespread dismay and criticism of the use of pellet guns against agitating crowds because these blinded hundreds of children and youth, the government made clear that its forces will continue to deploy these in Kashmir. The only concession to outraged public sentiment was an assurance that the guns would be fitted with a deflector to reduce – but not eliminate – chances of the pellets hitting the face and eye or sensitive organs in the abdomen. But these safeguards would depend on the soldier actually adhering to protocols of firing at the feet of the agitators. And even if he does, since each round of pellet gun fire would release a spray of hundreds of pellets, there is no guarantee that these will not blind or disable people, mostly young people, but also women in the crowds and bystanders. Small

post.in/2017/05/22/actor-paresh-rawal-has-scored-a-spectacular-self-goal-suggesting_a_22103238/
22 See Harsh Mander, "Spring is far behind", *The Indian Express,* 11 March 2017. Available at http://indianexpress.com/article/opinion/columns/spring-is-far-behind-kashmir-violence-pellet-gun-youth-bjp-bipin-rawat-4564103/
23 "Army chief warns of tough action against stone-pelters in J&K", *India Today,* 15 February 2017. Available at http://indiatoday.intoday.in/story/army-chief-warns-of-tough-action-against-stone-pelters-in-jandampk/1/883785.html
24 "Kashmir unrest: Modified pellet guns to prevent eye injuries, says CRP chief General K Durga Prasad", *Firstpost,* 27 February 2017. Available at http://www.firstpost.com/india/kashmir-unrest-modified-pellet-guns-to-prevent-eye-injuries-says-crpf-chief-general-k-durga-prasad-3305690.html
25 See Mirza Waheed, "India's crackdown in Kashmir: is this the world's first mass blinding?", *The Guardian,* 8 November 2016. Available at https://www.theguardian.com/world/2016/nov/08/india-crackdown-in-kashmir-is-this-worlds-first-mass-blinding

children watching from windows have been blinded by pellets. These proclamations signalled clearly that there would be no change in the Modi government's muscular Kashmir policy.[26]

But what is more worrying is that it is very rare, if not unprecedented, to hear India's army chief – normally fittingly apolitical – use the belligerent language of threats to target not enemy soldiers or armed militants, but the country's civilian populations. In the 1990s, the uprising in the Kashmir valley was fuelled by militants supported by the Pakistani establishment. However after an entire generation of Kashmiris have grown up under the shadow of the gun, the revolt has transformed increasingly into a mass movement. The government itself admits that the number of militants in Kashmir are only a few hundred. But young people have lost their fear of the soldier and the gun. They are spilling in thousands onto the streets, and there is no part of the valley that is untouched by their rage.

In any democratic country, the fundamental principle that must govern lawful crowd dispersal is the minimum necessary application of force. The force that is used against violent crowds should be unavoidable and proportionate to the violent actions of the crowd. It should be carefully calibrated, targeted and deliberate. Deadly force should be used as only the last resort, after all other measures are tried and fail, and after due warning to the crowd. Even when this last-resort lethal force is used, it should be deterrent rather than retributive, and should be followed by full medical attention to save the life and limb of the injured person.

None of these standards are met by pellet guns, therefore these are very rarely used against civilian populations anywhere in the world. Every time the pellet guns are fired, these spray five to seven hundred pellets. It is impossible for the pellets to accurately target a particular individual or the most violent sections of the mob, therefore the random hitting of innocent bystanders is highly probable when pellet guns are deployed. Pellets are made from lead, and are irregular in shape, and their rough edges cause unpredictable damage when they hit sensitive parts of the body. Pellets are particularly destructive when they enter the eye. The soft tissue of the retina is irreparably destroyed by the trauma of high-velocity lead pellets. Doctors in hospitals in Srinagar worked heroically almost without sleep for several weeks to try to save the eyes of hundreds of young patients. Often the lead pellets got embedded so

---

26 See Kashmir unrest: Modified pellet guns to prevent eye injuries, says CRP chief General K Durga Prasad", *Firstpost*, 27 February 2017. Available at http://www.firstpost.com/india/kashmir-unrest-modified-pellet-guns-to-prevent-eye-injuries-says-crpf-chief-general-k-durga-prasad-3305690.html

deeply in the skull that doctors could not extract these, and these can lead to poisoning and unpredictable disasters later in the patient's life. Bullets kill, but pellets leave them blinded or disabled for a lifetime. And many patients did not approach for treatment a government hospital for fear that merely having pellet injuries could mark you as a stone-pelter and the police would register criminal charges against you.

The instrument of violence deployed by the masses of Kashmir's youthful agitators is stones. The answer of the Indian security establishment to their stones is bullets and pellet guns. Last winter, I visited the valley with a solidarity team comprising Pamela Philipose, Tapan Bose, Navsharan Kaur and Dinesh Mohan. We encountered numerous young people blinded by pellets, and others with bullet injuries in their skulls and legs. Some of those felled and blinded may have been among those who pelted stones on the soldiers and policepersons who tried to block their processions. But many were too young to have even understood what was happening. Their families were utterly devastated with the suffering of many who were still children. The wanton blinding by security forces of children has wounded the souls of the Kashmiri people in ways that little else has in the past. The question that people asked us over and over again was this: 'You say we are equal citizens of India. Yes, some of our boys pelted stones. But we know of far more violent mobs in other parts of India this last year – the Jat and Patidar agitations, the Cauvery dispute and many others. To disperse those mobs, have security forces ever used pellet guns? In all those unrests, lathis, tear-gas and water-cannons were found to be sufficient by India' security establishment. But why is it that only for Kashmiri youth throwing stones, you use pellet guns?'

❀

The 'nationalist' duty to demonstrate your love for your nation, in the Hindutva doctrine, requires the ultimate litmus test of hating. This obligation to hate in order to establish that you love is part of a recurring binary. I can be a proud Hindu only if I hate Muslims. I can love the cow only if I am willing to pulverise all those who I believe do not. I can love India only if I noisily hate Pakistan.

Mahatma Gandhi, a deeply devout practising Hindu, refused to accept the binary that he must hate Muslims. On the contrary, he said that Hindus and Muslims were like his two eyes. He lived for many convictions, but died in the end for Hindu Muslim unity. I was speaking in a Literature Festival in Dehra Doon on a panel on nationalism with writer Nayantara Sahgal. She said at one point, 'But I am half-Muslim.' We were surprised, because we knew that her father was a freedom fighter Ranjit Sitaram Pandit who died in 1944 in Lucknow prison; and her mother Vijaylakshmi Pandit was Motilal Nehru's daughter and sister of Jawaharlal Nehru. She went on to explain. 'I was raised in Awadh. Half the food we ate, our music, poetry, dance, literature, all had Islamic origins. In that sense, I am half-Muslim.' On the same panel, human rights lawyer Nandita Haksar recalled that when she was around nine, her younger sister asked her mother, 'Am I Hindu or Muslim?' Her mother's spontaneous reply was – '*Aisi vahaiyat sawaal kyon pooch rahi ho?* Why are you asking such a worthless question?'

In the Hindutva nationalist world-view the good Muslim is loyal to India and respects Hindu values. But such Muslims, they are convinced, constitute a small minority. The bad Muslim lives in India, is contemptuous of Hindu scriptures and sentiments, and his (or her) heart beats for Pakistan. Pakistan unsurprisingly surfaces in every election campaign that the BJP runs, which always has communal overtones. In Modi's Gujarat, posters of Pakistan President were pasted on walls,[27] and election speeches charged that a victory for the Congress would be celebrated in Pakistan (presumably because the Congress is partial to the state's Muslims, and the Muslims are loyal to Pakistan). In the UP elections of 2017, hoardings appeared lauding India's military action called 'surgical strikes' on terrorist enclaves on Pakistani soil.[28]

The obligation to hate Pakistan to prove your love for India sometimes assumes almost comical proportions. As India's Defence Minister Manohar Parrikar claimed that going to Pakistan and going to hell are the same thing. Kannada actor Divya Spandana tweeted in response, 'I respectfully disagree. Pakistan is not hell, people there are just like us.' She was booked for the crime of *sedition*, no less!

This arraignment of sedition against the actor spurred me to write an article for Scroll.in. It was titled #SeditionThis Why I Believe Pakistanis are the Most Gracious People in the World'.[29] I wrote:

27 "'Friends of Pakistan!' Kejriwal features on Gujarat posters with Osama, Saeed, blames BJP", *The Economic Times*, 15 October 2016. Available at https://economictimes.indiatimes.com/news/politics-and-nation/friends-of-pakistan-kejriwal-features-on-gujarat-posters-with-osama-saeed-blames-bjp/articleshow/54864062.cms

28 "BJP banners across UP laud 'surgical strikes'", *The Hindu*, 5 October 2016. Available at http://www.thehindu.com/news/national/other-states/BJP-banners-across-U.P.-laud-%E2%80%98surgical-strikes%E2%80%99/article15425612.ece

29 *Scroll*, 29 August 2016. Available at https://scroll.in/article/815122/inviting-sedition-why-i-believe-pakistanis-are-the-most-gracious-people-in-the-world

My mother was forced to leave behind the city of her birth, Rawal-pindi, when she was just 18 years, because of the tumultuous ruptures of Partition. She had never returned. When she was to turn 75 years, I thought the best gift I could give her was to take her, if it was at all possible, to the city, and if possible to the home, in which she was born.

I emailed my friends in Pakistan tentatively with my plan. They were immediately very welcoming. 'Just get her visa, leave the rest to us', they said. I applied for visas for my parents and the rest of my family. It seemed then a small miracle that we got these easily. I booked our flight tickets, and before long we were on our way.

Our flight landed at Lahore, and our friends drove us from the airport to their home in Islamabad. I noticed that my mother was initially a little tense. Maybe it was memories of the violence of her exile; maybe it was just the idea that this was now a foreign land, and for many in India the enemy land. I watched my mother gradually relax even on the road journey to Islamabad, as she delighted in hearing my friends and the car driver speak the Punjabi of her childhood and she watched the altered landscape of her journey. Islamabad of course did not exist when she lived in the Punjab of her days.

In Islamabad, my friends invited to their homes many of their associates with their parents. They organised evenings of Punjabi poetry and music, which my parents relished. Our friends drove us to Marri, the hill-station in which my mother had spent many pleasant summers as a child. My mother had just one more request. Could she go to see the colony where she was born and spent her childhood in Rawalpindi? My father wanted to also visit his college, the famous Gordon College in Rawalpindi.

She recalled the name of the residential colony in which they lived was called Gawal Mandi. My friends knew it well; it was now an upmarket upper middle-class enclave. When we reached there, my mother tried to locate the house of her childhood. It seemed impossible. Everything was new: most of the old houses had been rebuilt and opulent new structures had come up in their place. She located the building that had housed their gurudwara. It had now been converted into a health-centre. But we had almost despaired of actually finding her childhood house. We doubted if it was even standing all these years later. We were leaving when suddenly my mother pointed to the fili-gree or jafri work on the balconies of one of the old houses. 'I remember it because my father was very proud of the designs. He said there was none like it in the neighbourhood.'

Taking a chance, we knocked tentatively at the door of the house. A middle-aged man opened the latch, and asked us who we wanted to meet. My mother said apologetically, 'We are so sorry to trouble you, and intrude suddenly in this way. But I lived as a child in Gawal Mandi, before Partition, when we had to leave for India. I think this maybe was our home.'

The house-owner's response was spontaneous and immediate. 'Mataji, why do you say that this was your home? It continues to be your home even today. You are most welcome.' And he led us all in.

Before long, my mother confirmed that this was indeed her childhood home. She went from room to room, and then to the terrace, almost in a trance, recalling all the while fragments of her childhood memories in various corners of this house. For months after we returned to Delhi, she would tell me that recollections of the house returned to her in her dreams.

Half an hour later, we thanked the house-owners and said that we would be on our way. But they would not hear of it. 'You have come to your childhood home, then how can we let you go without you having a meal with us here?' They overruled all our protestations, and lunch were prepared for around eight members of our party, including not just my family but also our Pakistani hosts. Only when they were sure that we had eaten our fill, and more, did they allow us to leave.

After we returned to India, news of our adventure spread quickly among family and friends. The next year, my mother-in-law, a wheel-chair user, requested that we take her also to Pakistan to visit her child-hood home, this time in Gujranwala. Given the joys of my parents' successful visit, I was more confident. But then many elderly aunts and an elderly uncle joined the trip, and in the end my wife and I were accompanying six older people to Pakistan. Our experience this time was very similar to a year earlier. The owner of their old ancestral haveli in their Gujranwala village took my mother-in-law around the sprawling property on her wheel-chair, and after we had eaten with them asked her, 'Would you not like to check out your farm-lands?'

On both visits, wherever my wife visited shops, for clothes, footwear or handicrafts, if the shopkeepers recognised her to be Indian, they would invariably insist on a hefty concession on the price. 'You are our guests', they would say. 'How can we make a profit from our guests?'

As news of these visits travelled further, my associates from an NGO Ashagram for the care and rights of persons living with leprosy in a small town Barwani in Madhya Pradesh – with which I had a long association since its founding – demanded that I organise a visit for them also to Pakistan. Once again, the Pakistani High Commission granted to them visas and they were on their way. There was only one catch, and this was that all of them were vegetarian. They enjoyed greatly the week they spent in Pakistan, except for the food. Every night they would set out looking for a wayside shop to buy fruit juice. Each night they found a new shop, and each night without exception, the shopkeeper refused to accept any money for the fruit juice. 'We will not charge money from our guests from India', they would say each time. This happened for a full seven days.

I have travelled to many countries in the world in the sixty years of my life. I have never encountered a people as gracious as those in Pakistan.

This declaration is my latest act of sedition.

CHAPTER EIGHT

The Multiple Betrayal of 'Secular' Parties

I regard the openly communally charged campaign in the 2017 spring Uttar Pradesh election; the unification of most Hindu caste and class groups against the Muslims including many sections of the Dalits; and the selection of one of BJP's most hate-mongering leaders who had raised a private Hindu militia against minorities to lead Uttar Pradesh; as further fruition of the vision for India of the RSS, less than a hundred years since the RSS was constituted in 1925. It is a victory for the RSS, its ideology and cadres, and the BJP. But the victory of a brawny politics of communal hectoring and name-calling, hate and division and the defeat of the constitutional values of fraternity and equality, cannot be laid only at their door. Equal credit, or culpability, lies with the parties of the opposition, which have long abandoned any real commitment to secular values, or even the defence of the country's minorities.[1]

I will illustrate first their multiple betrayals with the role they played, or did not play, in Muzaffarnagar, which I observed closely in the course of our work with the survivors of the mass communal violence of 2013. Muzaffarnagar in Western Uttar Pradesh had an unbroken history so far of communal amity, even during the Partition riots and the turbulent movement for the demolition of the Babri Masjid. It was again the cadres of the RSS, the Vishwa Hindu Parishad and the Bajrang Dal, that stirred the communal cauldron in these regions.[2] It has been established beyond doubt that BJP MLA Sangeet Som circulated a fake video of two youth being lynched by a crowd of Muslims. He claimed mischievously and dangerously that lynch mob was of Muslims of Muzaffarnagar, and the men who were brutally killed were two Jat brothers who were trying to defend the honour of their sister from

---

1 Portions of this chapter are reproduced from an article I authored for *Scroll*, "Yogi Adityanath is as much a creation of the so-called secular parties as the Sangh", 21 March 2017. Available at https://scroll.in/article/832292/adityanath-is-as-much-a-creation-of-the-so-called-secular-parties-as-the-sangh-parivar

2 Gaurav Vivek Bhatnagar, "BJP, RSS Leaders Caught Using 'Love Jihad' Bogey to Fuel Communal Polarisation", *The Wire*, 5 October 2015. Available at https://thewire.in/12409/bjp-rss-leaders-caught-using-love-jihad-bogey-to-fuel-communal-polarisation/

the sexual harassment of a Muslim youth.[3] It mattered little in the post-truth world of command prejudice that all of this were falsehoods, that the video was of a lynching in Pakistan, and that the Jat brothers and Muslim youth killed each other not because of any sexual predation but following a heated skirmish after a motor-cycle accident. These falsehoods resulted in the largest episode of anti-Muslim violence in a decade.

Anything between seventy and a hundred thousand Muslims fled from their villages in terror after their neighbours of generations suddenly turned against them, burning and looting their homes, raping women of their village, killing even elders and children. The role of the RSS was not different from what it has been since the Partition riots, of fomenting communal hatred and violence through deliberate and communally combustible falsehoods, hate propaganda and rumours. But the role of the Samajwadi Party government led by Chief Minister Akhilesh Yadav, and of other parties that claim to be 'secular' require much closer interrogation.

I found the character, the part played and the attitude of the state administration in Uttar Pradesh hardly different in most ways from that of the state administration in Gujarat in 2002. It could have prevented the scale of hate attacks on Muslims if it had been firm and steadfast in not permitting the mahapanchayats in which hate speeches were made against Muslims based on the RSS-created rumours. It is the mahapanchayat that led directly to massive crowds being mobilised and provoked and incited to inflict hate violence against their Muslim neighbours. The soft-pedalling by the state administration did not just suggest criminal administrative incompetence: if it was just this, it would be bad enough. The real doubt was that it secretly believed that it would benefit along with the BJP from the polarisation between Muslims and Hindus in a communal riot, a harvest that both parties would reap in the forthcoming 2014 general elections.

Even more shameful was the neglect, and even hostility, of the Uttar Pradesh state administration to the refugees from hate violence in camps. I visited the camps on many occasions and found them little different from the relief camps I had seen in Gujarat in 2002. In both, the state administration refused to establish and run relief camps for those displaced from their homes by hate violence. It left this mainly to the battered community itself,

---

3 Sreenivasan Jain, "Muzaffarnagar clashes: BJP MLA booked for fake video with inflammatory comments, evading arrest", *NDTV*, 10 September 2013. Available at https://www.ndtv.com/india-news/muzaffarnagar-clashes-bjp-mla-booked-for-fake-video-with-inflammatory-comments-evading-arrest-534156

as though the responsibility for taking care of these hate refugees was not of the state but of the Muslim people. With nowhere to go, people endured the winter cold, the hot dusty summers and the rains under plastics, with reports of children dying, but the state administration remained unmoved. As in Gujarat in 2002, we found little presence of the state in these camps: it did not organise sanitation, health care, child care or police outposts to record people's complaints.

The only real departure of the practice of the Uttar Pradesh administration from that of the Gujarat administration eleven years earlier was in the payment of five lakh rupees as compensation to those persons who undertook that they would not return to their original villages. This policy had no precedent in India. For people displaced by hate violence, the duty of the state administration should be recognised to be to create conditions that are conducive to enabling people displaced by hate violence to return to their original homes. This required the administration to take the lead in attempting to rebuild social bonds between the estranged communities, and to ensure the security of those who returned. Far from doing this, the action of the Uttar Pradesh state government in effect accepted that Muslim and Hindu populations would no longer live together peacefully, and even incentivised their separation. In earlier large episodes of rural communal violence like Bhagalpur and Gujarat we found that social fractures tend to be enduring, and Muslims are ejected from mixed settlements. A state government that claimed to be secular should have firmly fought and resisted this, promoting the restoration of mixed plural habitations, rather than for the first time in free India actually incentivising separate living on religious lines as official state policy. This was an utterly bankrupt state policy of the Akhilesh government, with communal underpinnings, one that has no precedents in past communal riots.

Just three months after the carnage, the state government officially terminated all relief camps, again as happened in Gujarat, even though several thousand displaced persons were still in fear and dread, and unwilling to return home because they continued to feel unsafe.[4] Whereas displaced persons in camps should be officially assisted and supported to return to their original homes by promoting reconciliation and security, to force them to

4 See Dionne Busha, "The crisis of the camps", *Frontline*, Volume 19, No 8, April 13 – 26 2002. Available at http://www.frontline.in/static/html/fl1908/19080220.htm. The People's Union for Democratic Rights filed a petition against the closure of the camps, which the Supreme Court refused to pass an order on. See "SC refuses order on Guj relief camps closure", *The Times of India*, 20 May 2002. Available at https://timesofindia.indiatimes.com/india/SC-refuses-order-on-Guj-relief-camps-closure/articleshow/10465232.cms

do so by premature closure of camps resulted only in thousands being left without even the meagre food and health support which the government had extended in the camps. The sense of fear and alienation of the survivors was enhanced by distressing reports of organised social and economic boycott of Muslims after the mass violence, once again on the model incubated successfully in Gujarat. Many men testified that they were told they should cut their beards off if they wished to live in their village. People also reported similar hate exchanges in buses and public spaces. Survivors recounted intimidation and boycott in employment as farm labour, or economic activities like *pheris*, or selling cloth and other goods from house to house.

The Akhilesh Yadav-led state government did little to create conditions in which survivors felt safe to return to the villages of their birth. Without any public remorse by their attackers, any official or community initiatives for reconciliation, and any attempts at justice, these hapless people were unable to return to the villages of their birth. Sometimes with small grants from government or NGOs, but mainly with usurious loans from private moneylenders, they bought house-plots in hastily laid out colonies in Muslim majority villages on what were cultivated fields. Seizing the opportunity to make windfall profits, local large farmers and real estate developers sold these plots at exorbitant rates to these luckless displaced persons. The indifference of the state government is reflected also in the fact that there is no official record of these mostly self-settled colonies, let alone official plans to ensure that they are able to access basic public goods and citizenship entitlements. In a survey undertaken by Aman Biradari and Afkar India Foundation, we discovered as many as 65 refugee colonies, 28 in Muzaffarnagar and 37 in Shamli, housing 29328 residents, described in our report *Living Apart*. In hellish slum-like settlements, these internal refugees are bravely building their lives anew. Perhaps our most striking survey finding was the almost complete absence of the state from these efforts to begin a new life of the refugees. Apart from the 5 lakh rupee grant given only to households directly hit by the violence who would not return to their original villages (and none to the much larger number who escaped their villages because of fear of attacks), the state took no responsibility for helping them resettle in any way. The displaced hate-refugees were forced to either abandon or sell at distress prices their properties in their villages of origin, and the state compensation for the loss of their moveable assets was negligible. The colonies were settled substantially with the self-help efforts of the impoverished and battered refugees themselves. This again strikingly mirrors the story of the violence-affected people of Gujarat.

The confidence of survivors to return to homes was further shaken because of the very low numbers of arrests and convictions of the men accused of murder, rape, arson and looting. Without justice, as we have learned from the survivors in Gujarat and every other site of communal violence, neither do wounds heal nor can fresh violence be deterred. Police and even the judiciary in Uttar Pradesh often displayed communal biases very similar to their Gujarati counterparts. Of 6400 persons accused of crimes in 534 FIRs, charges were ultimately pursued against only 1540 persons. Most of the cases of murder were closed without a charge-sheet or trial claiming the accused were 'unknown persons'. Even after a year of the carnage, only 800 people were arrested, and most of those who were arrested were quickly released on bail. One reason given for low numbers of arrests by the police administration was that large numbers of women blocked the entrance to the village entry whenever police vehicles drove there for arrests, or farmers parked tractors to thwart police passage. Survivors on the other hand believed that police themselves informally tipped off the villagers before arriving to make arrests, otherwise how would so many assemble at short notice to blockade village roads? This allegation was difficult to independently verify, but no self-respecting police administration could accept this kind of public blockades to persist when it came in the way of their fulfilling their official duties. Only three of the 25 men accused in six cases of gang-rape were held. In one rape case, all the accused men have been acquitted; in another after three years no one has been arrested; and in the other rape cases, all the accused men are out on bail. There was enormous pressure on the witnesses to rescind on their statements, and a large number of witnesses have turned 'hostile' in court. Although Indian criminal law does not permit 'compromise' in heinous offences, we observed in Gujarat that this remains a routine practice after mass communal violence. Since the accused freely roam the same villages, either evading arrest or on bail, they are free to intimidate the complainants and victims. It does not help that the majority of the complainants were impoverished farm workers or brick kiln labour, critically dependent economically on the large Jat landowners for work and loans. The police was particularly soft in acting against politicians who were allegedly directly involved in the rioting. They have at best been booked in very minor sections like Section 188 of the IPC. Most of them did not even see the inside of a jail. There were also other distressing signs of judicial bias, because most arrested persons have been granted bail almost the next day or soon after their arrests. This ignored the gravity of hate crimes, and the susceptibility of the survivors to intimidation because of their vulnerable situation after mass targeted violence has spurred large-scale fear, destruction of livelihoods and habitats and migration.

When the carnage unfolded, and in the crucial months that followed, the Congress Party headed the UPA government in the centre. But it never directed or advised the state government in Uttar Pradesh to fulfil its constitutional duties to the violence affected people more responsibly or compassionately, nor did it reach out to them directly in any way. As a party, I found Congress workers completely absent from the relief camps, in Muzaffarnagar as much as in the Gujarat camps a decade earlier. This is where the Congress Sewa Dal (does it even exist?) should have been visible, extending discernible solidarity and service to the people displaced by hate violence. Equally, BSP leader Mayavati never once reached out to the hapless violence-hit people. She mostly maintained her imperious silence, indicating indifference. What credibility would she carry if years later, she reaches out for an 'alliance' with the Muslim 'people' of the state? The only political party that did reach out in any way to the violence-hit people of Muzafffarnagar was the Communist Party (Marxist), which helped establish a resettlement colony. But even this assistance was much smaller and less visible than the role that the Communist Party played in the early communal riots after Independence.

The enormous tragedy of India's secular majority, as much as of India's minorities, is that India today lacks an authentically secular political opposition. I believe that it is these failures of parties that characterise themselves as 'secular' that ultimately emboldens a resurgent and triumphalist political right, led by Modi and Amit Shah, the selection of communal firebrand Yogi Adityanath as the leader of Uttar Pradesh, and the unleashing of lynch mobs against India's minorities across the country.

✳

Around the time I was trying to make sense of Yogi Aditynanath's selection as the Chief Minister of Uttar Pradesh, it was instructive to read Vibhuti Narain Rai's slim book *Hashimpura 22 May* (Penguin 2016).[5] It helped me understand starkly the roots and sources of the current communal juggernaut in Uttar Pradesh. This stirring book by a man who combines the clinical forensics of a trained and experienced policeman with the sensitivity and

---

5 This section is adapted from a review of the book that I wrote for *Scroll*, titled "Why the Hashimpura massacre of 42 Muslim men in 1987 is relevant in the polarised UP of today", 16 April 2017. Available at https://scroll.in/article/833915/why-the-hashimpura-massacre-of-42-muslim-men-in-1987-is-relevant-in-the-polarised-up-of-today

eloquence of a skilled novelist, and the outrage of a human rights activist, exposes from the inside the sordid communal rot of all of India's public institutions – its political leadership, its police, its civil service, its courts, even its media. It reminds us of why the Congress earned its terminal decline in Uttar Pradesh and increasingly across the country. Reading it again after the ascendancy of Yogi Adityanath with his hard communal rhetoric to the highest political office in Uttar Pradesh, we are reminded by Rai's account of how the cynical betrayal of the state's minorities and of the constitutional values of secular democracy had begun much, much earlier. We read of the communal duplicity of 'secular politics', of the political, administrative and media establishment for decades, that paved the way for unfolding tragedy of Uttar Pradesh – and India – today.

Rai describes one of the most horrific communal public crimes that we have erased from public memory and conscience. This is India's biggest episode of extra-judicial custodial killing after Independence: the slaughter by men in uniform in the night of 22 May 1987 of 42 young civilian Muslim men. These youths were rounded up from their homes in Hashimpura in Meerut on that humid midsummer night, allegedly picked from a larger crowd by security personnel, driven to a canal bank, shot in pitch darkness at close range, and their bullet-ridden bodies were thrown into the Hindon canal.[6] The men were guilty of no crime, and were chosen for slaughter allegedly by paramilitary soldiers only because of the god they worshipped, and their youth. Not a single person has been punished for this crime despite heroic and dogged battles for justice for three decades by the indigent survivors of the slain men. 28 years after the crime, all 16 persons accused of the massacre, all junior paramilitary personnel, were acquitted giving them the 'benefit of the doubt' as there was 'insufficient evidence'.[7]

Rai was the Superintendent of Police in the district on the opposite banks of the canal in which the bodies of the slaughtered men were dumped, Ghaziabad. It was he who first discovered the bullet-ridden floating corpses, rescued the handful of survivors, and helped first bring the story of the custodial massacre to the world. The memories of that horrifying night, he says, remain etched in his memory 'as if in stone', weighing heavily on his

---

6 Some survivor testimonies in Kaunain Sheriff M, "27 yrs after Hashimpura massacre, 4 who survived watch 16 cops walk free", *The Indian Express*, 22 March 2015. Available at http://indianexpress.com/article/india/india-others/27-years-after-hashimpura-4-who-survived-watch-16-cops-walk-free/

7 Nirnimesh Kumar, "Hashimpura massacre accused set free", *The Hindu*, 21 March 2015. Available at http://www.thehindu.com/news/national/other-states/16-acquitted-in-1987-hashimpura-massacre/article7018797.ece

conscience. Its nightmares continue to torment him – 'something that over-powered the cop in me..'

Rai's account is above all a reminder that the 'relations between the Indian State and the minorities are almost the same now as they were in 1987 or even earlier in the decades of the 1950's or the 1960's. The same absence of trust, the same hatred, the same prejudices, the same notions, and the same requirement as well as attempt to prove their Indianness. Nothing has changed, as though the more things change, the more they remain the same. Or perhaps, worsen.'[8]

He begins his account with the night that a shocked and frightened sub-inspector first brought him news of the massacre. Rai drove immediately to the canal bank with District Magistrate Nasim Zaidi. In the headlights of the vehicles and lit torches, they saw '(b)odies covered in blood, some in the ravine, some hanging precariously from the canal embankments partly in water, partly outside and some floating on the water. The blood had not even dried up.' He describes how they searched 'for those alive among (the) blood-soaked bodies...with a dim struggling torchlight while also ensuring that one doesn't trample upon bodies.'[9]

A cough revealed the first survivor – 'someone hanging between the bushes and the canal, half immersed in water... difficult to figure out at first whether he was alive or dead... shivering with fear...' Seeing men in khaki, 'it took us a long time to convince him that we were there to help. This was the man who was to later tell us the bloody and horrific tale of that night – Babudin. Bullets brushed his flesh at two places, but he had no injuries. In fact, after being helped out of the canal, he sat briefly on the culvert, rested and then walked down on his feet without any help to where our vehicles were parked.'

Rai describes Babudin as a 'frail, hollow cheeked boy of average height (who) stood before us, diffident and scared like a sparrow with wet wings. His trouser was muddied by slush on the canal embankment and the shirt was so drenched that you could extract a litre of water from it. Shivers passed his body even in that scorching summer. He had a stammer but a voice that was stone cold.' Babudin told Rai and Zaidi, the Superintendent of Police and the District Magistrate, that 'it was during routine searches that a PAC truck

8 Quoted from a *Scroll* article I authored, "Why the Hashimpura massacre of 42 Muslim men in 1987 is relevant in the polarised UP of today", 16 April 2017. Available at https://scroll.in/article/833915/ why-the-hashimpura-massacre-of-42-muslim-men-in-1987-is-relevant-in-the-polarised-up-of-today
9 Quoted from Vibhuti Narain Rai (2016) *Hashimpura 22 May,* New Delhi: Penguin Books.

picked up some 40 to 50 people and drove them away. They all thought they had been arrested and would soon be lodged in some police lock up or jail. While it appeared rather strange that it was taking too long for them to reach the jail from curfew-bound streets, everything else looked so normal that they had no inkling of what was in store for them. But when they were asked to step out at the first canal and started being killed one after the other that they understood why their custodians had been so silent and why they kept on whispering into each other's ears.'

When they reached the canal banks, in pitch darkness, 'Jawans standing outside ordered their colleagues inside the truck to catch by the collar of the 'circumcised' and throw out those hesitating to jump. They pushed their victims with the butt of their rifles and by holding their collars; those who were difficult to handle were virtually lifted and hurled outside. Every time somebody fell outside, he could hear gunshots and the painful cries of someone dying.'

'Imagine', Rai says, demanding from the reader that they try to empathise with a moment when death suddenly becomes your co-traveller. 'Imagine such a close encounter with death that when you open your eyes to bodies – dead and half dead – you may want to touch them to believe you are still alive. When molten lead rips through your flesh and flings you in the air like cotton balls, there is no pain, no fear and there is not even time for memories to torment you. There are rifles blazing around you and then there is the cacophony of abuses being sprouted by your killers. And with numbed senses, you wait for one of the bullets whizzing past you to enter your body in a way that you are tossed in the air for a moment and collapse on the ground with a thud. How will you describe such a death? Especially when you are seeing your killers for the first time and despite thinking hard your mind cannot just figure out why would they want to kill you.' He tries to imagine their state of mind 'when they must have seen their friends, relatives and colleagues getting tossed in the air and then falling with a thud, convulsing and writhing in pain, and their senses so numbed that they could not even dare to do the obvious thing of trying to run away?'

Every one of the few survivors who hit the ground after being shot at tried hard to pretend he is dead. 'They hung on to the canal's embankments with their heads in water and the body hanging precariously clutching on to grass and other foliage to show to their killers that they were dead, hoping no more gunshots are fired at them.'

But even more horrifying than Rai's haunting recreation of the massacre and its immediate aftermath is his graphic inside story of the many betrayals of the political, bureaucratic, police, judicial and media establishments to ensure that the guilty men in uniform would escape punishment.[10] The most gripping and telling is his blow-by-blow description of the meeting the next night that the District Magistrate and he had with the Uttar Pradesh Chief Minister Veer Bahadur Singh and a battery of senior officials of the state about how to deal with the massacre. Since District Magistrate Nasim Zaidi was a Muslim was therefore diffident the onus was on Rai to steer the discussions.

Rai records that 'Whatever happened for the next couple of hours in that room was a sordid saga of smarminess, opportunism and hedging so typical of the Indian bureaucracy.' Rai was clear that the only legal and ethical course after such a heinous crime would have been to lodge an offence of murder against the killers without bothering that they were armed policemen and to treat them in the same manner as any other accused person in a similar case. 'This meant we should have immediately raided the PAC battalion and seized the truck they used to execute the murders; it was imminently possible to find blood stains in the vehicle. We should have tried to arrest the PAC personnel who would have just returned to Meerut after committing the crime and confiscated their weapons, which could be key evidence during the trial.'

But this was stoutly opposed by all the other officials present in the room, 'none of who the slightest sense of constitutional, legal or moral responsibility towards the biggest custodial killing after Independence.' Instead the central issue of concern among the officials was on ways to wriggle out of the crisis. They were all dead opposed to the arrest of the PAC soldiers and seizure of their truck. 'There were more than 30 companies of PAC posted in Meerut and police officials present in that room with me remembered quite well the 1973 mutiny by the PAC which could be suppressed by concerted efforts only with the assistance of the Army... And nobody was sure what could be the possible reaction of the 3,000 armed PAC men deployed in Meerut'... Nobody could guess the possible reaction of the forces deployed in the city to any attempt to raid a PAC camp and arrest its men. Nobody supported my proposal, one doesn't know if this was actually out of the suspicion of a violent reaction from the PAC troops or it spawned from a hidden sentiment that Muslims deserved such a lesson.' Even more shocking were suggestions that the state erases evidence of the massacre, by pushing the bodies further down the canal, and killing the three survivors!

10 Saurav Datta, "How the Prosecution and the State Conspired To Deny Justice at Hashimpura", *The Caravan*, 28 March 2015. Available at http://www.caravanmagazine.in/vantage/how-lack-evidence-hampered-hashimpura-massacre-case

The only saving grace of the discussions that night was that the Chief Minister did not accept these last cynical suggestions, but also did not allow the arrest of the PAC killers. The dice was already cast against the possibility of eventual justice with that one fateful and cynical decision. Rai observes that Chief Minister Veer Bahadur Singh 'could not be bracketed among those leaders in the pedigree of Jawaharlal Nehru for whom secularism was a principle. For many Congress leaders secularism is more about political expediency and they swear by it only till it benefits them during elections. I would put Veer Bahadur Singh under this lineage... The custodial killing of 42 people was neither an administrative challenge for him nor did it matter that it was a harbinger of a danger for India's secular fabric that 42 Muslims were killed like this. He was the product of such breed of politicians for whom secularism was limited to being a ladder to electoral success.'

Rai goes on to describe how the state establishment ensured that there was no news in any newspaper about the massacre. For many days it was as though it did not happen. He describes how he was torn between his training as a police officer as his conscience as a citizen. The latter finally won, and he secretly leaked the news to his journalist contacts in a leading newspaper. He was shocked when the editor killed the story in what was clearly 'an uncanny criminal silence.' He found another smaller paper that finally published the story.

He records many other such historic betrayals, such as of Mohsina Kidwai, Union Minister, who refused to even give shelter to one of the survivors who was frightened he would be killed and first reached her door secretly. It was Syed Shahabuddin – recently deceased – who eventually gave the terrified man refuge. He also speaks of Prime Minister Rajiv Gandhi's betrayal. His 'political advisers would have impressed upon him that more important than justice and secularism at that time was the election that was just about one and a half years later. A nice human being but a political novice, Gandhi succumbed to the coterie of his advisers and first kneeled down to Muslim fundamentalists and reversed the Supreme Court's verdict in the Shah Bano case, and next, to appease aggressive Hindu leaders got the locks opened of a temple on the premises of the Babri Masjid in Ayodhya. Naturally the idea of punishing guilty policemen for ghastly Hashimpura incidence could not find due attention of the leader who was soon going to face a very difficult election of his life.'

He describes the sordid ways that the police investigation deliberately ensured that the guilty could never be punished, even though these were being monitored directly by the Prime Minister's Office. The report of the CID absolved senior police officers as well as those of the army of any wrong-doing. It stated: 'No evidence has been found during the investigation to indicate if a senior officer had issued any orders to kill the arrested persons. Evidence suggests that this crime seems to be the outcome of the perverse psyche of only the doers (those who actually committed the murders) and only they could be held responsible, nobody else.' It also erases all guilt of the commander of the army detachment, Major BS Pathania, whose roe in inciting the gun-toting PAC men Rai delineates.

He maps in detail the many profound betrayals of the criminal case, which after 28 years of the massacre, acquitted all 16 of the accused, though the court accepted that during searches in Hashimpura on May 22, 1987, Muslims were indiscriminately picked up, loaded in a yellow coloured truck and brought to two water canals where a team of PAC jawans killed 42 persons. These were foot soldiers, the senior officers and political leaders under whose command and in whose refuge they were assured of impunity, had never even been charged. He writes in white rage: 'a group of Uttar Pradesh's armed reserve police force select 42 youngsters among a crowd of more than 500 people in full public view, load them in an official police truck, take them near water canals, kill them one by one, throw them into a fast stream of water, hop on to the truck, reach their camp and go to a nice undisturbed sleep. Twenty-eight years later, the court says have fun. Yes, it all happened, but the investigators did not have enough meat in their material to make the killers sleep in the jails.'

In the closing chapters of his book, Rai returns again to his central torment: why did the Hashimpura massacre happen at all? If you are not psychologically deranged, how can you cold-bloodedly kill someone at point-blank range? Either you kill someone with a strong sense of revenge, his death gives you an unprecedented financial reward or a deep internal satisfaction. 'In Hashimpura, neither the killers nor the victims even knew other, either as friends or enemies. Nor were the killers expecting nor were they to be given any rewards for the murders.'

He concludes bleakly that Hashimpura is not just an aberration, and one instance of impunity that could be dismissed simply as the outcome of pathetic and unprofessional investigation. Hashimpura is a phenomenon that goes much deep into the mindset of Indian society that leads to communal violence. This violence may not always play out as blood flowing on the streets. But he believes that the rot has got imbibed into the psyche of ordinary people, an always lurking 'uncanny unspelt malignancy that is quietly gnawing at (social) relations (between Hindus and Muslims).' Some years after Hashimpura, Rai took leave to study the attitude of ordinary people to the police during communal riots. He found that the majority of Hindus saw the police as friends while the Muslims, in contrast, regarded them as their foes and not protectors. In normal circumstances even the Hindus would not call the police as their friend. An adage is popular among almost all Indian languages that one should neither have friends nor enemies with the police. Why is it then that an average Hindu sees the police as his friend and protector during communal riots? The plausible reason, Rai suggests, is that even under his khaki uniform the policeperson strongly retains his intrinsic Hindu identity. He also feels somewhere within that if he does not interfere and check the 'barbaric' Muslims, they would make the lives of 'non-violent' Hindus difficult.

❀

The lesson, then, from both Muzaffarnagar and Hashimpura, is that the runaway electoral victory of the BJP in the elections to the Uttar Pradesh assembly in the spring of 2017 was as much due to the BJP's polarising campaign and Mr Modi's charismatic but divisive leadership, as it is due to the failure of any authentic and credible secular alternative. 'Secularism' is not treating Muslim minorities as a hapless, powerless, dependent 'client' population whose votes can be taken for granted at election time and forgotten for the rest. 'Secularism' is not a selective, opportunistic policy, to be played with a continuous timid eye fixed on not upsetting majoritarian communal sentiment. It is an unshakeable, even sacred, article of faith, which rises above all immediate electoral considerations.

Remembering Hashimpura and Muzaffarnagar in the Uttar Pradesh of Yogi Adityanath and the India of Modi and Amit Shah, I suggest that the people of India find themselves in the present dangerous moment of history not only because of the openly communal politics of the RSS and BJP, through the Partition riots and the innumerable fires of communal hatred that followed, through the movements for the Ram Mandir and cow protection, through their systematic manufacture of hatred against India's Muslims and Christians. At least equal culpability lies with the parties which describe themselves as secular, but for whom secularism is not their central organising principle, an idea higher than any immediate considerations of electoral victory. On the contrary, after Nehru, the default mode of most such parties has been majoritarian. It is Hindu communal sentiment to which they have consistently pandered. It is under Congress governments that most major communal conflagrations have occurred, including the largest massacres of Nellie in 1983 and the Sikh massacre in Delhi in 1984. It is true that most judicial commissions and citizen tribunals have pointed to the central role in these communal riots to the RSS for fomenting hate against minorities and organising the attacks on them. But they could not have succeeded unless they were supported by the state, its politicians, its officials and its police. Rai is right that Hashimpura was not an aberration. It is under Congress governments that the perpetrators of communal violence and the organisers from communal organisations were assured immunity from punishment. It is under Congress governments that most laws criminalising cow slaughter were passed. It is under Congress governments that the idols of Ram were surreptitiously introduced into the Babri mosque in Ayodhya and the locks to the Ram Temple were opened to permit worship. It was on the watch of Congress governments that the Babri Masjid was demolished and a makeshift Ram temple built in its place.

When I say that every government was majoritarian, I underline that these governments did not respect Hindu sentiment but Hindu *communal* sentiment. These are not the same thing, although the unstated (and unjust) assumption is that most Hindus are communal and anti- Muslim and anti-Christian under their skins; therefore if governments were actually to adhere uncompromisingly to principled secular democracy as mandated in the country's constitution, they would anger the Hindu voter who is assumed to be the communal by default. This cynical calculus resulted in a long and disgraceful history of betrayals by successive governments – Congress, socialist, Bahujan, and to a lesser extent even at times communist. Betrayals of the constitution and law, of the country's minorities but also of the country's large liberal populations, of people who follow every – or no – religious persuasion in the country but are committed to equal rights, citizenship and protection of the law of people of all faiths, castes and gender.

The manner in which Mamata Banerjee, Chief Minister dealt with communal violence in Bengal in Basirhat in July 2017 – one of the very few communal conflagrations that was ignited by minority (read Muslim) communalism rather than majority communalism – was by being soft on reactionary elements of Muslim communalists. This is a textbook example of what secular politics is *not*.[11] A young teenager posted an offensive post on Facebook of Prophet Mohammed. Muslim mobs went on a rampage for a couple of days, attacking Hindus and burning their properties. The state government could have prevented the violence, but was weak-kneed in its response. As commentator Shamshul Islam observes, 'The mobs, which roamed freely, attacking their victims and destroying their property for a couple of days, claimed that they were doing so to save the honour of Islam. The honour of Islam seemed to be so shallow and vulnerable that a Facebook post would destroy it.'[12] The RSS and its functionaries also had a field day, using the social media to pose a range of fake news photographs, including an image from a Bhojpuri film of a rape, claiming that this was from Barishat, and also images of attacks from the 2002 Gujarat carnage and Bangladesh.[13]

Muslims constitute a significant 27 percent of the Bengali electorate.[14] Traditionally they voted for the Left Front. With the weakening clout of the Left in West Bengal, Mamata tried to woo them not with actual programmes to assist them to fight their poverty, poor education and poor heath indices. Her government announced measures like stipends for imams and free land and education for the children of these imams; and distributing sugar through the PDS during Ramzan. Hoardings of the Chief Minister with head covered and hands raised in prayer like a devout Muslim appeared in Kolkata. As Sabir Ahmed, a senior researcher at Pratichi Institute said to Indian Express, this is not what the Bengali Muslim needs or wants. The Muslims of Bengal continue to be among the poorest in the state, he says. 'If you see the figures, you will know that Muslims are still among the lowest wage-earners, the most trafficked victims, with dismal access to education, especially higher education. Their presence in government jobs also remains poor... We want proper education, participation in governance, employment, higher education, among others.'

11 See Apoorvanand, "Mamata's Opportunism and the BJP's Communalism are Pushing Bengal to the Edge", *The Wire,* 8 July 2017. Available at https://thewire.in/communalism/mamata-basirhat-muslim-hindu

12 See Shamsul Islam, "Competing communalisms", *The Indian Express*, 11 July 2017. Available at http://indianexpress.com/article/opinion/columns/west-bengal-violence-basirhat-facebook-hindu-muslim-communal-hindutva-west-bengal-4744763/

13 M Reyaz, "Basirhat riot: Why Bengal is different and why it still gives hope", *Daily O*, 8 July 2017. Available at https://www.dailyo.in/politics/bengal-basirhat-riot-communal-polarisation-bjp-rss-fake-news-mamata-tmc/story/1/18253.html. Also see Sam Jawed, "Basirhat riots – the vicious cycle of fake images", 7 July 2017. Available at https://www.kractivist.org/basirhat-riots-the-vicious-cycle-of-fake-images/

14 Esha Roy, "Almost 80% of rural Muslims in West Bengal are borderline poor: Report", *The Indian Express*, 15 February 2016. Available at http://indianexpress.com/article/cities/kolkata/80-rural-muslims-near-poverty-report/

The BJP is quick to describe the policies of the Trinamul government to be 'appeasement' of the Muslims. But the truth is that these appease communal elements of the community, not the people at large. Indeed all political parties, including so-called secular parties, have indeed followed a consistent policy of 'appeasement', but this is not the appeasement of minorities as alleged by the BJP. It is an appeasement of communal elements of both the majority and minority community. It is this appeasement of communal Muslims when even Sonia Gandhi goes to the Shahi Imam of Jama Masjid to seek Muslim votes for the Congress, as though Muslim people are sheep who follow the dicates of this disreputable cleric. The BJP only differs in restricting and exponentially enlarging its appeasement to only majority communalism. Sabir Ahmed is correct in observing that these policies do nothing to benefit the suffering people of the oppressed communities. 'All these populist measures have created a rift among Hindus and Muslims of Bengal,' he says.

※

Ironically the cynical policy of tacit soft-Hindutva (and occasional soft-on-Muslim-fundamentalism) has also proved suicidal electorally for these 'secular' parties. The near-terminal decline of the Congress in Uttar Pradesh and Bihar can be traced from precisely the period, especially since the mid-1980s, when it most dangerously compromised with its secular foundational principles, and most openly pandered to majoritarian and minority communal sentiment. From being the dominant political force in Uttar Pradesh and Bihar, it was reduced to fourth or fifth position, a pathetic after-ran scrambling for scraps, and there is little chance that they will revive their old standing unless they ever go back to their authentically secular roots of Mahatma Gandhi and Nehru. The policies of secularism cannot be practiced with one eye on the constitution and the other on the ballot-box. I tried to reason with senior leaders of the Congress whenever they were willing to hear me – which is not very often – that policies that are ethically right will also prove ultimately to be politically sound. This is a lesson the senior leaders of these parties refuse to learn. After the 2014 electoral debacle of the Congress, one of its senior leaders said to me: 'The trouble with the Congress is that we have done too much for the minorities and the poor. We need to change track if we are to return to power: for this we must now concentrate on the Hindus and the middle-class.' I replied, 'I wish it was true that the Congress had actually stood resolutely with the country's minorities and its poor. It would not have found itself in the humiliating situation that it finds itself today. The problem with the Congress is not that it has done too much for the country's minorities and it's poor but that it has done too little.' If the Hindu voter is communal, why should he vote for the Congress and not for the BJP which has always been open about its majoritarian politics? And if she is liberal and secular, or is from the ranks of the country's religious minorities, why should she have faith in the Congress which is notoriously weak-kneed and duplicitous about its professed secular ideals?

Apoorvanand observes, 'No political party in India, not even those who swear by secularism, has the courage any longer to call the murders (by lynching) by their name, to say that Muslims are being killed because they are Muslims. Various kinds of intellectual detours are being taken by politicians and, regrettably, by a section of the media in their nightly 'debates'. It is said that mobs are 'spontaneously' attacking Muslims, or that the violence was a case of 'mistaken identity', that the violence was an expression of 'legitimate historical anger' that took an 'unfortunate' turn. But no political party has the guts and honesty to say that these killings and assaults are *not* spontaneous, that a long, well-planned, cynical hate campaign is behind the formation of these lynch mobs. Nobody asks how is it that cutting across the linguistic and cultural diversity of India, it is a Muslim who gets identified and attacked everywhere. The harsh fact is that India's legislators and parliamentarians seem to have deserted the country's Muslims. The killing and brutalisation of Muslims fails to interrupt the routine business of our legislatures.'[15]

In all of this, the short end of the stick is borne by India's Muslim and Christian citizens. The 'secular' political parties believe that they are captive voters to them, held in permanent hostage by their dread of the BJP and the RSS. They need to actually deliver nothing to them, as they have nowhere else to go. The parties need to worry instead about the Hindu – and increasingly the Dalit – voter, but not the Muslims (and Christians except in Kerala and the north-east). And they make the same unjust assumptions about the sympathies of the 'Muslim voter' as they do about the 'Hindu voter'. Just as they assume that most Hindus as instinctively communal, they assume that most Muslims are like sheep led by their most regressive and backward-looking communal clerics. This homogenised Muslim voter who votes en masse in the thrall and on the directions of Muslim religious leaders is as

---

15 Apoorvanand, "Muslims Must Refuse To Be Killed", *The Wire,* 9 April 2017. Available at https://thewire.in/politics/muslims-must-refuse-killed-cow-beef

much a myth as the uniformly communally inclined Hindu voter. Come election time, and the leaders of 'secular' political parties all line up for photo-ops with bearded Muslim clerics who are voluble in their opposition to women's rights, and are indifferent to the real concerns of poor and low caste Muslims of the most developmentally disadvantaged populations in India – of education, public services, and jobs. When the Supreme Court during its summer recess in 2017 was hearing petitions to ban triple talaq or a verbal divorce by Muslim men in one sitting, the regressive and patriarchal Muslim Personal Law Board was represented by one of the best known faces in the senior Congress leadership, Kapil Sibal, who argued that matters of religious belief – in which he included both triple talaq and the Ram Temple in Ayodhya – are beyond court intervention. Kapil Sibal is generally progressive, and to see him pander to both Muslim and Hindu communal politics in one of the most closely-watched court proceedings in the country, only helped reconfirm the bankrupt politics of the Congress in recent decades, and underline the long way it has travelled from the secularism of Gandhi and Nehru.

All of this only further fuels Hindu resentment – among communal but even relatively moderate Hindus – against the 'appeasement of the Muslims'. Government after government has done nothing to assist and give their due to, let alone 'appease' the country's minorities. Each have appeased only communal sentiments of both Hindus and Muslims. No wonder that a section of Muslim voters have decided to vote for the BJP. They argue: If every party is communal, then why should we support the parties that claim to defend us but always betray us? Let us give the BJP a chance – at least it is honest to its brand of politics.

To say all that I have here about the multiple and unconscionable treacheries of 'secular' parties is still not to subscribe to the idea of the equivalence between the BJP and other political parties that claim faithlessly to be secular. I often hear friends say – 'what is there to choose between the BJP and parties like the Congress and the various socialist parties of Uttar Pradesh and Bihar or the Trinamul Congress in Bengal?' It is true that these parties have failed the secular idea and democracy, but they are still not simply the other side of the same coin as the BJP. A party whose stated ideology is pluralist, progressive and inclusive but whose everyday practice is disloyal to its creed is still one that can be challenged, held to account, fought and hopefully reformed. It still contains spaces for dissent and advancement. This differs from a majoritarian party wedded to the ideology of the RSS, which in turn is openly committed to the establishment of a Hindu Rashtra[16]. And the greatest danger to India's constitutionalism is not even from the muscular body of the BJP but from its soul – the RSS. An alliance of parties like those that joined hands in Bihar in the 2016 elections (only to have one of the two main parties walking out and cynically joining hands with the BJP to form a government with them in defiance of the electoral mandate) may defeat the BJP in 2019. But the real battle is not against the BJP, it is not even against Modi and Amit Shah. I believe that the battle of liberal, constitutional, republican Indians is against extremist ideologies of Hindu nationalism (rather than a humane, inclusive nationalism) that in effect seek to reduce India's minorities to second class citizens, and to crush dissent.

Our large 'secular' political opposition has betrayed us profoundly, and the people if India are paying the cost. The hot winds of communal hatred of the past three years can be expected to grow now into a blinding sandstorm.

It is ordinary people who must act as the opposition. The decisive battle for India's future will not be won, or even fought, merely in the hustings. It will be fought and won – ultimately – in the hearts and minds of its people.

16 http://rss.org//Encyc/2012/10/22/rss-vision-and-mission.html

CHAPTER NINE

'Anti-National' Conversions

It is a difficult time to be both Muslim and Christian in the India engineered by majoritarian politics. In the week leading up to India's seventieth anniversary of freedom in Augist 2017, a high constitutional functionary thought it fit to issue a stinging message to tame and intimidate a small religious minority, the Christians, comprising 4 percent of the population of Jharkhand state (in which a little over a quarter of the population is tribal). This was a front-page advertisement in most newspapers of Jharkhand on August 11, 2017, funded by the Government of Jharkhand, with a picture of a beatifically smiling Mahatma Gandhi, and a poisonous quote attributed to him, attacking Christian missionaries. The quote is: 'If Christian missionaries feel that only conversion to Christianity is the path to salvation, why don't you start with me or (my secretary) Mahadev Desai? Why do you stress on conversion of the simple, illiterate, poor and forest-dwellers? These people can't differentiate between Jesus and Mohammad and are not likely to understand your preachings. They are mute and simple, like cows. These simple, poor, Dalit and forest-dwellers, whom you make Christians, do so not for Jesus but for rice and their stomach.' On the same page is a picture of Chief Minister of Jharkhand, Raghuvar Das.

By sheer coincidence, I was in Jharkhand the day this advertisement appeared. An even greater coincidence was that I had accepted that morning an invitation to speak to a congregation of Christian nuns from all across India on the theme 'The Idea of India'. In the tea-break mid-morning in the middle of my lecture, several nuns came to be with copies of the newspapers, speaking in low voices of their anguish and helpless anger at what they saw as clearly an open official malicious attack on the people of their faith.

The central issue is not whether Gandhiji in fact made this statement or not. Apoorvanand, in an erudite article in The Wire, establishes that the quote from 1936 is a partial distortion and was deliberately pulled out of context. The larger context in which Gandhi made his observations, as Apoorvanand explains, was Gandhi's anti-untouchability temple-entry movement juxtaposed against Ambedkar's ringing call for fifty million Hindu untouchables to convert to an egalitarian religion like Sikhism, Islam or Christianity. Gandhi believed that untouchability is a distortion of Hinduism and sought to reform Hinduism, whereas Ambedkar was convinced that it is intrinsic to Hinduism and that therefore Hinduism is beyond reform. This is a debate that continues until the present day. Gandhi said some of the words attributed to him against this background in a debate with a Christian evangelist. He spoke indefensibly of Dalits being simple-mined like cows, but not Adivasis. Gandhi was not opposed to conversions if they arose from personal faith, but not as a political instrument. Even with these caveats, I am entirely at odds with Gandhi's views in this debate. Gandhi was a devout practising Hindu, was opposed to cow slaughter, and felt that caste inequality and discrimination were not an essential path of Hindu teachings. I am none of these, and on all these issues, I find myself much closer to Ambedkar's teachings.

But at the same time, taking a more expansive and comprehensive view of the life, teachings and practice of Mahatma Gandhi, I believe that there is no leader who better embodies the humanist spirit of secularism as imagined in our Constitution of equal respect for every faith than Mahatma Gandhi. A man sympathetic to the ideology of the RSS took his life for precisely this reason. Today it is a tragedy (and not merely a farce) to witness a political party that is wedded to the ideology of the same RSS trying to reinvent Gandhi as a mascot of hatred and intolerance against minorities.

And what is relevant here is not what Gandhi did or did not say about conversions, then or later. What is relevant is the Constitution. The Constitution defends the right of all Indian citizens to not just practice but also propagate their faith and beliefs. As Apoorvanand observes, it would be a different matter if the RSS had issued this advertisement. But this advertisement was issued, using public funds, by the elected state government, to openly foster hatred and division among the tribal communities and against the tribal Christian community and their priests and missionaries. It is a transgression of the Constitution by a constitutional functionary, and a hate crime under the law of the land.

Significantly, just a day after the advertisement appeared on the front pages of all Ranchi newspapers, the Jharkhand state cabinet approved an anti-conversion bill, which contains severe penalties for conversion through allurement or coercion. In characteristic double-speak, this bill has been called the Religious Freedom Bill, 2017. It provides for a minimum jail term of three years and/or a fine of 50,000 rupees, or both, for persons found guilty of converting people through allurement or coercion. In the case of a minor girl belonging to Scheduled Caste or Scheduled Tribe being converted, the punishment will extend to four years in prison and/or 1 lakh rupees, or both.

The Jharkhand state BJP spokesperson Pratul Shahdev said to the Indian Express in glowing defence of the Bill: 'Forces out to disintegrate the society have been indulging in conversions over a long time. It is good that the Bill envisages tougher punishment for those involved in converting the members of the SC/ST community.' He significantly added that even Mahatma Gandhi was not in favour of allowing conversion through allurement or coercion.[1]

The RSS and BJP view the conversions of Adivasis only to Christianity as covered by this Bill, but have a completely opposite view of the Hinduisation of the Adivasis, which they do not regard to be conversions (whether by fraud or allurement or without these). The traditional Sarna faith of the Adivasis is in fact not Hindu.[2] Ashok Bhagat of the RSS backed organisation Vikar Bharati said to the Indian Express that Sarnas are close to Hindus, arging: 'They worship nature, Hindus too worship nature.'[3] Sarnas constitute 12.84 per cent of the population of Jharkhand, whereas Christians are 4.3 per cent (according to the 2011 census). The same tribal families may have adherents to the Sarna faith traditions, Christians and people who worship Hanuman and Ram. The danger of a draconian anti-conversion law will be that it will divide tribal communities, even families, and in the end the BJP hopes to reap a rich electoral harvest from the hostility it is fostering against its small, peaceful Christian minority.

The hostility of the RSS and its affiliates to the Christian minorities has a long history. But the state government has openly declared war against them by recruiting Mahatma Gandhi as their talisman for this battle. The proposed anti-conversion law in Jharkhand has fostered enormous disquiet

---

1 Prashant Pandey, "Jharkhand cabinet approves anti-conversion bill; to be introduced in state Assembly this month", *The Indian Express*, 1 August 2017. Available at http://indianexpress.com/article/india/jharkhand-cabinet-approves-anti-conversion-bill-to-be-introduced-in-state-assembly-this-month-4777587/

2 See Saurav Roy, "Sarna a different religion from Hinduism, say tribal outfits", *Hindustan Times*, 1 September 2015. Available at https://www.pressreader.com/india/hindustan-times-jalandhar/20150901/281947426612625. See also Hansda Sowvendra Shekhar (2017), "Sarna-Hindu Theology: A Study of Some Cults, Gods and Worship in Jharkhand", *The Apollonian*, Vol 4, Nos. 1-2, pp. 94-106.

3 See Rajiv Singh, "RSS vs Church: How tribals in Jharkhand are being seen as potential leaders", *The Economic Times*, 19 November 2017. Available at https://economictimes.indiatimes.com/news/politics-and-nation/rss-vs-church-how-tribals-in-jharkhand-are-being-seen-as-potential-leaders/articleshow/61704979.cms

among Christian people everywhere in India. The BJP-RSS combine has long spoken to its Christian minorities with a forked tongue. The RSS regards Christianity to be a 'foreign' religion, and therefore its adherents worthy only of second-class citizenship.

Yet there are many states in India in which they form a majority or significant sections of the population, especially states in north-east India and Kerala. These are states in which the BJP nurtures towering ambitions to advance their political juggernaut to ensure nation-wide dominance. Attacks on Christian minorities also spark greater condemnation than attacks on Muslims by governments in North America and Europe whose opinion matters most to the ruling BJP-led government. This requires tactical alliances with Christian community leaders in some parts of India, such as Kerala and north-eastern states. One of the most horrific incidents of lynching – because it involved a mob breaking into a jail and pulling out a Muslim man accused of rape from the jail, stripping and brutally lynching him – occurred in Christian majority Nagaland.[4] The Catholic Church in Kerala was one of the early agencies that make the fanciful but dangerous charge of love jihad as a conspiracy by Muslim youth to 'entice' and convert Christian girls.[5]

But particularly in large tribal states of central India like Jharkhand, Odisha and Chhatisgarh, the political strategy of choice has been to target, defame and intimidate the Christian minorities, with violence against Christian shrines, priests, nuns and women, and with laws that criminalise conversions to Christianity.

The first years after Modi's election to the office of Prime Minister was scarred with a rash of attacks on Christian places of worship and priests and nuns, which resulted in international criticism. But these have not ended. In 2014, faith-based rights agencies recorded over 147 incidents where Christians were targeted, with many more going unrecorded[6]. The states of Karnataka, Madhya Pradesh and Chhattisgarh have recorded the most number of attacks in the past two years. The Evangelical Fellowship of India has recorded as many as 177 such cases in 2015. This includes physical violence, stopping

4   "India suspects charged over Nagaland mob lynching", *BBC News*, 9 March 2015. Available at http://www.bbc.com/news/world-asia-india-31792402
5   Naveen Nair, "The BJP and the Church find common ground on 'love jihad' in Kerala", *Hindustan Times*, 17 July 2017. Available at https://www.hindustantimes.com/india-news/the-bjp-and-the-church-find-common-ground-on-love-jihad-in-kerala/story-krCpAE2YLaxTLxLZuXAnhJ.html
6   'Hate and Targeted Violence against Christians in India – Report 2014, available at http://us8.campaign-archive1.com/?u=d85671af78bbf54876608a2de&id=e95d57b851

of worship in churches, attacks on churches, arrests of pastors and their companions, and rapes of nuns.[7] There were over 100 incidents across the country in the period of January-July, 2016. Another very common phenomenon is the social boycott being experienced by Christians in several parts of the country; local panchayats are also known to have imposed fines on Christians for practising their faith.

Christian advocacy groups have compiled several such incidents. In June 2016, a Catholic priest was brutally attacked with a machete in the state of Assam's Udalguri district.[8] In April 2016, an armed mob attacked a church in Parpa, in Chhattisgarh, set the Bible on fire and severely assaulted the pastor.[9] In March 2016, near the capital city of of Raipur, Chhattisgarh, a mob of more than 15 men, vandalized a prayer hall that served as a church, while a prayer meeting was in progress.[10] In March 2016, a church was vandalized in Coimbatore, Tamil Nadu.[11] In April 2015, a church in Agra, state of Uttar Pradesh, was vandalized and the idol of Mother Mary damaged.[12]

Women were particularly subject to sexualised hate crimes. There is an increasing number of rapes and sexual assaults on Catholic nuns and Christian women. Catholic nuns are attacked deliberately to teach a lesson to, shame and intimidate the Christian community in India, and to force it to a subservient status in Indian society. The UN Special Rapporteur for Violence against Women, after her country visit to India in 2014, also recommended to the Indian government: 'Numerous testimonies shared on recurrent episodes of communal violence against religious minorities, including Muslims and Christians, reflect a deep sense of insecurity and trauma of women living in those communities. Experiences included women being stripped, burned,

---

7 'Hate and Targeted Violence Against Christians in India', Report 2015, available at http://www.efion-line.org/the-news/persecution/645-efi-annual-persecution-report-2015
8 'Catholic Priest Injured in Machete Attack in Assam', *Hindustan Times,* 21 June 2016, available at http://www.hindustantimes.com/india-news/catholic-priest-injured-in-machete-attack-in-assam/story-6KMKz6jYelpV5Wu9eomM8N.html
9 'Armed Men Attack Chhattisgarh Church, Set Afire Bible, Thrash Pastor', *The Indian Express,* 19 April 2016, available at http://indianexpress.com/article/india/india-news-india/chhattisgarh-church-attack-armed-men-set-afire-bible-2760376/
10 'Mob Vandalises Church in Chhattisgarh', *The Indian Express,* 8 March 2016, available at http://indianexpress.com/article/india/india-news-india/bajrang-dal-men-allegedly-vandalised-church-in-chhattisgarh-five-injured/
11 5 Hindu Outfit Members Held for Vandalising Church in Coimbatore, *Indian Express,* 14 March 2016, available at http://www.newindianexpress.com/states/tamil_nadu/5-Hindu-Outfit-Members-Held-for-Vandalising-Church-in-Coimbatore/2016/03/14/article3326118.ece
12 'Agra Church Vandalised, Mother Mary Idol Damaged', *Hindustan Times,* 17 April 2015, available at http://www.hindustantimes.com/india/agra-church-vandalised-mother-mary-idol-damaged/story-MhXgo9FrWuMogcoa0RGyCO.html,

attacked with objects inserted into their vaginas and sexually assaulted in myriad ways because of their religious identity.[13]

Among the incidents compiled by Christian groups, in March 2015, a 71 year old nun who worked with the Convent of Jesus and Mary in Ranaghat town, close to Kolkata, state of West Bengal, was gang raped by dacoits, who also desecrated the chapel.[14] Surendra Jain, the general secretary of the Hindu right-wing Vishva Hindu Parishad (VHP) retorted: "It is a Christian culture to exploit nuns. We don't do such things."[15] In June 2015, a 48 year old nun in Kerala was gang raped at a nursing home where she was working, in Raipur, Chhattisgarh. She was found semi-clad, unconscious, with her hands tied, and bleeding. Two masked men entered her room, purportedly to in search of cash and valuables, and sexually assaulted her. Rs. 25000 cash was found in her cupboard, indicating that the attackers had clearly intended to sexually assault her.[16] No arrests took place even after two months of the incident.

Apart from such attacks, on July 2014, in Bastar, state of Chhattisgarh, 50 villages, through an order from their village councils, banned entry to non-Hindu missionaries, especially Christians, due to an aggressive campaign by VHP.[17]

But the gravest threat is posed by the anti-conversion laws. Members of the Constituent Assembly took great care to uphold the freedom of religious belief in India's Constitution. After extended debate, it decided that this freedom should not just be to practice and profess one's faith, but also to propagate it. KM Munshi declared that 'under freedom of speech which the Constitution guarantees, it will be open to any religious community to persuade other people to join their faith.'

However, Hindu nationalist organisations never reconciled to this fundamental guarantee of the Constitution. Their resistance derives from the larger running narrative of the RSS that the Hindu majority is persecuted

13 A/HRC/26/38/Add.1

14 'Rape of Elderly Nun Sparks Outrage in West Bengal', *The Hindu*, 14 March 2015, available at http://www.thehindu.com/news/cities/kolkata/nun-gangraped-in-west-bengals-nadia-district/article6993607.ece

15 'VHP Defends Attack on Haryana Church, Says Rape of Nuns is "Christian Culture", *Daily News & Analysis*, 17 March 2015, available at http://www.dnaindia.com/india/report-vhp-defends-attack-on-haryana-church-says-rape-of-nuns-is-christian-culture-2069494

16 'Nun Sexually Assaulted at Medical Centre in Raipur', *The Times of India*, 21 June 2015, available at http://timesofindia.indiatimes.com/city/raipur/Nun-sexually-assaulted-at-medical-centre-in-Raipur/articleshow/47753184.cms

17 'In Bastar, 50 Villages Ban Non-Hindu Missionaries', *The Hindu*, 5 July 2014, available at http://www.thehindu.com/news/national/in-bastar-50-villages-ban-nonhindu-missionaries/article6180825.ece

in 'their own country', by its minorities and political parties that are wanting in true nationalism that seek election by pandering to the minorities. The alleged threats they inventory from Muslim minorities are many, as have seen: historic violence and persecution, support for terror, reproductive excesses and sexual marauding. Against Christians, the single threat they speak of is of being erased by religious conversions based on 'falsehoods' and 'bribes' misleading 'innocent' tribals funded by big foreign money. It matters little that the facts don't bear out claims of the 'menace' of mass conversions. Christians constituted 2.5 percent of India's population in 1981, and 2.3 in 1991, 2001 and 2011. If large-scale conversions were indeed occurring, their numbers would have swelled. But when have hate propagandists been deterred by incompatible truths? This sustained misinformation has resulted in profound and sometimes violent schisms between Christian and other tribal people, and rich electoral harvests for the BJP.

After the gruesome burning alive of a Christian missionary and his sons in Odisha in 1999, Prime Minister Vajpayee with his masterly ambivalence, called for a national debate on conversions. The same discourse has surfaced with more open stridency after the ascendancy of the new government in Delhi in 2014. There is an open call for a national law banning religious conversions, in direct violation of the letter and spirit of the constitution.

Their contention of the RSS is that Hinduism is denied a level playing field for conversions because enormous overseas funds support the work of Christian missionaries. But the truth is that there is no shortage of resources for the RSS and its associate organisations, with the Indian diaspora funding for the work of these organisations in tribal India. A massive network of tribal educational institutions of the RSS family have grown in central India, and penetration of the north-east is significant. All of this is yielding rich electoral dividends to the BJP.

The real problem is that few can match the selfless quality of educational and health services which Christian missionaries offer, even to most despised and excluded peoples like leprosy patients. The even greater problem is the ritualised and religiously sanctioned inequality of caste inherent to the Hindu faith, which renders egalitarian faiths like Islam, Christianity and Buddhism attractive to those enduring caste violence and discrimination at the lowest rungs of the Hindu social hierarchy. TT Krishnamachari, Constituent Assembly member, remarked presciently that conversion 'depends on the way certain religionists and certain communities treat their less fortunate brethren.' The large majority of converts to egalitarian faiths are, not surprisingly, from the lowest Hindu castes, stirred by hopes of greater social dignity and the opportunities to study and escape socially humiliating caste liveli-hoods. It is their on-going collective tragedy that even Islam and Christianity in India have absorbed ideas of caste, therefore their journey to social equality continues to be hamstrung by old walls of caste.

But it must be stressed that Jharkhand will not be the first government to pass an anti-conversion law if this is voted for by the state assembly. Eight state governments have passed such laws since Independence, and in five states these are in force. Anti-conversion laws were passed in Orissa in 1967 under a Swatantra Party government; in Madhya Pradesh in 1968 under the Samyukta Vidhayak Dal coalition (which included the Jan Sangh); and in Gujarat in 2003 and Chhattisgarh in 2006 under BJP governments. The Jayalalitha government in Tamil Nadu passed the law in 2002 but repealed it in two years after its passage in 2004. The only Congress government to pass such a law was in Himachal in 2006. Rajasthan passed an anti-conversion law in 2006, again under the BJP, but the Governor refused to sign the law. Arunachal passed such a law in 1978 under the People's Party of Arunachal, but it was never enforced as rules have not been framed to date.

These laws criminalise religious conversions by what is described as force, inducement or fraud. The peril is that these terms could be expansively interpreted. Force could for instance include the threat of divine retribution, fraud the promise of rewards in an after-life, and inducement free services in school or hospital. Impoverished new converts and priests have actually been jailed under these clauses, and punishment can extend to three or five years. Prior permission of the District Magistrate is also required in some states, and whereas applications for conversion out of Hinduism are withheld for years, these are promptly given for conversions into Hinduism. The even greater problem is that Hindu nationalists and even officials assume erroneously that those Adivasi people who adhere to their traditional animist faiths are also Hindu. There is aggressive penetration of Hindu gods, forms of worship, and Brahmanical practices like abjuring meat, but these are not interpreted to be attempts at religious conversion, and therefore do not attract the stringent prescriptions and penalties of the law.

Criminalising religious faith carries grave dangers both for religious free-doms and minorities, especially in an aggressively majoritarian climate such as one which has risen today. It can reduce minorities into fear and submission in the way blasphemy laws have done in Pakistan. In this divisive competi-tion for the religious allegiance of India's poorest and most vulnerable people, marked by stridency and hate, it is important to recall the gentle counsel of one of the world's tallest public figures, the Dalai Lama. 'It does not matter which God you worship,' he declares, 'or even if you worship no God. What is important is to be a compassionate human being.'

CHAPTER TEN

Communal Violence, Lynching and Counterfeit Peace

Hate lynching is growing into a national scourge. More and more people today feel free, emboldened, even encouraged to violently act out their prejudices and hate as they find enabling climate for hate speech and violence-fostered and legitimised by our political leadership and a wider majoritarian social climate. Lynching is fast becoming the new normal in these times of orchestrated hate and rage that we live in in India.[1] The targets of furious and public bloodletting as have seen are most often Muslims, but Dalits are also in danger. From time to time hate violence also spills over to people of colour especially African nationals, and ethnic minorities particularly people from India's north-east. (Christians, as we have also seen, are subdued not but lynching but by attacking Christian shrines, nuns and priests).

The seemingly dispersed lynch attacks may be sparked variously by disputes over something even as trivial as a seat in an unreserved train compartment, or allegations of cow smuggling or slaughter, or carrying, cooking or eating cow meat, or rumours of cattle theft or child kidnapping, or charges of sex work and drug-trafficking. But make no mistake: these are targeted hate attacks. Whatever the ostensible trigger, murderous mobs gather to lynch people of hated identities often to death. These assaults are also characterised by crowds of bystanders who either actively support the killing, or do nothing to stop the strikes or to save the innocent victims.

The political response to these attacks also tends to follow a set pattern. The Prime Minister and BJP Chief Ministers mostly do not condemn the attacks, even less express sympathy with the victims. The Prime Minister does occasionally condemn the mob attacks, but well after they occur, in general terms, refusing to describe these as hate crimes, never expressing sympathy

---

1 "The New Indian Normal: Mob Violence and Lynching", *Sabrang India,* 17 May 2017. Available at https://www.sabrangindia.in/article/new-indian-normal-mob-violence-and-lynching

with the victims of these attacks, and not ensuring even in BJP-ruled states (where the majority of lynch attacks have occurred) that the men accused of these hate crimes are caught and punished. If he actually did not want these attacks to recur, or indeed for hate speech against minorities to end, he has the power and the reach to ensure that these end. His condemnation is more convincing when the victims are Dalits, never when they are Muslim.

Senior ministers and elected representatives come out in open defence of the attackers, charging the victims with crimes that provoke the attacks. The innuendo is that the victim, or at least the community to which he belongs and therefore the victim, is somehow guilty and the violence therefore understandable, even if regrettable. The police tends in most such instances to be absent or partisan. They come in too late to save lives, and very often register crimes against the victims and drag their feet to charge and arrest the attackers. On occasion, they are present even as the slaughter of innocents unfolds but still don't act, pleading later that they were outnumbered.

The main opposition parties especially the Congress are timid and equivocal in their opposition, especially when the victims are Muslim, as though they are afraid to be counted as standing with the targets of hate attacks: in abject and disgraceful fear of a majoritarian Hindu backlash. It is only the left parties that sometimes reach out in solidarity with the victims.

Many commentators suggest that lynching is not new, and hate attacks targeting minorities and Dalits have a long history in India. Are we then deliberately taking lynching out of context, ignoring mass communal violence and caste atrocities that have recurred in newly independent India since the bloody Partition riots of 1947? Some suggest that this is being done to discredit the government led by Narendra Modi.

There is no doubt that mass communal and caste violence have long targeted religious minorities and Dalits. But we need to understand what makes the present phase of lynching distinct. Communal violence in particular, however severe and lethal, is still bound by geography and time. A tempest of targeted hate hits a specified minority in a particular location, destroys lives, homes and livelihoods, but then it in time it passes. The numbers of persons injured and killed by lynching maybe much smaller than in many major communal violence episodes. (It is too early to confirm this conclusively, though, because a large number of lynch attacks are not acknowledged or recorded and these continue right through the time I am writing this book). But the social, political and psychological impact of lynching, when it becomes commonplace, is to make *every* person of the targeted community feel vulnerable at all times. Muslims in every corner of India that I visit tell me that at the back of their hearts a fear is now firmly lodged, an unspoken dread that they can be attacked anywhere – in their homes, at work, in a train, on a bus, or in any public place. This is the success of the political project of lynching, to reduce targeted people into a psychology of everyday lived terror. Not all Dalits, but those engaged in caste occupations of skinning animals are learning to live with the same fear. In tribal areas, Christian tribal people have been reduced to similar dread, not by lynching, but recurring and widespread attacks on Christian places of worship, on nuns and priests.

❁

I have handled many episodes of communal violence as a district administrator, and subsequently carefully studied communal violence in India. These religious bloodbaths are often described as communal riots. Episodes typically constitute targeted hate killings, gang-rapes, arson of homes and businesses, large-scale looting, and destruction and desecration of places of worship. But I have grave reservations with calling these riots, because the word 'riot' suggests that what transpires is that people of two communities battle each other, usually spontaneously. India's Partition did witness massive blood-letting in communal riots. But post-Partition India has seen very few riots; it has seen organised attacks on the country's religious minorities and vulnerable castes. For instance, it is especially a travesty to describe the violence against the Sikhs in Delhi in 1984 as anti-Sikh *riots*, because it was exclusively the Sikhs who were the victims of violence in almost all these attacks. The same is the case with many, if not most, other episodes of communal violence.

All communal 'riots' require first the systematic manufacture hatred against minorities, and then the organising of the logistics of the 'riots'. I use the word 'manufacture' of hatred consciously, because communal organisations like the RSS and its affiliates specialise in actively and malevolently creating hatred between communities who normally live in peace with one another, almost as though in a chemical laboratory or on a factory assembly line. Each large and small incident of communal violence requires the deliberate creation of hate, which builds on hate-inducing images, rumours and stereotypes of the 'other' minority community. The image of the Bengali Muslim as a foreign infiltrator from Bangladesh spurred the incredibly brutal slaughter in Nellie; the Sikh as the unpatriotic sympathiser of Prime Minister Indira Gandhi's assassins fanned the anti-Sikh carnage in 1984; Advani's Rath Yatra fuelled across the country a hateful demonisation of Muslims as temple destroyers, and this was inflamed further by rumours of killing of Hindu students in Bhagalpur in 1989; the same temple destroyers and mafia stereotypes of Muslims were deployed to burn Bombay in 1992-92; the certainty that Muslims deliberately killed women and children in a train compartment burning in Gujarat led to retaliatory violence across large parts of the state in 2002; the credence that Christian missionaries convert hapless people by fraud and bribery kindled Kandhamal in Odisha in 2008; the improbable fiction of love jihad estranged communities in coastal Karnataka from the mid-2000s and burned Muzaffarnagar in 2013; and the old 'foreigner' taboo resulted in attacks on Bengali Muslims in Lower Assam in 2012. The systematic role of organisations like the RSS, VHP and Bajrang Dal has been critical in creating an on-going social climate of revulsion and suspicion against religious minorities around stereotypical themes such as enemies of one's religious faith, terrorists, sexual predators, and forced conversions. These prejudices help create what Ram Punyani describes as an alternative 'social common sense'.[2]

Each of these massacres are sought to be explained, and at least rationalised – if not 'justified' – as spontaneous and understandable public anger among a persecuted majority against minorities because of provocations listed above. But the evidence from each of these riot sites is that none of these major carnages are spontaneous. There is systematic preparation for the conducting of riots including deploying men and vehicles, distributing weapons, bombs and gas cylinders and so on. Commissions of enquiry as well as citizen investigations suggest extensive planning for communal massacres such as in 1984 and 2002, and in many others. Most preparation is by communal organisations, but there is open or tacit support by the state.

Beginning with a communal conflagration in 1961 in Jabalpur, 14 years after India's freedom, many parts of the country have witnessed sporadic episodes of hate violence which victimise people due to their religious identity right up to the present day. There have been periods during which this targeted sectarian violence has spiked, especially since the 1980s, targeting Bengali Muslims in Assam in 1983, the Sikhs in the nation's capital after

2 See Harsh Mander, "The truth about love jihad", *Live Mint*, 16 October 2014, available at http://www.livemint.com/Opinion/LeB6Xvk205tYUq1x0ZW9wL/The-truth-about-love-jihad.html; see also Harsh Mander, "Made in India", *The Hindu*, 1 November 2015, available at http://www.thehindu.com/opinion/columns/Harsh_Mander/made-in-india-by-harsh-mander/article6555269.ece; and see Harsh Mander, "Eight years after Kandhamal violence, justice still evades many", *The Hindu*, 14 September 2016, available at http://www.hindustantimes.com/columns/eight-years-after-kandhamal-justice-still-evades-many/story-Al880zQZ6K9g0GyApXvcEM.html

Prime Minister Indira Gandhi's assassination in 1984 and subsequent years of Khalistani militancy, and Muslims in many parts of India during the Babri Masjid movement since the late 1980s, beginning with the massacre in Bhagalpur in 1989 and peaking in the carnage in Gujarat in the spring of 2002.

While the deliberate manufacture of hatred, the systematic planning if the massacre, and an enabling role of the state are essential elements of every episode of communal violence. I observe three distinct phases in India's troubled history of periodic mass attacks on Muslims and other minorities since India became free in the bloodbath of Hindu-Muslim riots in 1947 that took a million lives.

❋

The first phase of communal violence beginning with Jabalpur in 1961 declines after 1983 (the year which saw the bloody and mostly forgotten Nellie massacre). In this early phase of communal violence, we see more localised and mostly urban communal violence spurred ostensibly by local disputes involving Hindus and Muslims. These local disputes were often connected with places of worship and religious celebrations and processions, including allegations of desecration of these places of worship or provocations such as using loud-speakers to instigate persons of the other community. Disputes typically involved playing of loud music before mosques and temples especially during prayer or festivals, disagreements about routes of religious processions, competing claims on religious places by different communities, desecration of a place of worship, alleged killing of cows – an animal held sacred by Hindus – by Muslims, desecration or disruption of religious congregations including by setting into these animals abhorred by a community (especially by pigs among Muslims), and construction of new mosques or temples.[3]

To take just a few examples, one of the most gruesome riots in this phase was in Ahmedabad, in 1969, memories of which still haunt its survivors and their descendants. This was sparked by a series of disputes over religious congregations and processions. In Jalgaon in 1970, the Rashtriya Utsav Mandal decided to take a procession through a Muslim-dominated area, near an important mosque, which was allowed to continue despite protests by Muslims. The procession passed through, chanting anti-Muslim slogans.

3 Ministry of Home Affairs

In Varanasi, 1977, a Durga Puja procession tried to pass through a Muslim locality that did not wish to allow it for fear of setting a precedent; Muslim residents resisted and a clash followed between both groups which were armed.[4] Many other disputes, beginning with the Jabalpur riots, related to consensual or non-consensual relations between young men and women of different communities, anxieties relating to which have evolved into the idea of love jihad in the new century. Disputes between people of different communities were also often given a communal colour, such as the assault on a member of one community by a member of the other community, quarrels between a tenant of one community with a landlord of the other, commercial rivalry, road accidents involving the members of the two communities, fights among youths (almost always young men) of the two communities, land disputes involving Hindus and Muslims, and clashes between criminal elements of the two communities. Many riots were fanned by rumours of violence planned or instigated by Muslim people. Some were caused by disputes around alleged cow slaughter by Muslims.[5]

It was less common in this phase for non-local causes to fan communal violence, but there were exceptions to this as well: for instance, in Rourkela, Jamshedpur and Calcutta, in 1964, around 2000 people, mostly Muslims were killed as retribution for atrocities committed against Hindus in East Pakistan; likewise the Ranchi and Hatia riots in 1967, according to a Ministry of Home Affairs report, were stirred when news of atrocities committed against Hindus in East Pakistan reached the area.

In these episodes of communal violence – which were largely, as we noted local and urban – a great deal of loss of life and property occurred in both communities – Hindu and Muslim – in successive episodes of communal violence. The 'social common sense' was (and remains in present times) that in most of these 'riots', Muslims were the main instigators and Hindus suffered the greatest losses of life and property. What the Commissions of Enquiry report – and independent scholarship and painstaking documentation by that indefatigable chronicler of communal violence Asghar Ali Engineer and others – reveal is an entirely different story. The majority of the riots were found to be instigated by the RSS and its affiliates, usually by demonising and blaming Muslims for initiating as well as sustaining the violence.

---

4 Violette Graff and Juliette Galonnier, "Hindu-Muslim Communal Riots in India II (1986-2011)", 20 August 2013. Available at http://www.sciencespo.fr/mass-violence-war-massacre-resistance/en/document/hindu-muslim-communal-riots-india-ii-1986-2011
5 Ministry of Home Affairs

And majority of the loss of life was of Muslims, both by mass violence and in police firings, as well as much of the property loss. Vibhuti Narain Rai studied numerous episodes of Hindu-Muslim violence since the 1960s, and basing his claim on official records, has not found a riot in which less than 90 percent of those killed have been Muslims. 'These are official figures and no government on earth would release false data', he says in an interview. In the first post-Partition communal violence in Jabalpur in 1961, all people killed were Muslim (16 – of whom 4 were killed in police firing) and property loss incurred by Hindus was marginal (damage to 4 houses), compared to 156 damaged houses of Muslims.[6] In Rourkela, Jamshedpur and Calcutta, in 1964, 2000 people, mostly Muslims, were killed.[7] Likewise in Ranchi and Hatia in 1967, violence claimed 19 Hindus and 164 Muslims.[8] In Ahmedabad in 1969, about 413 of the 512 persons killed were Muslim;[9] other reports variously estimate fatalities of about 660 or even above 1000[10] in which at least 80 percent of the people killed were Muslim. Out of 6742 buildings destroyed, 6071 were owned by Muslims.[11] In Jalgaon, in 1970, 1 Hindu and 42 Muslims were killed.[12] In Bhiwandi and Jalgaon, in 1970, 120-165 people were killed, of who over 80 per cent were Muslim.[13] In Bhiwandi, almost all material losses amounting to over 33 lakh rupees were borne by Muslims.[14] Sexual violence is also recorded in some of the major episodes.[15]

But the important point about this phase of communal violence is that there were also significant – although notably much smaller – losses of life and property among the Hindu community. This means that Muslims were the much greater victims of violence, but also both fought back and perpetrated much smaller but often not insubstantial amounts of violence against the 'other community'.

....

6 (MHA report).
7 B Rajeshwari (2004), "Communal Riots in India: A Chronology (1947-2003)", Institute of Peace and Conflict Studies.
8 (MHA, AR Desai, 1984)
9 (ref)
10 B Rajeshwari (2004), "Communal Riots in India: A Chronology (1947-2003)", Institute of Peace and Conflict Studies.
11 (AR Desai)
12 B Rajeshwari (2004), "Communal Riots in India: A Chronology (1947-2003)", Institute of Peace and Conflict Studies.
13 (Desai; Violette Graff and Juliette Galonnier, "Hindu-Muslim Communal Riots in India II (1986-2011)", 20 August 2013. Available at http://www.sciencespo.fr/mass-violence-war-massacre-resistance/en/document/hindu-muslim-communal-riots-india-ii-1986-2011
14 (Gupta 2000)
15 It is worth remembering that there was sexual violence in the Ahmedabad riots of 1969 as well, but these are poorly documented. More in Megha Kumar's book *Communalism and Sexual Violence in India* on this.

Two other features of this phase may be also noted. The first is that the Muslims were the only socio-religious minority community to be targeted by hate communal violence in the first quarter-century of communal violence – not Sikhs and Christians. The second is that almost all these 'riots' were urban in character. Urban riots are easier to curb by any administration. But rural riots are much harder to control administratively, because there are limits to the amount of force which can be deployed when riots spill from cities into villages, and from village to village. Also, the rupture in social relations is much more profound in rural riots, because unlike cities where often one does not know even one's neighbour, in villages there are intimate social relations between members of a village, therefore the sense of betrayal when one group of villagers attack another in targeted hate violence runs much deeper.

Although there were far greater losses among Muslims during this phase, police action including firing and arrests tended to mostly target Muslims. In Jabalpur itself, all the deaths in both the riots and the police firing were only of Muslims. In Bhiwandi in 1970, 17 Hindus and 59 Muslims were killed, but 1286 Muslims and 323 Hindus were arrested after the violence. In many instances the police and para-military forces directly killed Muslims: 15 were killed by the PAC in Moradabad in 1980.[16] The Jagan Mohan Reddy Commission report into the Ahmedabad carnage of 1969 noted that the violence appeared to be orchestrated; and that voters' lists were used to identify Muslim households, a chilling prequel to patterns observed in Delhi in 1984 and again in Ahmedabad in 2002.

※

A new phase in communal violence began with the gruesome but mostly forgotten massacre in Nellie in Assam in 1983. In this phase, we see overwhelming losses of life and property among people of the targeted religious minority, and much smaller losses among the majority Hindu community. These are even much less in the nature of riots than in the first phase, but because of the decisive role of state functionaries, are more in the nature of targeted hate massacres of religious minorities, or pogroms.

This phase is characterised by massive slaughters, and even more brutal violence than in the first phase, with extensive targeting of children in places

---

16 B Rajeshwari (2004), "Communal Riots in India: A Chronology (1947-2003)", Institute of Peace and Conflict Studies.

HARSH MANDER

like Nellie and Gujarat, and of women by sexual violence. Other major massacres in this phase are: the anti-Sikh carnage of 1984 in Delhi and other cities, Hashimpura in 1987, Bhagalpur in 1989, Bhopal and many other cities in 1992, Mumbai in 1992-93, and climaxing in Gujarat in 2002.

A committee set up by the Ministry of Home Affairs also observes that the nature of violence changed in the 1980s. It states that in previous decades, violence had been sporadic, spontaneous and short-lived. The report recognizes the Ram Janam Bhoomi movement as a major watershed in communal relations in India, which led to communal mobilization and polarization on an unprecedented scale. Unlike in the first phase of communal violence of the 60s and 70s, the violence is rarely spurred by local disputes. People are attacked due to national issues, such as the anger against Sikhs for the killing of Prime Minister Indira Gandhi and the later wave of Khalistani terrorism, and against Muslims for the alleged history of Muslim rulers destroying Hindu temples which drove the Ram Janam Bhoomi movement. Nellie was a massacre resulting from the anger in Assam against Bengali Muslim immigrants from neighbouring Bangladesh.

Nellie was the first site of violence that resulted in the scale of fatalities characteristic of Phase 2. Attacks on 14 villages resulted – in the space of barely a few hours – in the deaths of 1800 children, women and men, according to official estimates (but unofficial estimates put the number at 3000),[17] and over 2.5 lakh people in this and related violence in the state took shelter in relief camps. This was followed the next year by mass violence targeting Sikhs in the nation's capital, killing more than 3000 persons, in what is probably the largest single episode of communal blood-letting after the riots of Partition. Hashimpura saw massive communal tensions[18] before the cold-blooded execution of 42 young Muslim men by the Provincial Armed Constabulary. Under the protection of the PAC, Hindu crowds looted and burnt Muslim houses in poor localities of Meerut.

Under the leadership of Lal Krishna Advani, the BJP launched a powerful national movement in the late 80s to build a Ram Temple in Ayodhya by

17 Prita Jha (ed. 2014), "On Their Watch: Mass Violence and State Apathy in India", Gurgaon: Three Essays Collective, p. 55.
18 Between April and May, 1987, several incidents involving inflammatory speeches, arson, looting, bomb blasts and murder occurred in different areas of Meerut. Victims were both Hindu and Muslim; panic was created among the Muslim community, by the police, which searched their houses on the pretext of looking for explosives (2 boys suspected of killing a Hindu man, because of burning his shop were executed by the police). A crowd of Muslims gathered also, in response to a speech 'exhorting people to save Islam', which was followed by a 'carnage', when Hindus were murdered, torched and their properties looted and burnt.

demolishing the Babri Mosque there. After this, communal tempers against the Muslim minority rose in the country to levels unmatched since Partition. In the inflamed national climate, many mass communal attacks on Muslims ensued, the largest of which was the violence in Bhagalpur, a district in Bihar, which continued intermittently for about six weeks from 24 October 1989, and spread from the town to villages – some of the worst massacres were in fact, in rural areas.[19] Engineer[20] reported that about 896 Muslims and 50 Hindus died; 50-60,000 became refugees. The numbers were likely to be much higher, close to 2000 people, mostly Muslim.[21]

Between 1989 and 1992, as the movement for the Ram Temple gathered steam, the country continued to be wrenched by a series of communal mass attacks. The triumphal demolition of the Babri mosque in 1992 by a massive rampaging mob led by BJP leaders like Advani was then followed by another frenzy of communal blood-letting in many parts of the country. The worst episode was in Bombay, in which the Srikrishna Committee confirmed that the majority of the estimated 600 deaths was of Muslims, and a great part of these killings were in police firings. Bhopal also saw around 143 persons killed, and 30,000 people displaced, again mostly Muslims, both slum dwellers and middle class residents of the BHEL township. Within two weeks of the destruction of the mosque, 227 were killed in Gujarat, 250 in Maharashtra, 55 in Karnataka, 14 in Kerala, 42 in Delhi, 185 in Uttar Pradesh, 100 in Assam, 43 in Bihar, 100 in Madhya Pradesh, and 23 in Andhra Pradesh.[22]

'The response of the Central Government was marked by unbelievable inertia. The political preoccupations of the ruling party, Congress (I), took precedence over the need to come to grips with the situation, which was assuming the proportions of a communal holocaust.... As a result, police firings seemed to have claimed more lives than the communal clashes did. This indicates a plain inadequacy of deployments and the absence of directions from Delhi and the State capitals.'[23] This phase of massacres climaxed in Gujarat in 2002.

19 Prita Jha (ed. 2014), "On Their Watch: Mass Violence and State Apathy in India", Gurgaon: Three Essays Collective, p. 116.
20 Asghar Ali Engineer (1990), "Grim Tragedy of Bhagalpur Riots, Role of Police-Criminal Nexus", *Economic and Political Weekly*, 10 February 1990, Vol 25, No 6, pp. 305-307.
21 Refer to Prita Jha and Warisha Farasat (eds.), *Splintered Justice* (2016), Gurgaon: Three Essays Collective.
22 "Communal Violence and Denial of Justice", *Human Rights Watch*, April 1996, Vol. 8, No. 2. Available at https://www.hrw.org/reports/1996/India1.htm#P284_65932
23 See above.

The second major feature of this phase of communal violence is the even much more openly partisan role of the state. There is not just institutional bias which we see here, which widely prevailed also in communal violence of the 1960s and 70s. We see evidence of active state planning of many of these massacres, facilitating and fanning the climate of hate from Nellie to Delhi to Bhagalpur to Bombay to Gujarat, deliberate and culpable criminal inaction, and even active participation in the violence such as in Hashimpura. Therefore in addition to being communal massacres, these are also communal pogroms, state-enabled if not state-sponsored massacres.

In addition in this phase, we find that whereas Muslims remain the major target in this new phase of communal violence, there is also violence targeted against Sikhs and later – in Phase 3 – against Christians. We also find the worrying re-emergence after the Partition riots of *rural* riots, in Nellie, Bhagalpur, Gujarat, – and also in the Phase 3 episodes in Kandhamal, Lower Assam and Muzaffarnagar; and this contributed further to their prolonged runaway character, in addition to the deliberate culpable delays by the state.

This phase is characterised, especially in the rural riots, with a much deeper and enduring social divide after the carnage, sustained often by economic and social boycott, continued hate propaganda, discouraging people from returning to their homes, imposing conditions of second class citizenship on those who still choose to return (to live in segregated colonies, without social interaction and reduced religious and cultural rights); cleansing of many habitations from their erstwhile Muslim residents, and the engineered and forced separation of populations. Riots in the first phase were more short-lived, and people tended to return home in larger numbers after each episode of violence settled down. People of goodwill would reach out from both sides of the communal divide, and the social ruptures between the estranged communities would slowly and at least partly heal.

But not in this new phase. Now the attempt is to not just strike at the time of violence, but to continue to nurture and deepen the social divide between the estranged communities. Normal social healing processes which lie within all pluralist societies are deliberately thwarted through sustaining hate propaganda and social and economic boycott, as I have demonstrated here. People from the minorities are not welcomed to their old homelands, and if they still return, they are forced to live segregated and isolated, as second class citizens. Many have no option except to seek the safety of Muslim ghettoes. This pattern is observed in both Bhagalpur, Gujarat and now Muzaffarnagar (all three major rural riots), where we estimate that more than half the displaced persons will never return to their homes. Sadly this feature of sustained social divides is what also characterises the emerging third phase of communal violence, described below.

☼

We see post-Gujarat the emergence of a new phase, with much in common with the phase stretching from Nellie in 1983 to Gujarat in 2002 – the creation of hatred around issues such as cow protection, religious conversions and alleged sexual predation, one-sided targeted pogroms, rural riots, sexual violence, violence also against other minorities than Muslims, social and economic boycott, sustained social divides and population divisions, and so on. The big difference in this stage is that there is now much less loss of life than in the worst massacres of 1983, 1984, 1989, 1992- 93 and 2002, but significant damage to property and far greater displacement of populations from their original homes. I speculate that the intense legal accountability enforced by actions of many organisations, and the international odium and disrepute which resulted in the aftermath of the Gujarat violence, has resulted in a shift to attacks with far fewer deaths but with extensive hate social mobilisation, huge attacks on property, and much larger displacements of human populations.

In this phase, we see first the Kandhamal violence of 2008. We also see the extensive low-intensity hate mobilisation in coastal Karnataka from around 2006. The violence in Lower Assam in 2012 saw comparatively fewer deaths, but half a million people were displaced, the largest displacement by targeted violence after Partition. (I must add strong caveats here that Assam did not see communal violence of the kind found in other parts; here oppressed minorities attack other oppressed minorities, and in this case Muslims did to Bodos in Muslim majority areas exactly what Bodos did with them). And Muzaffarnagar in 2013 again saw limited deaths (in a two-digit range) but 50,000 people displaced in just 2 districts (remember that Gujarat saw 2 lakhs displacement in violence which affected 20 districts and 2 large cities). In each of these, we witness the deaths in two digit figures, but displacement – often permanent – on a scale rarely witnessed in the communal violence of the 60s and 70s. There are numerous other even smaller such communal cashes. The hatred and social divides that they foster are even more stubborn that after the large mass communal violence of the past.

It is too early to confirm this, but perhaps we have seen the end of large massacres and their replacement with more invisible, pervasive communal attacks. But this has proved a brilliant political and social strategy for majoritarian politics. It accomplishes stirring and settling hate in the majority community; as well as in targeting and displacing minorities from their home-lands and livelihoods, reducing them to a life of everyday normal fear. This is the stuff of *making second-class*, and without the odium of international and domestic scrutiny, criticism and accountability.

⁕

The current phase on lynch attacks on religious minorities and Dalits is yet another mutant of low intensity localised episodes of communal violence. It is too early to say if this is evolving into an independent fourth phase in the waves of communal violence after Independence in India, or whether lynching will continue to coexist with low intensity, mostly under-the-radar dispersed communal episodes.

Meanwhile, lynching is emerging as a new convention, or routine, in these times of orchestrated hate and rage that we live in in India. The targets of furious and public bloodletting are as we have seen most often Muslims, but Dalits are also in danger. It has become increasingly common for mobs to gather, and to publicly attack, lynch and murder people who they claim have broken the law or hurt their (Hindu) sentiments. The excuse for the mob kill-ings are often claims that the victims were transporting cows for slaughter. In Jammu, in April 2017 even women and a young girl from pastoral nomadic Muslim tribal communities who traditionally rear livestock attacked when they were travelling with their animals to the higher mountain reaches, where they migrate ever summer. If the animals being transported turn out not to be cows, the vigilantes claim instead to be animal rights activists, and beat the transporters for alleged cruelty to the animals. In Assam in May 2017, two young Muslim men were killed by villagers because they suspected them to be cow thieves. But the claimed love of cows is not the only reason for murderous attacks. In Jharkhand, rumours of child kidnapping circulated on social media and led to mobs to brutally kill seven men. In Bulandhahar, six men alleged to be members of the private militia raised by the Uttar Pradesh Chief Minister Yogi Adityanath, the Hindu Yuva Vahini, killed a 59 year-old Muslim villager only because he was the neighbour of a Muslim man who eloped with a Hindu woman. One of the most sensational instances of mob lynching occurred in 2015 when a mob broke into the Dimapur Central Jail in Nagaland, pulled out a 35 year old Muslim man who was charged with the rape of a Naga woman and beat, stripped him naked, paraded him, and beat him to death in the city square.

Only a small fraction of the most dramatic of these mob killings actually make it to the front pages of newspapers or television screens. In most of these contemporary instances of mob lynching, the police is absent or if present merely stands by, and defend themselves later by claiming later that they were outnumbered. Both in cases of cow vigilantism and those in which Muslim men and Hindu women have even consensual relations, the police are seen to tacitly or openly encourage these attacks.

Sanjay Subrahmanyam, historian at the University of California, Los Angeles (UCLA), agrees in an interview with the Indian Express that these lynchings are a form of communal violence different from what we have seen before. 'Firstly, they are apparently decentralised. Earlier, organised acts of mass violence were repetitive in character and there was a pattern, e.g. processions were attacked or the violence was timed with public festivals....(P)ost-Independence, there have been largely urban, organised forms of violence, where various political parties have provided protection to the perpetrators... But what we are seeing now is not at a single place, there are fewer numbers attacked and it is decentralised, done by little groups all over the place. These groups are either being told, or imagine that they have been told to act in this way. Further, after the event, no one in authority is clearly telling them the contrary... It is low-level... if journalists don't choose to report it, it may not even register if one isn't vigilant.'

Very often the attacks of these lynch mobs are recorded on mobile phone cameras and uploaded on the social media, because the attackers gloat over what are they see to be acts of valour. The humiliation or intimidation of the victim is broadcast as a lesson in subjugation to every member of the targeted community. When they are seen pleading for their lives, this is a public display of their status in the country as second class citizens.

Subramaniam again concurs that 'the curious thing is that the perpetrators want it to be known. After all, some of the people doing this are even videotaping it. They make sure the information is circulating, intended as a warning, as a signal and controlling device for the social behaviour expected of minorities. It is a form of violence which can pop up here one day and there on another. It is never mass killings, but based on the existence of grassroots kind of organisations which believe in doing this, and also to an extent on copycat behaviour. So even if it is decentralised, there is a larger context...The actors seem to know that for all intents and purposes, nothing will happen to them, and they know they are implicitly meeting approval from higher-ups. People are using this to probably build political careers, a CV-builder of some kind. It is in part aspirational and cynical violence, of killing because you can do it.'

In the political and social enterprise of reducing minorities to second class citizens, lynching is therefore a critical instrument. Large mass communal and caste violence also created fear among the targeted communities, but in a certain space and time. However lynching as we observed respects no boundaries, of either space or time. Every person of the targeted community feels vulnerable everywhere and at all times. For them no place feels safe anymore – they can be attacked in their homes, trains, buses, or public roads.

The culpability for each of these clashes – lynch attacks as well as small decentralised communal clashes – lies with the communal organisations bent on fomenting communal animosities. But it is shared equally by the shamefully weak-kneed (or actively prejudiced) responses of the state and district administrations in each of these states. Each of these episodes could have been prevented or rapidly quelled, if only local officials had effectively publicly dispelled hate rumours and expeditiously arrested those who spread these falsehoods and organised violence. After lynch incidents it is commonplace for the police to charge the victims for crimes through which they seek to construct a rationale for the mob violence, and the attackers are recorded as anonymous men enraged by the illegal activities of the victims.

However blame also lies with the ruling central leadership. It is true that law and order is primarily the responsibility of state governments. But it is no secret that the BJP rose to power with active support of invigorated RSS cadres, and the adrenaline of their huge decisive victory has led them to feel emboldened to pursue even more vigorously their intensely divisive agendas. Raised on a staple diet of anti-Muslim propaganda, and encouraged further by the open deployment of these sentiments to reap a profoundly polarised vote in states like UP and Assam, high-pitched communal tempers are not a genie which can be released and then pushed back in a bottle at will.

I have referred earlier to the *India Spend* survey of cow related violence reported in the English-language press after 2010 which found that 97 percent of these attacks happened after Modi was elected in midsummer 2014, and more than half in BJP-administered states.[24] It is a device by which the ruling establishment out-sources violence against minorities to mobs, creating an enabling environment that encourages people to violently act out their hate

24 Alison Saldanha, "99.38% Indians Now Live In Areas Under Cow Protection Laws", *India Spend,* 14 April 2017. Available at http://www.indiaspend.com/cover-story/99-38-indians-now-live-in-areas-under-cow-protection-laws-42787

against minorities with assured impunity, and yet permits governments to free themselves of any responsibility for these attacks.

A sense of dread slowly therefore mounts almost invisibly over the country as communal tempers are cynically and perilously being overheated for a series of electoral harvests, and for drawing larger and larger sections of low caste Hindus to stand with their upper caste oppressors against the Muslim 'other' who is cultivated as their common enemy. The Congress, socialists and the Left are too decimated and dispirited – and most importantly too weak in their convictions – to convincingly take to battle.

※

Many ask, maybe the time has come for a new, stronger law to deal with hate crimes? Others disagree, because although lynching is not specifically recognised to be a crime, the Indian Penal Code recognises all the criminalities perpetrated by lynch mobs. Section 223(a) of the Code of Criminal Procedure also provides for persons or a mob involved in the same offence in the same act to be tried together.

But still, is there a case for a special law recognising that these are not just violent crimes but *hate* crimes which target people because of their identity? India already does have some laws to deal with forms of hate violence. The SC and ST (Prevention of Atrocities) Act recognizes the particular nature of violence that targets Dalit and tribal people, and therefore fittingly creates new crimes and higher punishments. But there have been very low rates of conviction under this law, sometimes as low as 4 percent, because of the extensive and often malevolent upper-caste bias of criminal justice institutions. If lynch crimes mainly target Muslim and Dalits, there is little reason to believe that the experience of a special lynch law would be different.

Anti-terror laws also deal with certain kinds of hate crime, by abridging the protections that the law normally accords to persons accused of crimes. The innovation of laws such as Prevention of Terrorism Act, 2002 was to take away some of the normal rights of a accused persons, such as by allowing pre-trial detention for 180 days and by admitting confessions to police officers as evidence. This is not allowed in normal law, because even colonial governments recognised that this enables confessions accomplished through torture. This is not a course I would recommend. We have seen the monumental injustice to innocent accused persons from religious minorities, and Dalits and tribal people, enabled by such laws, with recent reports of numerous men tortured and jailed for as long as 23 years before they are found innocent. I fear that any such enhanced power in a criminal justice system driven by majoritarian bias would tend to work against these very vulnerable people and minorities.

If we don't need to create new crimes of lynching, or reduce the rights of the accused, then why would one need a new law? In the past, I have advocated for a different legal approach to dealing with hate. From 2010 to 2012, when I was a member of India's National Advisory Council, I was part of a team which proposed the Communal and Targeted Violence Bill. This dealt with still another kind of hate crime, namely mass communal violence. The previous UPA government did consider – but never even introduced in Parliament let alone pass – this special law to deal with these crimes.

This law would have created new crimes for public officials who fail to prevent or control targeted mass communal violence, or obstruct the process of justice subsequently. There is a systematic pattern by which the criminal justice system is subverted during cases of both mass communal violence and individual hate crimes.[25] For these reasons, the centrepiece of the NAC draft of the Communal and Targeted Violence Bill was the creation of a new crime of 'dereliction of duty by public officials' punishable with up to five years' imprisonment. Combined with 'command responsibility' – the provision that the officials on the ground and the ones who commanded them are both liable for criminal dereliction – the law would have made criminally culpable senior political or administrative authorities who direct officials not to act when hate attacks occur, or to act with bias. The proposal was bitterly attacked by the BJP, which claimed that it was pro-minority. The UPA government never mustered the political will to steer it through Parliament.

The mounting scourge of targeted hate crimes by lynch mobs does require the creation of a similar crime of dereliction of duty by public officials. This, and not simply creating a new crime of lynching or enhanced punishments, would actually ensure that public officials act firmly and fairly against hate crimes, and not with majoritarian prejudice.

25 This was confirmed by On Their Watch, our report by the Centre for Equity Studies (CES), published in 2014. We found that in 42 percent FIRs in Nellie, 35 percent in Bhagalpur, and 76 percent in Gujarat, officials didn't record the names of the accused even when the victims know them. We found cases in which police filed charges against the victims to bully them into compromising, and deliberately weakened police investigations, while prosecutors acted in a partisan manner. All of these tendencies combine with the judiciary's upper-caste bias to lead to nearly complete impunity from those who commit communal hate crimes. Authorities have specifically ensured that most perpetrators of communal and caste violence are never punished. The CES carefully studied four of the largest post-Independence communal massacres — Nellie 1983, Delhi 1984, Bhagalpur 1989 and Gujarat 2002 — and found that, in each of these cases, very few of those guilty were penalised. Most cases were closed without even a trial. Nellie is the extreme case of a communal massacre in which not a single accused to date even faced trial, let alone conviction.

But even this will not be enough. No law, new or old, will in itself guarantee an end to this mass affliction of hate lynching that if unchecked can tear apart the fraternity of the country. The challenge ultimately is not of law, but of our collective humanity. What is it that goads us to join or incite lynch mobs, or to turn our faces away when people are targeted by hate attacks, or to justify these attacks as explicable, even righteous fury?

It is imperative that people do not allow hatred and bigotry to get routinized into a new 'normal' that would have been morally and politically unacceptable in the past. Solidarity with and between religious, ethnic and sexual minorities, oppressed castes and tribal peoples, women, poor and dispossessed people, immigrants and working class people, and people of colour, must be forged and strengthened. And above all, in these times of normalising hate, a new imagination must be nurtured, of people of difference of religion, caste and gender, within and across borders, bound together by love and respect.

CHAPTER ELEVEN

Hate Attacks and a Journey of Love

To speak to the gathering darkness of hate, to our collective silences, some comrades and I embarked during the month of September 2017 on a journey of shared suffering, of atonement and of love. We called it Karwane Mohabbat, or a Caravan of Love.

It was imperative to respond to mobs violently and feverishly acting out visceral hatred everywhere – on highways, in train compartments, inside homes – targeting people only because of their faith and caste. Our own offerings in this journey were modest: a lamp lit is a tempest of hate. We resolved to travel across the country, to meet families who lost their loved ones to hate lynching and hate violence, placing a garland of empathy across the land. With pain and shame, to seek from them our collective forgiveness, an atonement, to try a little to share their suffering. And to speak to them of our solidarity and love, and our resolve that justice must be done.

Within just a month after my appeal was first published, the Karwan set off on 4 September 2017. Entirely crowd-funded, and with an exceptional group of volunteers – writers, journalists, social workers, teachers, trainee priests, lawyers – we intersected India from east to west over a month, traversing Assam, Jharkhand, Karnataka, Delhi, Western Uttar Pradesh, Haryana, Rajasthan and Gujarat. As we travelled, I wrote an update late every night as we tried to catch a few hours of sleep.[1]

The Karwan found lynching events in every state we visited, and minorities in all these places living with intense and settled fear, hate and state violence, resigned to accept these as normalised elements of everyday living. We encountered widows, mothers, fathers and children, numbed with incomprehension of the loathing and violence that snatched from them their loved

---

1 Harsh Mander, personal communications, dated 5 September, 6 September, 7 September 2017, 9 September 2017, 10 September 2017, 11 September 2017, 13 September 2017, 14 September 2017, 15 September 2017, 16 September 2017, 17 September 2017, 18 September 2017, and 19 September 2017.

ones. As I wrote later, 'How could parents of two teenaged boys in Nagaon, Assam come to terms with not just with the lynching of their sons by a mob from their neighbouring village, accusing them of being cow thieves? Why would they gouge their eyes out and cut off their ears? Why would complete strangers stab Harish Pujari fourteen times near Mangalore, pulling out his intestines, only because they mistook him for a Muslim when he was riding pillion behind his Muslim friend?'

We found Dalits viciously attacked by upper caste neighbours to crush any assertion. Single women remained vulnerable to incredible medieval cruelty by family and neighbours, branded as witches. But the foremost targets of hate violence by lynching and police killings were Muslims, and it is they who have most abandoned hope.

Against Muslims, the hate weapon of choice is a very public lynching. We read of lynching of Blacks in America as public spectacles, watched by white families in picnics. In today's India, this same objective of lynching as public performance is accomplished with the video camera. Most lynch attacks are filmed by the attackers, with images of their victims humiliated, cringing, begging for their lives. In a particularly horrifying incident in Jharkhand, in a busy market square in Ramgarh, a mob stops the car of a Muslim man. A huge pile of red meat – the size of the body of a full cow – appears on the street, the mob claiming that they 'seized' this from the car. He is filmed as they beat him to death. Laughing faces of attackers appear in the video. They upload the videos even as they lynch the man and torch his car. His young son on his mobile receives the video of his father being lynched even as the lynching is underway.

We found that lynch videos are widely and avidly shared among young Hindutva activists. As evidence of what they see as their valorous exploits. As proof that the state will protect them. As public exhibitions of the humiliation of their 'enemy' communities. And for drafting new recruits to militant Hindu supremacist formations.

We found consistently that Muslim families hit by hate violence were bereft of hope of either protection or justice from the state. The police in almost all the over fifty families we met during our travels in eight states registered criminal charges against the victims, and treated the accused with kid gloves, not opposing their bail or erasing their crime altogether. A lynch mob, for instance, attacks a vehicle transporting cattle, killing some of the transporters. The police registers criminal cases of illegal cow smuggling, animal cruelty and rash driving against the victims. It obliterates completely the fact that the men were lynched. Or in other cases it mentions anonymous mobs

who are never caught. The families of people attacked by lynch mobs sometimes do not even file a complaint with to the police, because far from getting
justice, the police would register criminal charges against them.

Even more worrying, we found that the police has increasingly taken on
the work of the lynch mob.[2] There are tens of instances in which the police
itself kills Muslim men, charging them to be cattle smugglers or dangerous
criminals, and claiming that they fired at the police. In Gujarat, policemen
publicly lynch a tribal man charged with cow slaughter on two market squares
until he soils his clothes with his excreta and then dies. And unlike lynching,
this has barely registered in the national conscience.

And we found in all these local communities profound and pervasive
failures of compassion. We encountered very little acknowledgment, regret
or remorse amongst the upper-caste Hindu communities in any of the states
we travelled. They remain convinced that somehow their Muslim and Dalit
neighbours deserved their cruel deaths to lynch mobs or police bullets.

They expressed their anger and hostility to the Karwan at many points.
In one leg, they became violent. I extract from my update: The tenth day (of
the Karwan) was marked by news of anger and hostility to the advance of the
Karwan to Behror, the highway crossing where Pehlu Khan had been lynched
on the highway by a cow vigilante mob some months earlier. The Karwan
had resolved the next morning to place flowers at the site of his lynching,
in his memory and the memory of others like him who fell to hate violence.
Hindu supremacist organisations[3] announced that they would not allow the
Karwan to enter Behror and pay tribute at the lynch site. The local organisers were told that we would be met with sticks and stones if we entered. We
resolved in the Karwan that we would proceed to Behror to remember Pehlu
Khan despite any mob opposition. In Alwar, where we arrived to spend the
night, senior police and administrative officials tried to persuade us to bypass
Behror. We courteously but firmly refused. We argued – how can an administration block a Karwan that has set out to try to offer a little solace to families
bereaved by hate lynching from paying tribute to lynched man's memory.

The next day the Alwar district administration again tried hard to persuade
us to bypass Behror, where Pehlu Khan had been lynched on the highway. The
district officers who met me said that violent mobs had gathered with stones
to block our passage. The administration said that a furious mob had gathered

2 "Remember Hashimpura Now, When Majoritarianism is Eroding Democracy", *The Wire*, 22 May
  2017. Available at https://thewire.in/136648/hashimpura-may-22-custodial-killings/
3 Namely the Vishwa Hindu Parishad, the Hindu Jagran Manch, and the Bajrang Dal.

there with stones and sticks and would cause me harm. I said I was prepared for it, and would not agree to discard the plans of a floral tribute to extend solace to the loved ones of the man who was lynched there. I said I would go there alone as I did not want to risk any of my Karwan colleagues being attacked or hit by a stone. A senior police officer said to me hotly, the mob 'have the constitutional right to protest'. I answered – 'I am not sure that anyone has a constitutional right to protest with stones. But even if you so believe, then surely I have at least the same constitutional right to protest armed with nothing other than flowers.'

I began to walk to the site, but the police physically blocked me. I then sat on the ground in a spontaneous dharna (sit-in). They would have to either arrest me, or allow me to walk to the location and make my floral tribute. I sat for about half an hour, as they confabulated. Finally they relented.

With two fistfuls of marigold flowers, and surrounded by a few policepersons, I walked the couple of hundred years to the spot where the ageing cattle trader Pehlu Khan had been cruelly lynched by a mob. It was a dirty nondescript stretch of a sidewalk. I knelt down there, and said, 'I am not a believer, so I cannot pray. But I believe in *insaniyat aur insaaf* – humanism and justice. Therefore, for humanism and justice, I place these flowers here. In memory not just of Pehlu Khan, but of hundreds of others like him who have fallen to hate violence across our land.'

I returned to the bus, and the police bundled us rapidly into the bus. As we drove past, the protesting men threw a few stones at the bus. On the way, people of the small town Kothputli had planned a small welcome to the Karwan. But in the presence of the police, a bunch of young men arrived, tore down the banners and threw away the flowers. The police said they were helpless to stop them. The police then asked just two organisers to meet the bus outside the police station. I emerged with a couple of colleagues, and the policemen said we had only a couple of minutes. They handed over packets of packed breakfast, and a few men gathered. One of them took off his shoe to throw, as the bus drove away. We stopped the bus long enough to throw out flowers.

The Karwan now had police escort vehicles both ahead and following its bus. It was only with this that the state administration would allow the Karwan to travel through Rajasthan. A sad day when a caravan of love can travel only with the protection of the police. We don't need or deserve protection; it is the bereaved families who we have met these days of the Karwan who the police should protect, but it is they who they fail so profoundly.

It was clear that the government was troubled by the Karwan, its discourse of love, and the evidence it gathered about how widespread was the fear and hate that its policies had fostered. We learnt that all big newspapers and TV channels were advised to blank out news of the Karwan. Many, but not all, complied with these pressures. Despite everything, many stories – my daily updates, and several articles by Karwan travellers – appeared both on-line and in print. The most liberal of the major TV channels, NDTV, have slotted a very rare one-hour slot for a documentary on the Karwan, and its two reporters became precious members of the Karwan.[4]

In a television debate when the Karwan was being blocked from placing flowers, a leader of the RSS angrily decried my credentials (following up with many tweets describing me as a scoundrel, and the social media soon filled with abusive trolls slandering my work). He also said that the funds of 'my' NGO must be investigated thoroughly. Not wasting time, just four days later, the Centre for Equity Studies, of which I am a founding member and Director received tax notices. (The Centre for Equity Studies, a think tank which also works with homeless people, incidentally had nothing to do with the Karwan). The Income Tax Department may claim that this is just a routine notice. But the timing of the notice shortly after the public threat for getting the funding of 'my' organisations investigated, and the fact that less than 1 per cent of returns are scrutinised, suggest that this could well be an act of state vengeance and intimidation.

I issued a press-note, stating, 'We are happy to subject ourselves to any scrutiny, as we believe in public accountability. But I would like to state categorically that no amount of state intimidation of the organisations that I am associated with, would succeed to silencing my public dissent with policies and ideologies that I believe are detrimental to India's constitutional values.' The work that the Centre does is precious to me. But at times like this, I believe that there is no higher duty than public dissent. As I wrote to my colleagues, 'They can cancel our FCRA (permission to receive foreign funds). Shut down the organisation. How does it matter? This would be an infinitely small fraction of the suffering we bore witness to in the Karwan.' This is not an act of particular valour, just that no other option is acceptable.

※

---

4 "Atonement: The Karwan-e-Mohabbat Journey", *NDTV*, 6 October 2017. Available at https://www.ndtv.com/video/shows/india-matters/atonement-the-karwan-e-mohabbat-journey-469373

Did the Karwan accomplish anything? None of its fellow-travellers have been left untouched by this odyssey. Of this we are sure. Of one other thing also the Karwan members are sure. That their travels did offer precious solace to the more than fifty families we met across India who were struggling often very alone with the consequences of incredible hate and colossal state injustice. This alone made the voyage of love worth its while.

But we found a singular and worrying lack of remorse in the majority communities where hate violence against Dalits and minorities unfolded. At moments like the stoning of the Karwan by an angry mob that did not want us to pay a floral tribute to Pehlu Khan where he had been lynched, the Karwan feared that it needed to do much more to appeal to the conscience of the majority community in many local areas that they visited.

But we still took heart that not just stones and footwear were thrown at us, but also rose petals, in so many places that we journeyed, by ordinary people who joined the Karwan of love. There was a great response to the Karwan call for crowd funding, and the Karwan was entirely resourced by individual contributions. We started with no money. In a month, more than 200 people contributed 20 lakh rupees for the Karwan. Large numbers turned out for the peace meetings and to greet the Karwan, even when it was travelling late and arrived at night.

Hearteningly, we found that the Dalits in all three states were angry, proud, organised and fiercely determined to fight back. In Shabbirpur, the Dalits have converted en masse to Buddhism, immersing their Hindu idols in the village ponds. Jai Bhim was their resounding slogan everywhere. This was in stark contrast to the Muslims, who are today crushed, isolated and despairing.

We encountered very little acknowledgment, regret or remorse among the upper-caste Hindu communities in any of the states we travelled. They remain convinced that somehow their Muslim and Dalit neighbours deserved their cruel deaths to lynch mobs or police bullets.

※

During its travels, the Karwan bore witness to such intense and pervasive suffering and fear fashioned by hate violence, and such extensive state hostility to its most vulnerable citizens, that we resolved that the caravan of love must continue its journey. Even during the month that we travelled, news filtered in of one Dalit boy lynched for watching *garba* and two battered for sporting moustaches, a woman branded and killed for being a 'witch', continued police killings of Muslim youth, as also mob attacks in the name of the cow. Until collectively, all of us are able to bring an end to this, we resolved that our Karwan cannot end its journey.

Its journey must continue not just metaphorically but also literally. We committed that every month, some of us will visit families in at least one state.

The members of the Karwan resolved to chronicle – through books, films, photo exhibitions and public talks – the rise of hate and fear that we bore witness to during the Karwan, and would continue to do so as we continue to travelled during the coming months, with pictures, videos and words. In order to inform and appeal to our sisters and brothers across the country, to care, to speak out, and to resist. We felt this is imperative to inform, stir and appeal to the public conscience.

There is also a strong ethical commitment of the Karwan to ensure support to each of the families affected by hate violence. Human rights and humanitarian groups, both religious and secular, are extending such support to some families. The Karwan would come in only in cases where there are gaps. There are four kinds of support that families require. The first is for legal justice. The second is for psycho-social care, to help them cope and deal with their suffering. The third is to access their entitlements, such as compensation from government, as well as other needs such as education, pensions and health-care. And the fourth is for other material needs, such as to rebuild their livelihoods, often destroyed due to the loss of a breadwinner and of live-stock, or fear.

In Nuh in Haryana, a young Muslim man said, 'A poisonous wind is blowing through our country. I feel a stranger in my own homeland.'

There is an evil stalking our land, of hate and fear engineered by cynical politics. The gathering darkness in our land is less and less penetrated by the light of compassion and solidarity. As India is fast mutating into a republic of hate, we just watch from the side-lines. To fight these, to restore compassion and constitutional values to our country, not just this Caravan of Love, and many others, must continue their journeys, into India's troubled interiors as much as into the shadows of our troubled hearts and minds.

CHAPTER TWELVE

The Unmaking of India

India is being unmade, one lynching at a time. The core of our pluralist secular democracy has survived the assaults of mass communal violence. But I fear that it may not survive the current normalisation of hate and bigotry.

I have observed that Prime Minister Modi's brief and generalised periodic condemnations of mob violence do not reassure India's minorities and Dalits. Following countrywide spontaneous protests against lynch violence under the banner Not in My Name, on 29 June 2017, for instance, he said at the Sabarmati Ashram in Ahmedabad that killing in the name of gau bhakti, or devotion to the cow, is not appropriate as no one had the right to take law and order into his own hands. He added that Mahatma Gandhi would not have approved of it. Only because this broke a long silence after the brutal lynching of teenaged Junaid Khan on a train near Delhi, this was welcome. But as the *Indian Express* observed in an editorial, this just did not seem enough. He did not mention Junaid, or express any personal anguish and horror about the way the boy was killed and *why* he was killed. 'The PM had spoken of cow vigilantism and lynchings as disembodied events,' the editorial notes. 'He did not name the victims, call the crime by its name. He did not say that what India is seeing, across states, is a rash of hate crimes.' The editorial rightly observes that 'lynchings, mostly in the name of the cow, mainly targeting Muslims, cannot be treated as mere law and order disturbances generally left to the governments in the states.' It notes the role of the police in most instances of lynching: it reaches late, or becomes a bystander, or demonstrates greater zeal in filing cases against the victims. Yet it importantly underlines that even beyond the partisan role of the state administrations and police, what 'sets these lynchings apart, what makes them a hate crime, and what contributes to the police abdications is that, though separated by time and geography, they draw upon a common and centralised pattern of political understandings, cues and messages.' Lynch mobs which target minorities are 'emboldened by a perceived open season on Muslims.' They perceive and count upon 'a climate of impunity, presided over by a political regime that appears to speak more in defence of the cow – including through the plethora of laws, rules and notifications curbing and banning the sale and slaughter of cattle – than on the equal rights and special protections that governments in a constitutional democracy owe to their most vulnerable groups of citizens.'

It concludes fittingly that 'What the PM needed to say, what he still has not said, is that his colleagues in the Sangh Parivar must no longer deny the gravity of these crimes, or condone them. As the party that rules the Centre and in a large number of states, the BJP must send out the unequivocal message that these mobs do not act in its name. That its governments in the states will act firmly and fairly whenever such violence happens, and the Centre will use all the direct and supervisory powers and mechanisms at its command to ensure that they and other state governments do so.' But this political message is entirely missing in the country's highest leadership today.

As the months pass, the majoritarian political establishment, in a mood of mounting triumphalism, shows the country's two 'foreign' religious minorities – Muslims and Christians – their place in the country, in their on-going project of making them 'second class'. Even Ashutosh Varshney who was earlier willing to give Modi a chance after his election, voices his anxieties about where India under Modi is fast heading, 'India badly needs communal peace. Lynchings have shaken the Muslim community. If not stopped, it is not clear what domestic peace India can obtain. Over the last two months in India, I have travelled a lot, talked a lot, listened a lot. I have not come across a single Muslim who is not feeling insecure.'[1]

Senior journalist Samar Harlankar speaks of how in this new legitimised majoritarian social climate of rumours, lies, violence and political support for bigotry, many Hindus are feeling emboldened to reveal hidden prejudices.[2] And as anti-Muslim rhetoric spreads, he describes – as attacks based on rumour and lies increase and Hindu groups believe local administrations will back them – that there is a growing fear of living and travelling among Muslims in India. 'I never thought there will be a day when I will live in fear in my country,' his former colleague tells him. Her 80-year-old father, who lives in a Hindu-majority area, told her he never imagined living in such

1 Ashutosh Varshney, "More accountant, less visionary", *The Indian Express*, 16 August 2017. Available at http://indianexpress.com/article/opinion/columns/more-accountant-less-visionary-narendra-modi-independence-day-speech-4798607/

2 Samar Harlarnkar, "'Maybe it is time to change my son's name': The new reality of being Muslim in India", *Scroll*, 8 July 2017. Available at https://scroll.in/article/843074/maybe-it-is-time-to-change-my-sons-name-the-new-reality-of-being-muslim-in-india

times. 'And this from a man who has witnessed the Partition riots,' she says. 'I tell my house help never to disclose her identity when she is travelling alone in a train. Yes, it has come to this.'

His colleague tells Harlankar that she does not call her son by his name when they are out of the house. 'I prefer using J, it doesn't have a Muslim ring to it,' she says. Her son's name in Junaid. Junaid was the name of a teenaged boy lynched on a suburban train near Delhi a day before Eid in 2017 for the singular crime of looking Muslim.

Harlankar speaks of Nazmul Hassan, an Aligarh power-plant engineer detained by the police on July 2 2017 after being found on a railway station in a burqa. The police questioned him closely to determine if he was in any way connected to terrorism. 'When Hassan was handed over to the GRP [government railway police], he was crying and shaking and kept repeating that he is a simple man who has never done anything wrong,' Senior Superintendent of Police Rajesh Pandey fortunately felt sorry for the frightened man, and let him go. He told the *Times of India* that Hassan was in a burqa because he was recently threatened by a fellow passenger he accidentally jostled when alighting from a train. The man insulted his Islamic faith, and – joined by others – said Hassan would be driven out of Aligarh. 'I was scared for my life after the threat.' So, he wore a burqa, believing no one would harm a woman.

Harlankar notes sadly that he was wrong even in his belief that Muslim women, particularly those in burqas and hijabs, are safe. A year earlier, two Madhya Pradesh Muslim village women were kicked and slapped, first by cow vigilantes and later by a crowd that gathered, on the suspicion (later proved false) that they were carrying beef. The women were arrested, the attackers untouched.

※

The Madhya Pradesh police filed against fifteen Muslim men in Mohad village a case of sedition – which if proved could have kept them in jail all their lives. Their alleged 'crime' was of lighting firecrackers, chanting pro-Pakistan slogans and distributing sweets after Pakistan won the Champions Trophy final cricket match against the Indian cricket team on 18 June 2017. They spent ten traumatic days in Khandwa jail on these charges.

The First Information Report of the police against these men claimed that one Subhash Koli, who repairs satellite dish antennae in the village, was the one who lodged this complaint against his Muslim neighbours. But Koli denied that he made any such claim to the police. He said to NDTV that he did visit the police station late on the night of 18 June, but only to request the police to release one of the young Muslim men from his village who they had rounded up. He said he thought that since he is Hindu, the police would be more likely to believe him when he told them that his neighbour had not celebrated Pakistan's win. His friend Anis did not even know who won the match. 'He was asked his name and picked him up because of that,' Koli alleged. He further charged that he was now being threatened by the police "even inside the court." He went into hiding from the police for a few days.

The 15 harried men who spent around 10 days in jail, spoke after their release to the Hindustan Times of the trauma and humiliation that they had to endure in prison. 'We were made to clean toilets and drains in the Khandwa jail and were called traitors by the jail inmates. When we entered the jail, nearly a dozen senior jail inmates slapped each one of us and abused us,' said Mansoori, a tailor, showing bruises on his leg where he said the police had beaten him. The 25 year-old insists that they did not burn crackers after Pakistan's victory. 'We are Muslims, but also Indians,' he declares. Mansoori is a graduate in Education had applied for a job in the forest department. 'I was about to apply for a job with the police as well. Now with such charges, who will give me a job?" he despairs.

The men said that the worst treatment was reserved for a man with the misfortune of sharing his first name with Pakistan's cricket captain Sarfraz Ahmed. 'They had fun with me as for them, I was the captain. I was beaten up mercilessly by the police. In jail the inmates did the same,' Sarfraz Khan told Hindustan Times. Idbar Gulzar Tadvi, 24, lamented to the reporter that his days in prison were going to hurt and haunt him for a long time. His cotton crop wilted while he was behind bars. 'Most of us work in the fields as farmers or labourers. We have the most to lose,' he said.

❂

Another even more bizarre story from another part of India unfolded exposing communal (and patriarchal) biases not of the police but of the country's highest judicial institutions. An adult woman named Akhila Ashokan from Kerala, while studying homeopathy, felt drawn to Islamic teachings after she shared an apartment with two Muslim students. It is from them that she first heard and discussed Islamic teachings, and took from them a copy of the Quran to study. In time she resolved to convert to Islam, changed her name to Hadiya.

She created a stir when she returned to college wearing a headscarf. One of her classmates called her father, KM Ashokan, an ex-servicemen. Ashokan commanded his daughter to return home, and she refused, moving in instead with a Muslim girlfriend. Her father filed a habeas corpus petition with the Kerala High Court alleging that her daughter's conversion and marriage was part of a well-oiled conspiracy of love jihad to convert innocent women and recruit them to the Islamic State.

The court initially permitted her to stay with her friend. But her father appealed to the court again that he was worried that she was being trapped into converting to Islam. Hadiya refused again to return to her father, and the court directed that she should not stay with her Muslim girlfriend and be sent instead to a women's hostel. She decided to get married. She met a 27 year old Muslim man named Shafin Jahan employed in Muscat on a Muslim matrimonial site. When they both consented to this arranged marriage, she was 24 years old at that time, and a homeopathic doctor. They invited Hadiya's parents to the wedding, but they refused to attend. Ashokan instead again approached the High Court, charging that this was a conspiracy to move her out of India.

Two days after her wedding, Hadiya Jahan appeared in court with her husband, affirming that she was an adult woman of 24 years, and that she had converted and married according to her wishes and free will. She appealed therefore that her decisions should be respected. The Kerala High Court refused, and instead sent her back to the women's hostel in Kochi. It prohibited her to meet her husband, who had to leave his job in Muscat as the case stretched on. The High Court asked the Kerala police to investigate the matter to see enquire if her conversion and wedding was connected with any terror links. The police reported that it could find no connection of Shafin Jahan with any criminal activity (except one complaint connected with student politics), let alone terrorist endeavours.

Despite this, the Kerala High Court annulled her marriage. It observed, 'A girl aged 24 years is weak and vulnerable, capable of being exploited in many ways.' It therefore awarded custody of this adult woman to her father. 'She shall be cared for, *permitted* to complete her house surgeon course...Her marriage being the most important decision in her life, can also be taken *only* with the active involvement of her parents.' 'The marriage, which is alleged to have taken place', the learned judge maintained, 'is a sham and is of no consequence in the eye of law. Her husband has no authority to act as the guardian.'

By awarding 25 year old Hadiya Jahan's 'custody' to her father, it gave credence to the communally charged conspiracy theory of 'love jihad', a conspiracy to covert Hindu women to Islam to ensnare them into terrorist organisations. It refused to recognise Hadiya's voluntary conversion to Islam, referring to her in its judgment only as Akhila. It refused to recognise the agency of an adult woman, and maintained that her choice of marriage had no legal weight because her parents had not consented to it.

Shafin Jahan tried unsuccessfully to communicate with or meet Hadiya. 'I had sent a letter to her, but her father returned it with the acknowledgement "rejected by the guardian"', he told the *Indian Express*. 'Once I went to TV Puram (her parents' home in Kottayam) to visit her, but police did not allow me to enter the house.' Jahan said Hadiya is an adult and has every right to practice a religion of her choice. 'By confining her within the house, her family is now attempting a forced conversion. That is why Hadiya is not allowed to speak. She is still my wife,' he declared. The *Indian Express* reports, 'Hadiya has not been allowed to step out or meet anyone. Policemen watch her every move, and monitor the neighbourhood.' A police officer in Kottayam defended depriving Hadiya of her freedoms, by telling the reporter, 'We have intelligence reports that the woman and her parents face serious threat from Islamic fundamentalists. We have advised the family not to let the woman outside as it may endanger her life.'

Shafin Jahan appealed against this order, extraordinary both for its patriarchal and communal prejudices, to the Supreme Court, and the matter was heard by a bench which included the Chief Justice Khehar. But initially he got no relief from the country's highest court.

The Supreme Court instead directed the state police to share its investigation reports with the National Investigation Agency. 'The NIA's involvement is necessary to ascertain if this is really an isolated case or is there something more... something wider...,' the bench said. The learned Chief Justice referred mysteriously to the internet game, Blue Whale Challenge, to explain his decision! This internet game was making the headlines because it leads players to take a series of self-destructive steps over 50 days before finally committing suicide. When Shafin Jahan's lawyer Kapil Sibal requested the top court to interview the girl before reaching any decision, the chief justice mysteriously alluded to the Blue Whale Challenge internet game to elaborate his apprehension that 'such things can drive people to do anything.'

I am not clear what the Chief Justice meant when he enigmatically spoke of 'such things' which can drive people to do 'anything'. But he seemed influenced by the NIA claim that Hadiya's conversion and marriage was not an isolated case but part of a growing pattern of converting women from

Hinduism to Islam as a vehicle to recruit them for terror crimes in the Islamic State. It appears to me that asking India's top counter-terror investigation agency to enquire into the voluntary conversion to Islam by an adult woman and her subsequent marriage to a man against whom the police has found no evidence of any criminal or terror connections, smacks of astounding and whimsical prejudice at the highest levels of the judiciary.

The Supreme Court in later hearings made some amends, but at the time of writing, Hadiya's marriage is still annuled, her freedom to move out of her father's home still is restricted, and investigations continue into whether her conversion to Islam was linked to terrorism.

※

This is not the only matter in which India's highest courts have accepted stunning communal rationalizations for hate attacks. The first hate lynching of a Muslim after Mr Modi's election in May 2014 was of a young visibly Muslim man, Mohsin Sadiq Shaikh, an IT professional in Pune on June 4, 2014. Apparently provoked by the alleged uploading of derogatory pictures of Shivaji and Bal Thackeray, members believed to be associated with the Hindu Rasthtra Sena, a radical outfit active in the state, was killed brutally only for being Muslim.

In January 2017, the Mumbai High Court accepted bail of the accused, on the grounds that they 'otherwise had no other motive such as any personal enmity against the innocent deceased Mohsin. The fault of the deceased was only that he belonged to another religion.' The Court surprisingly considered this factor '*in favour*' (my italics) of the accused men. It observes that they 'do not have criminal record and it appears that in the name of the religion, they were provoked and have committed the murder.' The implication is simply that being provoked because the victim was of another religion is a mitigating factor, meriting the award of bail to the men accused of lynching.

※

These are just a few straws in the wind which reflect which was the wind blows today for India's minorities. In all of this, the predicament of Kashmiri students outside the valley is particularly acute, because they are both Muslim and Kashmiri. Niha Masih reports some glimpses of their trauma. She lists incidents involving Kashmiri students, drawn from reports in national newspapers, from just the one preceding year in Rajasthan, Haryana and Madhya Pradesh: 'Shakib Ashraf was arrested after a mob alleged he had cooked beef in his university hostel. The meat was later revealed to be mutton after a lab test by the police. Umar Rashid was thrashed after he told two people that he was from Kashmir. Kaleemullah was called a "terrorist" after an altercation with another student. Mujahid Zahid was beaten with wooden sticks and logs. Bahar Ahmed Giri was told to go back to Kashmir by locals at a market.' Kashmiri students report that prejudice against them has amplified in the current surge of hyper-nationalism in India. Masih reports that a few days after a video of a CRPF jawan being beaten by youth in Budgam went viral on 12 April 2017, a mob calling them terrorist attacked half-a-dozen Kashmiri students at Mewar University in Chittorgarh, Rajasthan, with hockey sticks, seriously injuring three of them. When they went to the local hospital, a group went there as well and told then, 'You are all Kashmiri militants. We won't allow you to live here.' The campus authorities did not let them out for two months, fearing for their safety.

❄️

Prime Minister Modi chose to resoundingly remind Muslim minorities of their place in the Indian nation by implication in his response to a speech by India's Vice President, Hamid Ansari to law students in Bangalore days before he remitted office after ten years, and an interview he gave thereafter to television anchor Karan Thapar. To law students, Hamid Ansari spoke of the Constitution of India and its Preamble as 'an embodiment of the ideals and principles' that he holds dear.[3] He talked of 'Indianness' 'not as a singular or exhaustive identity but as embodying the idea of layered Indianness, an accretion of identities.' He believed that the challenge today 'is to reiterate and rejuvenate secularism's basic principles: equality, freedom of religion and tolerance, and to emphasize that equality has to be substantive, that freedom of religion be re-infused with its collectivist dimensions, and that toleration should be reflective of the realities of Indian society and lead to acceptance.'

He went on to ask how do we go about 'creating conditions and space for a more comprehensive realization of the twin objectives of pluralism and secularism and in weaving it into the fabric of a comprehensive actualization of the democratic objectives set forth in the Constitution?' A commonplace suggestion, he observed, is advocacy of tolerance. Tolerance, he asserted 'is

---

3 "Full text of Hamid Ansari's final speech as vice-president: Why pluralism and secularism are essential for our democracy", *Firstpost*, 7 August 2017. Available at http://www.firstpost.com/india/full-text-of-hamid-ansaris-final-speech-as-vice-president-why-pluralism-and-secularism-are-essential-for-our-democracy-3902451.html

a virtue. It is freedom from bigotry. It is also a pragmatic formula for the functioning of society without conflict between different religions, political ideologies, nationalities, ethnic groups, or other us-versus-them divisions. Yet tolerance alone is not a strong enough foundation for building an inclusive and pluralistic society. It must be coupled with understanding and acceptance. We must, said Swami Vivekananda, "not only tolerate other religions, but positively embrace them, as truth is the basis of all religions." He spoke of the urgency to cultivate both tolerance and acceptance of difference in the light of the 'enhanced apprehensions of insecurity amongst segments of our citizen body, particularly Dalits, Muslims and Christians.'

He elaborated his concerns about this insecurity even more explicitly and poignantly in an interview to Karan Thapar on Rajya Sabha TV on his last day in public office.[4] He said he felt troubled by the direction that Indian society has taken. He voiced his worries about the ever-mounting violence that targeted minorities with claims of cow protection, and the rise of majoritarian-cultural nationalism. He said he often spoke of these concerns to Prime Minister Narendra Modi and his cabinet. Asked what their response was, he replied, 'Well, there is always an explanation and there is always a reason. Now it is a matter of judgement, whether you accept the explanation, you accept the reasoning and its rationale.'

Hamid Ansari held the only high office in the country that was occupied by Muslims, who are India's largest minority of over 172 million people, the third largest population of Muslim people in any part of the world. With his exit, there would be none. The ruling BJP did not file even one Muslim candidate to contest the Lok Sabha in the 2014 general elections. Persons committed to the ideology of the openly anti-minority RSS now hold the three highest offices in the country – the President, Vice President and Prime Minister.

It would have been healing to India's minorities if Prime Minister Modi would have used this moment when the urbane and dignified Ansari felt compelled to voice the fears of his community, to reach out to and reassure them. But even if Prime Minister Modi did not wish to speak words of reassurance and encouragement to India's minorities, he could merely have remained silent. What Mr Modi chooses to be silent about are as strategic as what he chooses to speak, lecture and hector about. But silence at least could have been subjected to more than one interpretation.

4 Karan Thapar, "A sense of insecurity is creeping in among Muslims: Hamid Ansari", Business Standard, 10 August 2017. Available at http://www.business-standard.com/article/economy-policy/a-sense-of-insecurity-is-creeping-in-among-muslims-hamid-ansari-117080901815_1.html

Instead the Prime Minister mentioned Hamid Ansari's long association with the Congress (read minority-appeasing) party; and also his family's support for the Khilafat Movement. He spoke of his career as a diplomat in West Asian (read Muslim) capitals, and his responsibilities in 'certain circles' (read as Vice Chancellor of Aligarh Muslim University and Chairperson of the National Minorities Commission). He said he interacted only occasionally with the Vice President, but when he did it helped him realise 'that things are not always what they seem to be.' And that 'In last 10 years your responsibility changed considerably and you had to confine yourself strictly to Constitution. You may have been internally agitated by this, but from today can speak will have the freedom to speak your mind and to think, speak and act according to your core set of beliefs.' In this way he chose a frontal assault – deploying his trademark razor-sharp sarcasm and barely disguised communalised innuendo – to respond to Mr Ansari's words spoken from the heart, in a four-and-a-half minute diatribe.

The innuendo was clear as if he had said this explicitly. 'You think and feel like a Muslim rather than as an Indian, and this has characterised your family legacy and your entire career before you took office of the Vice President.' He forgot that Hamid Ansari's father Abdul Aziz had rejected Jinnah's offer of a senior position in Pakistan and chose to stay back in India. He spoke of Ansari's postings to Muslim countries, as though this was his own deliberately sectarian career choice rather than the peculiar policy of the government of India to post Muslim officers to Muslim majority countries. He forgot that Ansari was also High Commissioner to Australia and India's Permanent Representative to the United Nations. He neglected that Hamid Ansari was India's UN Permanent Representative in the turbulent time when the Babri Masjid was demolished, and he played a key role in isolating Pakistan in the UN when it tried to internationally corner and embarrass India because of the demolition. Hamid Ansari was also at the forefront of protests against the exile of Kashmiri Pandits from the Kashmir valley.

Instead, the Prime Minister suggested by implication that Ansari's 'core beliefs' are Islamic, if not Islamist, and he was constrained by constitutional office to act on these beliefs. He also spoke of his sympathy for the Congress, which is in any case a pro-Muslim party. He did nothing at all to acknowledge that there is a real and mounting fear among Muslims, Dalits and Christians spurred by mounting vigilante and mob attacks on them and their places of worship. These were merely dismissed by the Prime Minister in his sarcasm-heavy speech as the jaundiced view of a Congress-sympathetic non-nationalist Muslim, not the lived reality of millions of Muslims in the openly anti-Muslim, anti-Christian (and sometimes anti-Dalit) environment that his government, other BJP-led state governments, and the RSS and its affiliates have fostered.

Many BJP leaders added their voice to that of the Prime Minister. Even his successor to the office of Vice President could not resist taking a pot shot at him, dismissing his claim (without naming him) that minorities are insecure as mere 'political propaganda'. 'Minorities in India', he contended, are 'more safe and get their due' compared to every other country in the world, The RSS was even more explicit in the acerbity and derision of its rejoinders, with open insults and taunts. 'For all these ten years, he (Ansari) didn't feel insecure. He should point out any country in the world where Muslims are secure. I don't feel Ansari should remain in trouble (*taklif*). So, he should head for any country where he feels he will be secure,' declared RSS leader Indresh Kumar in a press conference after attending a Raksha Bandhan programme organised by RSS-leaning Rashtriya Muslim Manch, according to an Indian Express report. His attack drew even more blood – 'He was secular for ten years when he was in chair. Now he has become a fundamentalist (*kattarpanthi*) Muslim. He was Bharatiya now he has become communal. He was a leader of all parties but has now become a Congressman.' Trolls in the social media outdid even these attacks. The charge of being a fundamentalist Muslim is appalling to apply to a man of dignity, grace, learning and moderation, who both embodied and was so explicitly committed to the values and spirit of India's pluralist Constitution.

The denials and insults by the RSS, the Prime Minister, and several leading lights of the BJP including the man who succeeded Mr Ansari to the office of the Vice President, were directed not simply at Hamid Ansari but to every Muslim who dares complain about discrimination, violence and fear; that they are feeling insecure in the land of their birth, a land they love, and a land who's Constitution had promised them equal citizenship. The message was loud and clear. That every 'good Muslim' must learn silence and acquiescence, or else she or he would be labelled in the way even an outgoing Vice President was, as a person culpably wanting in love for the country.

CHAPTER THIRTEEN

Partitions of the Heart

I took Usman Ansari's one good hand in mine. I said that I came with a message, of sharing his pain and seeking his forgiveness, on behalf of all of us.

In hiding, his crushed arm in a sling, the old man was manifestly broken. Not just in body, but in spirit. He sobbed many times as he spoke with us. When he talked of the nightmare of his neighbours' lynch attack, accusing him of killing his cow. Of how much he loves his cows. Of his family begging for money to pay for his medical expenses and food. Of his son losing his mental balance after his lynching. And of his resolve to return to his village one day. Even though he knows no one wants him there; but there is no other place he can call his home.

We met Ansari on the third day of our Karwane Mohabbat, or Caravan of Love, our journey of atonement and solidarity with those who are targets of hate attacks across our land. Ansari still so feared another attack that his family did not disclose his hide-out. People met us instead on the main road, from where only a few of us left in a jeep, driving through many villages before we reached his secret refuge.

His story had chilling echoes of Akhlaq in Dadri. Ansari lived, the only Muslim home in a Hindu neighbourhood, in village Barwadah in Giridih district. He reared ten cows and sold milk to both Hindu and Muslim customers. Some ten days before the attacks, one of his jersey cows fell ill, and ultimately died. The custom of the village is that dead cattle are not buried, and instead thrown in a designated yard. Ansari contacted the man from a disadvantaged caste who usually disposed of dead cattle. But they could not settle on a price. Therefore Ansari decided to drag the corpse of the cow himself, with his sons, to the dump-yard.

There it lay for two days. The day of the lynching, two days after Eid on 27 June 2017 the corpse was found mysteriously without its head and a leg. The rumour quickly spread like fire that Ansari had killed his own cow to eat during Eid. A mob of hundreds of angry men from the village and a nearby weekly bazaar surrounded his home baying for his blood. A terrified Ansari pleaded with the multitude that the cow had died of sickness. If he had wanted to eat her meat, why would he take away its head and leave the body which contained the meat? And none loved their cows as much as he did.

But no one heeded his pleas. The mob dragged him out, stripped him and thrashed him until he lost consciousness. They locked his son and daughter-in-law in a room in the house and set it on fire. They sprinkled the old man's comatose body with petrol and were about to set him on fire, except for the timely and firm intervention of the young Deputy Commissioner and the police force he commanded. They rescued the unconscious man, but the throng then turned its rage on the police, attacking their vehicles. The police opened fire, injuring one man in his leg. Ansari's son and daughter-in-law also had a miraculous escape, because the village chowkidar broke down the door of the room in which the horde had locked them before torching their house.

Ansari regained consciousness only eight days later. Discharged from hospital after two months, he continues in hiding. He has no police protection; and dreads his neighbours may still take his life. His one son has lost his mind, and his other two beg in mosques because they have lost all their cows, are too frightened still to work, and have not been helped by the administration or local organisations. No one from their village came even to meet him when he was recuperating in hospital. The old man is determined tenaciously to fight for justice. He does not know how, amidst so much hate, but still he hopes, hopelessly, that he can return one day to his village.

As part of the Karwan, wherever we travel, we request local organisers to arrange if possible a peace meeting. We were encouraged that they had organised one after we met Ansari. Although we arrived two hours late, we were heartened to find hundreds of men gathered there, including local officials.

But our optimism did not last long. Speaker after speaker declared that the attack was an unfortunate 'accident' that was best forgotten. Peace could be restored easily. All that was required was that Ansari should tell the police that the men they had arrested were innocent, that he did not recognise the men who tried to kill him. When their men were set free, they would allow Ansari to return. John Dayal, who accompanied the Karwan, and I took the mike, to reason with the gathering. 'If it was your own father who was stripped and nearly killed by his neighbours based on false hate rumours'- I asked them – 'would you even then say it was a minor incident that should be forgotten?' I appealed to them to go to Ansari, seek his forgiveness, assure him of his safety without conditions, and pool money to rebuild his home.

Tempers rose hotly. Speakers challenged me why we did not display the same sympathy with the Hindu man who the police had injured while firing to disperse the mob. They claimed Ansari was an evil man, a murderer. (We enquired later and learnt he had been involved in a violent property dispute with his brother). They said we were unconcerned that Ansari had provoked the anger of the Hindus of his village by beheading a cow.

The organisers of the programme were members of a leftist organisation, so we expected differently. But they too said they were sorely disappointed with our visit. They had hoped we would restore peace by brokering a compromise that set the Hindus free. Instead all we could do was to 'take the side of the Muslims.'

We could have been in Dadri. We could have been in living rooms across the land. The arguments are always the same. Muslims always provoke violence against them, they are by definition always guilty, even when they are lynched. Hindus are by definition innocent and non-violent, roused into understandable violence only by the perfidy of Muslims.

The Karwan could not make place for love in the hearts of the Hindus assembled in the village there. Love that is inseparable from justice. Love that does not differentiate between 'Hindu suffering' and 'Muslim suffering', incensed only by the first, indifferent to the latter.

Heavy in heart, we realized that it will take many journeys for love to prevail, to overcome. Until then we must continue to journey.

※

Gopalkrishna Gandhi,[1] grandson of Mahatma Gandhi and one of the most credible voices in public life in India, worries about a second Partition, a division this time not of the country but of the mind. He reminds us that the Two Nations Theory had not just Muslim but also Hindu adherents. These are now 'wandering over the Indian countryside looking for, thirsting for, disembowelling the Indian earth for the acquifers of hate... They want in India a partition of the mind within the partitioned nation... a Hindu Rasthra.'

'Two ways of life,' he declares in another interview, 'are now before us. One, that which wants Indians to have freedom of conscience, thought and speech so that the best ideas and energies can be devoted to raising the poor, the marginalised and the discriminated, making India a republic for all its

---

1 Gopalkrishna Gandhi, "We're witnessing a second Partition", *The Navhind Times*, 20 August 2017. Available at http://www.navhindtimes.in/were-witnessing-a-second-partition/

citizens. Second, that which wants India to be dominated by one political ideology, one religious order, one majoritarian grip on all, making India a nation of stark, severe and strict uniformity. A subtle fear pervades our politics today. This converts a majority from an honest weightage of democratic opinion into majoritarianism, the very antithesis of democracy.'

This violent, triumphalist majoritarian dominance is on lurid display across this new India. As lynching threatens to grow into a national pandemic, Indian Muslims are learning to endure a sense of foreboding – a lurking, unnamed, unspoken, everyday fear. This is the insecurity that the Vice President Hamid Ansari felt compelled to speak of in his last days in office, only to be diminished in return with the taunts of the Prime Minister, the BJP and the RSS. This is not simply to have to live with the apprehension of discrimination, of being treated the 'other': in classrooms, in public spaces, in residential colonies. This Indian Muslims have long become accustomed to over many decades as India's secular promise was systematically eroded. What is new is the sense of persisting danger of *imminent violence*, of being vulnerable to attack anywhere – on a public road, in a bus or train, in a marketplace, even in their homes – only for looking and being Muslim. In tribal regions, Christian people are also feeling a mounting dread, by attacks on their places of worship and their missionaries. There is another community as well that has long lived with everyday violence and humiliation, the Dalits. But they too are now fearful of attacks for pursuing their socially demeaning caste vocation of skinning cows.

As this fear grows like a cancer in a permissive political environment, there is very little resistance from the rest of the Indian people. Too little outrage, too little empathy and compassion.

I think today of Babasaheb Ambedkar, recalling his counsel that the core of democracy and our constitution is fraternity. That justice, liberty and equality can never become the natural order of things unless there is fraternity. Our shared sisterhood and brotherhood. Solidarity. Love. But of all our founding constitutional principles of our republic, it is fraternity today that is most under attack.

I recall today Mahatma Gandhi's last and finest months. In 1947, a million people had died in in a tempest of hate in Hindu-Muslim riots. Yet he risked his life repeatedly for love, for Hindu-Muslim unity, for the right of minorities to live in India as their homeland, as equal citizens in every way, with their minds without fear, and their heads held high. He walked bravely, alone and unmindful of his safety, and fasted again and again until peace was restored, consecutively in Noakhali, Bihar, Calcutta and finally in Delhi. He did this even as the entire country was engulfed and ripped apart by hate.

His epic fast for 40 days in Calcutta succeeded in dousing the inferno of communal killings of Hindus and Muslims. Lord Mountbatten wrote to him that what 55000 armed soldiers could not accomplish in burning Punjab, one man did in Bengal, battling with only the weapon of his frail body and his steely moral resolve. Gandhiji had resolved to proceed from Calcutta to Punjab to fight the communal madness that had gripped it on both sides of the new border. But when he reached Delhi, he found that Hindu and Sikh refugees had gathered in tens of thousands, bitterly enraged by the killings of their loved ones and the loss of their homes and homelands to Muslims there. Spurred and encouraged by the Hindu Mahasabha, the RSS and the Akalis, they began to attack Muslim settlements and violently occupied Muslim homes, and placed Hindu idols in more than a hundred mosques and dargahs in the capital.

It was both Nehru and Gandhi who would go to these refugee camps, braving the anger and hatred of refugees, to try to persuade them to restore peace and amity. Gandhiji said the Hindu faith would be destroyed if a single mosque was forcefully turned into a Hindu temple. He reminded angry Sikhs that love was central to the tenets of their faith. He said India's soul would be hollowed out if Muslims could not live in India as equal citizens, without fear. His last fast, a fortnight before he was killed, was for all mosques, dargahs and homes to be returned to the Muslims. Irfan Habib reminds us that in effect he was asking Hindu and Sikh refugees escaping murderous Muslim mobs in Pakistan, who had occupied Muslim homes in Delhi, to vacate these and return to their refugee camps. It required utmost courage of love to make such a demand on one's people. Only Mahatma Gandhi could do this. His moral force prevailed over the bitter rage of the refugees and the poisons spread by the RSS and Hindu Mahasabha. Irfan Habib believes that if Muslims could live in free India as equal citizens without fear and perse-cution, and if India chose to be a secular country that belonged equally to people of every faith, this became possible because of Gandhiji's last battle. Another historian Dileep Simeon describes the last months of his life aptly as Love at Work.

I worry about many things. Majoritarian governments that cyni-cally create an enabling environment that tacitly encourages hate attacks on minorities. The social ideology of the BJP and the RSS which poisons social association with prejudice and suspicion against minority groups. The morally weak-kneed response of parties across the political establishment which claim only for electoral gain what they call the 'secular' space. And the shamefully partisan role of the police, which does little to protect the victim, often criminalising those it is charged to defend, and subverting justice.

I worry also about the ease with which mobs gather, and the rage and hatred that drives them as they knife or pulp strangers, sometimes children, only for their faith or caste.

There is therefore much that we must do to fight this rising darkness. We must resolutely fight majoritarian political parties and communal social organisations; parties for which secularism is a strategy rather than a conviction; governments and policepersons who betray their constitutional duties; and the hate attackers, ensuring that they be tried and punished under the law of the land.

But more than all of these, I worry about the bystander. Lynch assaults across the land are characterised almost without exception by bystanders who either actively support the killing, or do nothing to stop the battering or to save the innocent victims. I worry about us who watch and do nothing. Starkly, I worry about you and me, and our complicities by silence and inaction. I believe our greatest, hardest battle will have to be with the bystander. With ourselves. And with our own. We need to interrogate the reasons for our silences, for our failures to speak out, and to intervene, when murderous hate is unleashed on innocent lives. We must interrogate our collective silences. We must ask ourselves how culpable are we when our brothers and sisters are lynched and we stand by?

Today lynch attacks barely register, or linger in the public memory, a blip in our consciousness until the next outrage. My idealistic young friend in Assam, Abdul Kalam Azad, asks in anguish in a recent article 'Has fear lynched my conscience?'[2]

I worry even more profoundly – Has *hate* lynched my conscience?

We need our conscience to ache. We need it to be burdened intolerably.

There can be only three reasons for our silences today as hatred and fear prevail. Either we are too frightened to speak, or we don't care. Or most worrying of all, somewhere in our hearts, is it that we too secretly nurture some of the hatred of the mob, and are happy to outsource to the lynch mob to do our work for us.

---

2 Abdul Kalam Azad, "Has Fear Lynched My Conscience?", *The Citizen*, 26 June 2017. Available at http://www.thecitizen.in/index.php/en/newsdetail/index/1/11101/has-fear-lynched--my-conscience

From Gandhi's last months we need to learn and claim a love that burns, that aches, love born from the defiant conviction of the equal worth of every human being, love that is fierce and brave, love founded in courage, in the willingness to sacrifice everything, even one's life, for love to overcome, to prevail. In the rising darkness in India, it is this radical love that has been lynched – whether by fear, indifference and hate, I do not know. But we must fight, before it is too late, to locate within ourselves our collective capacities for radical love.

Darkness can never be fought with darkness, only light can dispel the enveloping shadows. And so also a politics of hate can only be fought with a new and radical politics of love and solidarity. In battling ideologies that harvest hate, we can win only equipped with this love. We need to garner across our land a plenitude of acts of love.

If I Could Turn Back Time

Junaid rolls over, shakes off grave dust,
and starts walking home to his Ammi,
adjusting his skullcap

Mohammad Akhlaq opens his fridge
to pour a glass of tarboozi Rooh Afza

Pehlu Khan pushes away steel rods
like opening a window and walks on;
his cows mooing beside him

The tank rolls on in Kashmir,
no one would dream of tying
a man in front

The bus to Amarnath drives on,
voices raised in devotion

Bricks come flying back
to create standing walls –
children in Peshawar
turn the pages of history books

The car does not bloom
into fire in the crowded
market

Bullets dislodge themselves
from spines and bellies
and ricochet back
into muzzles

Everything continues
as God planned

And there are no more killings
in His name

218

INDEX

Other books of interest

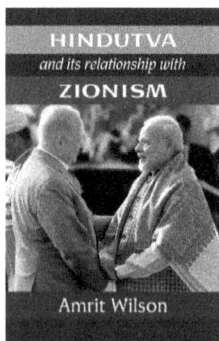

Hindutva and its relationship with Zionism
Amrit Wilson

The subject of this pamphlet is Zionism, the ideology of the Israeli apartheid state, and Hindutva, the ideology which drives the Hindu-supremacist Bharatiya Janata Party (BJP) regime of Prime Minister Narendra Modi. In this era of rising fascism, these two remarkably similar ideologies cement the economic and military alliance between two of the world's most repressive right-wing states.

ISBN 9781990263767 · 40 pages · $11

Domains of politics and modes of rule
Political structures of the neocolonial state in Africa
Michael Neocosmos

A brief attempt to study the neocolonial state in Africa through the manner in which it rules its people. The state deploys different politics over different parts of the population so it can combine a genuinely democratic rule in the image of the West over some while subjecting the majority to colonial forms of domination.

ISBN 9781990263774 · 44 pages · $10

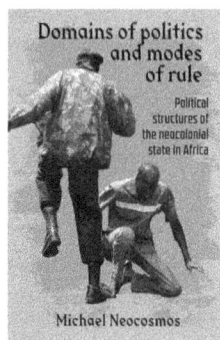

Left Alone
On Solitude and Loneliness amid Collective Struggle
Hjalmar Jorge Joffre-Eichhorn, Patrick Anderson

Left Alone brings together 15 authors and seven visual artists from Africa, Asia, Latin America, Europe and North America to individually and collectively reflect – in words and images – on an urgent psycho-political issue that has not yet been explicitly addressed through a left-political lens, that is, Left Loneliness.

ISBN 9781990263705 · 238 pages · $28

Fanon Today
Reason and Revolt of the Wretched of the Earth
Nigel C Gibson, editor

Fanon Today provides a solid overview of the relevance of Frantz Fanon to the work of those of us who still believe that a just and humane world is both necessary and possible. Throughout the volume the contributors provide space and examples of a Fanonist development of radical humanism, which provides for the psychological development of the person. – Timothy Wild, *Review of African Political Economy*

ISBN 9781990263019 · 488 pages · $32

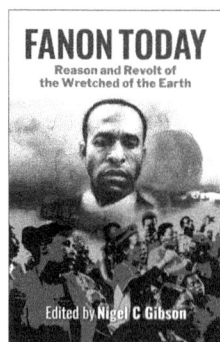

ALL PRICES IN U.S. DOLLARS

www.ingramcontent.com/pod-product-compliance
Lightning Source LLC
Chambersburg PA
CBHW050646270326
41927CB00012B/2897